Legal Consciousness and the Rule of Law in Post-Conflict Societies

This book considers how legal reforms and awareness raising associated with building the rule of law have engaged the popular legal consciousness, producing contradictions that have in turn shaped the nature of the resultant legality.

How are popular legal-justice beliefs and practices transformed when legal reforms encounter local contexts and cultures? For over a decade, scholars have engaged with the argument that legal reform through rule of law building is the answer to the various ills of countries transitioning from war to peace or authoritarianism to democracy. Yet, scholars have also repeatedly critiqued rule of law building projects: The rule of law, in theory and in practice, is a product of Western liberal thought and development and provides limited space for local culture, norms, and practices. This tension has been playing out in multiple locations and in the Democratic Republic of Congo for about two decades. This book examines how rule of law reforms in the Democratic Republic of Congo shape local understandings and practices of law and justice. Instead of focusing on their so-called successes and failures, it explores popular legal consciousness—how people think about, perceive, and engage with the law—to draw broader conclusions about the practical, everyday outcomes of attempts to build the rule of law.

This book will appeal to comparativists, Africanists, and socio-legal scholars who study post-conflict reconstruction, rule of law building, legal consciousness, access to justice and legal pluralism, as well as those with practical interests in these areas.

Holly Dunn is Assistant Professor of Political Science at the School of Interdisciplinary Global Studies, University of South Florida, USA.

Legal Consciousness and the Rule of Law in Post-Conflict Societies

Emergent Hybrid Legality in the Eastern Democratic Republic of Congo

Holly Dunn

Routledge
Taylor & Francis Group
a GlassHouse Book

Designed cover image: Holly Dunn. The cover image depicts the road to reach the research site in Kiliba. The state of the road is shaped by complex local realities and is often difficult to travel. However, like the road to justice, people forge a path, even if an imperfect one.

First published 2023
by Routledge
4 Park Square, Milton Park, Abingdon, Oxon OX14 4RN

and by Routledge
605 Third Avenue, New York, NY 10158

Routledge is an imprint of the Taylor & Francis Group, an informa business
A GlassHouse book

British Library Cataloguing-in-Publication Data
A catalogue record for this book is available from the British Library

Library of Congress Cataloging-in-Publication Data
Names: Dunn, Holly, 1985– author.
Title: Legal consciousness and the rule of law in post-conflict societies : emergent hybrid legality in the eastern Democratic Republic of Congo / Holly Dunn.
Description: Abingdon, Oxon ; New York : Routledge, 2023. | Includes bibliographical references and index.
Identifiers: LCCN 2022034314 (print) | LCCN 2022034315 (ebook) | ISBN 9781032267432 (hardback) | ISBN 9781032267449 (paperback) | ISBN 9781003289715 (ebook)
Subjects: LCSH: Rule of law—Congo (Democratic Republic)—Kivu (Region) | Customary law—Congo (Democratic Republic)—Kivu (Region) | Law reform—Congo (Democratic Republic)—Kivu (Region) | Postwar reconstruction—Congo (Democratic Republic)—Kivu (Region)
Classification: LCC KTX2020 .D86 2023 (print) | LCC KTX2020 (ebook) | DDC 340.11096751—dc23/eng/20220720
LC record available at https://lccn.loc.gov/2022034314
LC ebook record available at https://lccn.loc.gov/2022034315

ISBN: 978-1-032-26743-2 (hbk)
ISBN: 978-1-032-26744-9 (pbk)
ISBN: 978-1-003-28971-5 (ebk)

DOI: 10.4324/9781003289715

Typeset in Bembo
by Apex CoVantage, LLC

In memory of Mulangwa Lumeka François

Contents

Acknowledgements

After a decade of working on this project, there are so many people to thank for their support, feedback, and friendship.

First and foremost, I owe a debt of gratitude to my partner organizations in Uvira. CEEDECO, and its founder, Eric lwa Mwenge, as well as FOCHI, and its founder Floribert Kazingufu, were both exceptional partners throughout my research. They helped me find accommodations, interpreters, and contacts, and they were always concerned about my well-being and safety. My ability to conduct this research was greatly facilitated by all the members of both organizations, notably, Ibra, Sifa, Méma, Nzobé, Mésack, and Emmanuel.

I give my love and appreciation to Chantal Musafiri, François Mulangwa, and their families for providing a home while I was in Uvira, as well as in Bukavu and Goma. They welcomed me into their lives and shared their extensive and extended families with me. I never lacked for a family because I was invited into theirs, which I am sure was not always easy. I only wish I could come near to repaying the kindness I was showed.

Walter James, Charlie Walker, and Maya Doyon-Hanson were my first family in Uvira. Our few months together went quickly. They shared in the ups and downs of my first trip to Uvira and my first attempt at research. Charlie, in particular, helped me through various moments of analysis paralysis. Thank you to Luca Bigger and Annabelle Grassini for the mini-getaways while I was in Uvira.

Beyond CEEDECO and FOCHI, I am grateful to all the organizations and people who participated in and supported my research. Although I cannot include names here, the narratives, experiences, information, and advice that were shared with me were invaluable. I wish nothing but the best for you all in your daily lives, work, and future ventures.

This research would have not been possible without the participation of numerous people who were willing to share their stories and experiences with a stranger. I still struggle with how to show my gratitude and make something meaningful out of what was shared with me. This book is a small contribution to that idea.

The cultural and linguistic interpretation and translation provided by Ibra, Méma, Imaja, and Pélagie went above and beyond. They all worked through difficult conditions—rain, heat, mud, fatigue, and beyond—to make this research possible. I am so appreciative of their time and for all the effort each of them put into helping me understand the context, culture, and realities of life in Uvira.

I have also been fortunate to have some wonderful mentors and advisors along the way. At the University of Minnesota, Lisa Hilbink took immense time and energy to labour over my writing and ideas. I always felt that she really believed in me and my research, even when I did not. Lisa profoundly shaped my ideas about what it means to be a scholar. My meetings with Gabrielle Ferrales always uplifted and inspired me. I am grateful to Raymond Duvall, Joan Tronto, and Fionnuala Ní Aoláin for all their comments on various iterations of dissertation chapters and journal manuscripts. Their contributions were always thoughtful and helped me improve my ideas and arguments.

It was at Carleton University where the idea for this research first started with the much needed guidance and oversight of Augustine Park. Augustine made me a better scholar by bringing a critical eye to my writing and arguments and supporting my fieldwork. Thank you to James Milner for the support and feedback during my first attempt at research and writing during my MA. I benefited greatly from the opportunities provided by Doris Buss and Blair Rutherford. Working with them on the 'Economies of Sexual Violence Workshop' shaped my understanding of the power dynamics underlying research on conflict and sexual violence. They provided an example of 'engaged scholarship' that stuck with me. Their feedback on my early writing was also invaluable.

I would like to thank so many people who read different iterations of my work, as well as those who participated in countless conversations over the years—conversations about justice, the law, the Congo, methods, ethics, and beyond. In particular, Christopher Day introduced me to SERSAS and provided the space to workshop my book manuscript. His feedback, along with that of Kevin Fridy, on the book manuscript provided a needed confidence boost. Richard Matthew offered me with many opportunities to develop and share my research over the years. These opportunities helped me grow as a scholar. I appreciate everyone who offered feedback on manuscripts, presentations, and ideas, including Monica Williams, Emily Burrill, Farrah Tek, Oahn Nguyen, Whitney Taylor, Ore Koren, and especially Bridget Marchesi. Bridget always provided a different way of thinking about things.

I have been fortunate to join a wonderful group of scholars at the School of Interdisciplinary Global Studies at the University of South Florida. I am grateful to the SIGS faculty who supported my research in various ways, through ongoing discussions, feedback, and comments on written work, especially Aaron Augsburger, Peter Funke, Cheryl Hall, Tatsiana Kulakevich, David Ponton, Scott Solomon, Steve Tauber, Nick Thompson, and Manu Sammotra.

This book draws on research supported by the Social Sciences and Humanities Research Council of Canada. It was further made possible by the financial support of The University of Minnesota's Political Science Department and the Humanities Institute at the University of South Florida. I am grateful for this financial support, which made months of fieldwork possible.

Finally, I owe a world of gratitude to my family. Angela Rogers and Renee Malcom both played such an important role in my intellectual development. I thank them immensely for believing in me and supporting this work over the years. They offered much needed balance and opportunities for ongoing reflection.

Charles Skelton made it through the fieldwork years with me, sharing in the difficulties and achievements. It was not always easy, but I am so grateful for that time and encouragement provided.

To my immediate family, thank you for your ongoing support and caring, and for respecting my path even if it was not what you had expected. My parents raised me to have an open mind and to consider people's unique experiences and motivations with understanding, not judgement. Their influences profoundly shaped the way I see the world and do research.

And, finally, I have so much gratitude for my chosen family, my husband, Stephen Boyes, and Olive Palmer-Boyes. They have both been unconditionally supportive. Stephen is my number one supporter and critic. Thank you for always believing in this book and never giving me a hard time when I had to disappear to 'go write'. Our conversations and your thoughtful comments have helped bring this book into being. I even look forward to the next one!

Maps

Map 1 Democratic Republic of Congo

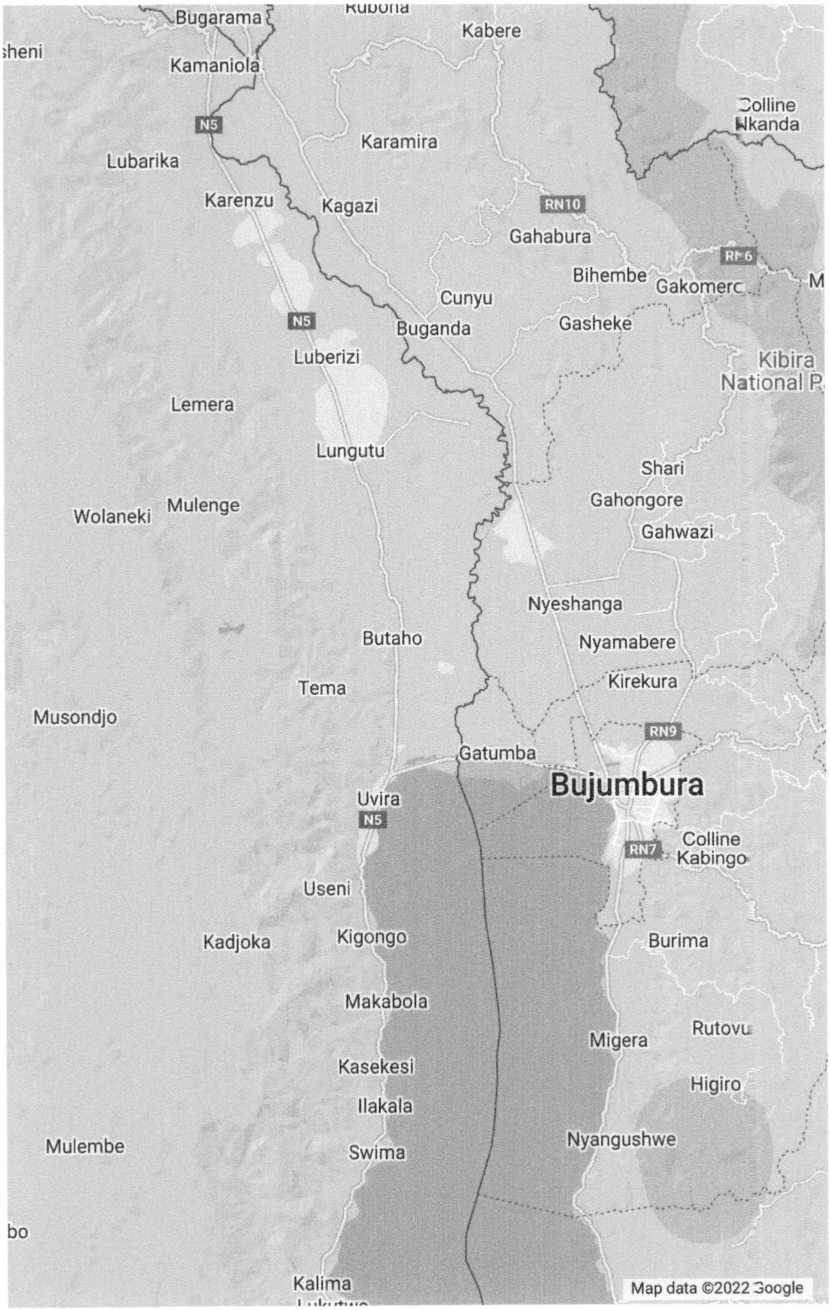
Bugarama
Kabere
Kamaniola
Colline
Nkanda
N5
Karamira
Lubarika
Karenzu
Kagazi
RN10
Gahabura
Bihembe
Gakomero
Cunyu
N5
Buganda
Gasheke
Luberizi
Kibira
Lemera
Lungutu
Shari
Gahongore
Wolaneki
Mulenge
Gahwazi
Nyeshanga
Butaho
Nyamabere
Kirekura
Tema
Musondjo
RN9
Gatumba
Bujumbura
Uvira
N5
Colline
Kabingo
RN7
Useni
Kadjoka
Kigongo
Burima
Makabola
Rutovu
Migera
Kasekesi
Higiro
Ilakala
Mulembe
Swima
Nyangushwe
Kalima
Map data ©2022 Google

Map 2 Uvira

Chapter 1

Problems with the Rule of Law and Research in the Eastern Democratic Republic of Congo

In one of the first group interviews[1] I facilitated in 2015, my interpreter, Marise, and I located a couple of *motaris*[2] and took the bumpy National Rt. 5 south to Makobola. We had arranged to meet with local security officials, but were greeted by four local *chefs*[3] of various levels, and one wise elder. I had been informed that Makobola was still governed as a *chefferie*[4], so the *chefs* we met played an important role in regulating everyday life in the area. We sat in a circle in a small hall on the shore of Lake Tanganyika; the breeze off the lake made the rather enclosed space of the room more bearable. We went around the circle doing introductions as a small child lingered silently in the doorway showing, and presumably trying to sell, a fish in a metal dish. After some general conversation, I asked the group what kinds of conflict occur locally. This question opened the door to a lengthy discussion about harms, disputes, the law, and justice.

Our exploration of these topics foreshadowed some of the complexities of understanding harm and justice that came to define my research. These *chefs* outlined several sources of local conflicts, from land ownership to inheritance to domestic disputes. Beyond the outlined conflicts, they raised a number of points that I proceeded to spend months delving into and trying to make sense of. For example, when I asked the group how life had changed since the wars, I was intrigued by the discussion that developed. Paraphrasing from my fieldnotes, the participants said,

> The problem is the law and women's rights. They are disturbing our customs. Before, everything was resolved through custom, and now there is both the law and customary justice, but people are not well informed. Instead of going to the *chef* or *sage*[5], they go directly to the *parquet*. Before, people didn't know the law, it wasn't promulgated, and they were happy with customary justice. After some movement, with non-governmental organizations (NGOs) and people travelling, people now have some information. Now, they no longer go to customary justice because they view it as a partial solution—because there are no sanctions, and people resolve the issue. People think there is more to win at the *parquet*[6]. But, it is not

DOI: 10.4324/9781003289715-1

> good to go to the *parquet*. Imagine, a woman takes her husband to court. How can they live together after that? The more women are informed and claim their rights, the more divorces there are, which is bad.

These *chefs* were putting forth arguments about both the limitations of the law and women's rights in contrast to the benefits of relying on customary justice, understood as emphasizing a role for *chefs* and wise elders in dispute resolution. The statement about people not being well informed was linked to their perception that people turn too quickly to the legal system, the *parquet*. Yet, this contrasted with arguments I had heard from other sources about people not knowing the law and that being a point of concern. Similarly, the idea that customary justice is seen as a partial solution also stood out as contradictory to other points I had heard raised about the importance of restorative justice and reconciliation for bringing people together so they can continue to live peacefully, as family or neighbours. In other words, the discussion I had with the *chefs* reflected one approach to understanding the law and justice, amongst a variety of understandings that I encountered over the course of four trips to Uvira. While it is not surprising that people might have different understandings of law and justice, I wanted to draw out these tensions and try to understand and theorise where they came from, how they shape and are shaped by people's consciousness, and what this means for the terrain of legality that is constructed in Uvira.

The *chefs'* remarks further highlighted some internal contradictions in understandings of harm and justice. Beyond the earlier outlined comments, they shared ideas about where custom is problematic or goes too far. For example, someone said,

> If a man dies, typically there is someone in his family who is supposed to marry his wife[7]. But, is it really ok to just give her to another person? Here, the custom goes too far. She should not be given away to others. This practice was done without women's choice before. Now, they see that it is not always good, and the woman has to want to do it.

They also added that some conflicts or harms should only be handled by *la justice*, such as rape. Thus, these *chefs* at first appeared to hold homogenous preferences for custom and customary justice, but actually demonstrated more nuanced views of legal-justice. The complexities in their analysis of the intersection of women's rights and justice suggest some maintenance of previously held views as well as an openness to rethinking these and even accepting a profound role for the state in justice delivery. The nuances, complexities, and contradictions in popular understandings of justice thus appear to manifest both socially and within individual legal consciousness. In a place that has experienced international pressure and support for legal reforms and implementing the rule of law (ROL), how did these interventions also shape people's experiences and understandings of harm and justice for quotidian harms and disputes?

Underlying daily life—hardships, marriage, illness, work—is the terrain of legality—ordering, punishing, resolving, rectifying, neglecting, overstepping—both looming large and hidden in the interstices of everyday life. Legality is reflected in the internationally funded prosecutions of accused war criminals, just as it is in the regulation of marriage, inheritance, sexual relations, and witchcraft. In Uvira, people's lives are shaped by a plurality of legal-justice systems, practices, institutions, norms, and actors. These include elders, wise people, local leaders, NGOs, administrative *chefs*[8], traditional *chefs*, police, military, and courts. These systems can be rooted in the past *and* reflect current strategic and pragmatic decisions. They can be imported from elsewhere and implemented by the state . . . or not. In legally plural contexts, scholars have long sought to outline, and problematize, the relationship between traditional justice and the state legal system, recognizing this distinction as a legacy of colonialism[9]. While that legacy persists, the realities on the ground continue to evade easy categorization and simple relationships due to their emergent, hybridized, and contextually defined forms.

At its core, this book is about the continuity, disruption, and the construction of legality through legal encounters, in particular through ROL building endeavours, as they play out in localized contexts. The ROL is now a long-standing buzzword in the international humanitarian world and is viewed as the key to successful interventions aimed at creating peace, liberal democracies, and market economies around the world[10]. Classical ROL notions of an independent judiciary, equality before the law, and publicity of laws (Raz, 2015) help define the goals of these interventions and substantiate the indicators used to measure their success. The United Nations (UN), for example, views the ROL as essential to three major areas of their work: Human rights, peace and security, and development (United Nations, n.d.). Not only has this been the case in the practitioner realm but in more abstract spaces. For example, liberal ideology often implies congruence between 'civilized life' and law, reinforcing the importance of the ROL as a symbol and practice of civilization, development, capitalism, and Western democracy (Fukuyama, 2010). In practice, this has led to extensive programming and funding by international organizations engaged in ROL building activities, especially in conflict-affected settings, to construct some version of liberal legalism.

The eastern Democratic Republic of Congo (DRC) has been a lively host to these legal transformations forged by, on the one hand, international humanitarian actors, their ROL programming, and their local partners. And, on the other hand, through the population's understandings and engagements with legal reforms; their intentional and unintentional acquiescence, resistance, and vernacularization[11]. In this book, I am interested in the *making* of legality and the role that legal consciousness plays in this process. The creation of legality emerges through people's everyday lives and through common harms and disputes and how people understand and address them. As these meanings and understanding of law circulate through social relations (Silbey, 2008), legal practices and institutions take form. The nuances of this emergent legality tend to be understudied, as the focus of research is frequently directed at how and why they fail to measure up to the liberal legal standards.

I argue that defining legal reforms and ROL building by its failures and deficiencies, vis-à-vis Western notions of liberal legalism, misses the whole array of creative ideas, practices, and engagements that are being constructed through people's everyday interactions with legal pluralism. Popular legal consciousness integrates newly emphasized areas of state law with popular worldviews and experiences. These elements of legal consciousness are frequently in tension, producing a more diverse and complex terrain of law that I call *emergent hybrid legality*. This concept reflects how I theorise the construction of legality through legal encounters and shifts in legal consciousness. The legal terrain is not predetermined because it cannot be manufactured or imposed in the way that ROL builders often attempt; the specifics emerge out of the more localized realities.

Therefore, in this book, I highlight the role of local NGOs and their awareness-raising practices in shaping legal consciousness, which manifests in the population in contradictory ways as a result of the integration of different understandings of law and justice. I make clear two important areas of contradictory legal consciousness: *Disconnect in harm naming* and *different logics of justice*. The former is a way to conceptualize the complexity of legal consciousness in situations where the state defines something as a harm but the population does not, and vice versa. The latter similarly reflects the tensions of legal consciousness, where the state understands justice for a harm or dispute in a way that is distinct from the population's understanding. These concepts are further developed in the next chapter and throughout the book. By exploring these areas of contradictory consciousness, I conceptualize the constructed legal terrain as *emergent hybrid legality*, which means the hybridization of different understandings of harm and justice in unexpected, emergent ways. This approach is further detailed in Chapter 2.

By exploring legal consciousness, I highlight the *friction* (Tsing, 2005) between globalized, liberal standards of law, as they manifest through ROL building, and more localized approaches to justice that may be rooted in tradition but are far more varied and complex than one might imagine as a unified traditional system. This book brings popular legal consciousness to the forefront of understanding why practices of legality have not become the same across different sites of ROL intervention. In other words, it provides a different approach to understanding the so-called failures of building the ROL in conflict-affected settings. In so doing, I seek to illustrate how the unanticipated outcomes of legal reforms are patterned and related to developments in popular legal consciousness. Importantly, I argue that the shifting terrain of legality reflects the encounter between globalized law and localized justice. As such, it is *emergent*—a process of coming into being—and hybrid—heterogenous in both origin and composition. Thus, what I call *emergent hybrid legality*, although unpredictable, is the *expected* outcome of legal reform. Moreover, it may actually serve the needs of the population and need not be framed primarily as a failure in liberal legality. The quotidian harms and disputes that arise in this context of generalized hardship are, perhaps surprisingly, frequently addressed peacefully through the variety of legal-justice mechanisms available. This is not a romanticization of the *emergent hybrid legality*, which can take violent forms, but a critical exploration of outcomes of legal encounters.

This book adds to our understandings of legal pluralism and legality in post-conflict settings, as well as the more practical scholarship on ROL building. I elaborate on the nuanced and unanticipated outcomes of legal encounters to provide insights into the unique outcomes of legal interventions and reforms in the eastern DRC. Although my fieldwork is in the eastern DRC, the theoretical developments linking legal consciousness to *emergent hybrid legality* are applicable beyond this case, most obviously other transitioning contexts in Africa, where the internationalized ROL building project is underway. More broadly, we can think about legal encounters in any context where external actors are playing an active role in constructing, reconstructing, or reforming the legal system of another country to align with liberal legalism.

Yet, the globalization of liberal legalism is glaringly evident in contexts of limited state capacity. Massoud (2013) argues that, in fragile states, ROL building is based on two assumptions: First, that law is lacking or highly problematic, and second, that capacity building is the way to transition to a modern, liberal society. These assumptions hold in the DRC, where the international community interprets the Congolese state as unable to provide order, law, and justice (Derks, 2012; Mobekk, 2009). Yet, they also see a window of opportunity for reforming the legal system as part of ROL building projects. Key components of these projects include strengthening state legal institutions, rewriting laws in line with international standards, and educating the population about these reforms.

The United Nations Organization Stabilization Mission in the Democratic Republic of the Congo (MONUSCO)'s mandate emphasizes ending impunity and building the state justice system through the broader agenda of security sector reform, under which ROL programming is advanced (Mobekk, 2009). Additionally, the international community's influence in shaping approaches to addressing sexual and gender-based violence (SGBV) has been remarkable and analysed from a multitude of different perspectives (eg. Lake, 2018; Freedman, 2016; Baaz & Stern, 2010). Indeed, Lake (2014) has illustrated that state weakness has provided a space for international actors to profoundly shape the provision of legal-justice. Legal reforms are seen to support the goal of addressing SGBV through new and updated laws, prosecutions, and legal aid (Lake, 2018).

However, in conflict-affected areas, ROL proponents have encountered a repeated problem: The precepts of liberal legalism rarely take root in the way and to the extent that international interveners expect and desire. The results seem to fall short, creating outcomes that scholars and interveners consider ambiguous at best (eg. Channell, 2006; Haggard & Tiede, 2014; Stromseth et al., 2006; Zurn et al., 2012). The conventional wisdom of ROL proponents blames a lack of expertise, time, resources, and the limitations of the local population's knowledge of the law, which I elaborate upon later in the chapter. Additionally, corruption is understood to be a major barrier to ROL building. Corruption[12] certainly plays a role in the functioning of the legal system in Congo, and throughout the book I include various quotes from people who talk about bribes, the legal system privileging the wealthy, and the importance of having connections. Yet, corruption is not a central analytical theme of the book. As I attempt to map out the terrain of legality, I include these aspects, but they are not the sole or even the most prominent reasons for why people engage with legal-justice in the ways that they do. Felices-Luna (2012) argues that there are multiple techniques the population uses to deal with corruption in the formal legal system, such as refusal to engage with the system, relying on knowledge of the system to seek out contacts to serve as intermediaries or even sometimes reporting corruption to NGOs. All of these can be situated within explorations of legal consciousness and the construction of *emergent hybrid legality*, which is how I approach them in this book.

Looking critically at the role of international actors in contexts of transition, I argue that their post-conflict ROL interventions have been defined by a cycle of assumptions, failures, and reinvestments. Yet, few studies seek to make sense of and theorize what these interventions *do* produce outside of the ROL metrics. Their effects and outcomes may not reflect a Western, internationalized, indicator-based understanding of ROL, but that does not mean that they are without consequence for the production of legality.

This book thus takes a different approach; I try to understand and make sense of the unexpected outcomes of legal reforms associated with ROL building. My conceptualization of legal reforms includes shifts in how the local legal complex[13] mobilizes around the law and *which* aspects of state law they prioritize in their work. Instead of relying on ROL measures to analyse the legal developments in the area, I highlight the local population's legal consciousness, their everyday engagements and experiences with the law, as well as the network of formal and informal justice systems, to understand the terrain of legality. Legal consciousness can be understood as common sense, taken for granted, and 'everyday' engagements with the law and, by extension, with legal pluralism. Therefore, I focus on 'everyday' harms and disputes that arise, probing various issues that commonly involve marriage, sexual relations, and witchcraft. In Uvira, these issues are cited as areas of dispute or harm, often with a clear gender dynamic that I will explore, yet they do not receive the same attention as more 'exceptional' harms have in transitioning contexts. My analysis lends insight into this construction of contextualized legality rather than providing a measure against a supposedly universal standard.

Finally, the local legal complex and related civil society organizations play a crucial role intermediating between the internationalized legal norms and practices that manifest in the state legal system and the more localized worldviews and understandings of what justice means in certain contexts In other words, members of the local legal complex are key players in the construction of *emergent hybrid legality*, often through the provision of justice that functions in some way outside the formal state legal system. As a result of local inputs, manifestations of *emergent hybrid legality* may actually provide justice in contextually relevant ways that grapple with universal legal standards, as well as women's rights, without passively accepting, or translating, these globalizing forces but through unanticipated and uncoordinated hybridization.

Perhaps the more interesting part of the role played by local organizations, however, is that they cannot impose their approach nor can they enforce it. Thus, popular consent and participation is essential for these actors to have a meaningful impact. This is not to romanticize *emergent hybrid legality*, which, as I illustrate in later chapters, can also encompass vigilante justice. However, the possibilities for advancing ROL goals, such as organizing everyday life and addressing harms in a consistent way, are both present in Uvira's legal context.

The eastern DRC is a meaningful place to explore the construction of legality, given its recent history of armed conflict and its internationally defined 'weak state' status and concomitant peacebuilding and statebuilding endeavours. But, it is also a unique case in that international attention and activism that have been directed at the eastern DRC have been oriented towards ending and addressing wartime SGBV, specifically wartime rape. This focus and its broadening to other forms of SGBV play a unique role in the construction of legality, which I am attentive to and elaborate on in my analysis of the case of the Congo.

Context: The Case of the Congo

I draw on nine months of immersive fieldwork in Uvira (city) and its surrounding towns to understand the relationship between legal reform, popular legal consciousness, and the nature of legality. The eastern DRC (formerly Zaire) has been devastated by protracted violence, armed conflict, and instability, with varying levels of intensity since at least 1994, when effects of the Rwandan genocide spilled across the borders. Both refugees and génocidaires lived in refugee camps in eastern DRC (Prunier, 2009a). Bouts of violent conflict, including two civil wars, have been defined by local, intrastate, regional, and global dimensions (eg. Autesserre, 2010; Lemarchand, 2008; Prunier, 2009a, 2009b; Stearns, 2011). Notably, the eastern DRC has housed one of the largest and most expensive UN missions—MONUSCO (previously MONUC) (Koddenbrock 2012). As a result of these years of instability, international actors have been concerned with legal reform and ROL building[14], understood as conceptually and practically bound with peacebuilding and prosecuting wartime rape.

Prosecuting wartime rape has been at the centre of the transition in the Congo. In 2010, Margot Wallström, the United Nations Special Representative of the

Secretary-General on Sexual Violence in conflict, called the DRC the 'rape capital of the world' (United Nations, 27 April 2010). The international sensationalization of wartime rape in the mid-2000s to 2010s made the eastern Congo the site of intense research, activism, media attention, and humanitarian action focused on the issue of women and armed conflict (Baaz & Stern, 2010; Freedman, 2016; Kirby, 2015; Lake et al., 2016). However, all this 'hype' can "produce [a] reductionist, singularly focused storyline for outlining a problem and offering a certain solution" (Hilhorst & Douma 2018, p. S81). International resources—directed at supporting female victims and taking the form of medical, psycho-social, legal aid, and developing the legal system's capacity—were often channelled through local NGOs and international organizations with local offices. Internationally funded justice projects thus prioritized building state legal institutions and prosecuting SGBV (Autesserre; 2012; Freedman, 2016) as well as improving the legal system's ability to function in line with international standards (Lake, 2014). The link between legal reforms and prosecuting SGBV has had a profound impact on the post-conflict interventionist/humanitarian terrain (eg. Freedman, 2016; Lake, 2018). This has been a rather distinctive phenomenon. While other countries have indeed addressed SGBV in the wake of armed conflict, such as Rwanda (eg. Koomen, 2013) and Sierra Leone (Kelsall & Stepakoff, 2007), the international 'hype' of the Congo case is relatively unique, providing an insightful case for exploring the localized gendered dimensions of legal reforms in a post-conflict context. Thus, while this case can speak to the situation in many other transitions and beyond, it is also firmly anchored in the particularities of its context and experience.

Upon critical reflection, part of my interest in the eastern DRC was likely influenced by the increased international activism, awareness, and growing 'hype' around conflict minerals, such as coltan, and prosecuting wartime rape as a mode of transitional justice. I believed that there was a need to explore other areas of justice beyond the state legal system and aside from wartime rape. When I started conducting my research in 2011, I became more interested in the common, everyday harms and disputes that people experienced because these were the issues that *they* emphasized in my early interviews. In day-to-day conversations with people, and even in *baraza*, a traditionally informed, NGO-run justice mechanism I was studying, people were looking for support to address quotidian harms and disputes, not the exceptional crimes that happened during the war. For example, in one *baraza* meeting that I attended, two young couples were brought together because one couple could not conceive, and they accused the other woman of witchcraft. In another case, a woman had gotten support from *baraza* mediators in a dispute that she had with the person she rented her field from. This dispute included several moving parts, from corrupt local police to a local NGO that had promised to help but had made things worse. In both cases, mediators helped resolve the dispute *and* engaged with law while doing so. These are just a couple examples of many, but they reflect the types of issues that people regularly experience and that were not receiving much research attention. My focus is obviously not meant to downplay the gravity of war-related crimes, but as I noted in the beginning of this chapter, everyday life persists, and the population regularly deals with a variety of 'ordinary' problems. At the same time, years of conflict, instability, and post-conflict international involvement shifted the nature of the available justice options.

As my research question shifted, my decision to do fieldwork in Uvira solidified. In Uvira, many local organizations have partnerships and receive funding from international and foreign organizations. These entities in turn play an important role in defining the nature of their justice-oriented projects. These international and domestic actors working on legal reforms comprise the internationalized legal complex. The internationalized legal complex is diverse, yet, in effect, it is the authoritative community that interprets the law and wields the power to name 'the law' and what it means (see Sarat, 1990). Major international actors involved in these 'building'—statebuilding, peacebuilding, ROL building—projects include MONUSCO and the European Union. Other international, governmental, and non-governmental actors have also had an impact, such as the American Bar Association, Kvinna till Kvinna, and Women for Women International. In some areas, these actors have had direct involvement in ROL building activities, but in Uvira, many have partnered with local organizations to fulfil their missions. Uvira is nowhere near as inundated with international organizations as the regional capitals Bukavu and Goma, but the international influence is clearly present, even if indirectly, and the ROL building project is alive.

While Uvira is a context that illuminates how legality comes into being through legal encounters, it is worth noting here that this phenomenon is not limited to eastern DRC or even to transitioning contexts. The processes of legal encounters, emergent practices, and hybrid structures are common across the globe. Yet, due to recent disruptions—colonialism, conflict, and intervention—Uvira allows us to see the different moving parts in the formation of legality; they are more visible. One may be able to transport this analytic framework more readily to other transitioning contexts, but there is also the potential to explore these dynamics in established democracies to look at how contradictory legal consciousness produces practices around the law and legality. This might challenge the powerful hold the ROL concept has in shaping our vision of ideal legality. For now, I offer the trend that I see in how the ROL is 'done' in transitioning contexts and return to the broader question about the ROL in the Conclusion.

The Rule of Law Cycle

In transitioning contexts, I understand ROL building to more or less follow a four part cycle. The first part of the cycle is defined by the underlying assumptions of ROL programmes and programmers: Failed states are essentially lawless, defined by violence, and are at risk of devolving into violence again if this is not addressed

(Massoud, 2013). When actors, such as the UN and EU, and other national and international humanitarian organizations perceive the law as broken or absent in a country, they respond with foreign assistance and capacity building (Massoud, 2013). Reformers often argue that if courts are functional and laws exist, people will prefer the state system (Stromseth, 2008, p. 1452). Thus, the need to build the ROL, the foundation of peace and democracy, has become the common sense of peacebuilding, giving it an axiomatic power that is nearly impossible to contest (Donais, 2013; Rajkovic, 2012).

Second, given these assumptions and expectations, interventions undertaken to build the ROL largely focus on state institutions; this includes drafting and amending laws and constitutions, training legal professionals, and developing infrastructure and materials from courthouses and computers to papers and pens (Carothers, 2006; Golub, 2006; Kleinfeld, 2006; Stromseth et al., 2006). This dominant framework also assumes that there is a particular checklist of institutions and practices that make up the ROL (Hertogh, 2016) and, once implemented, stability, justice, democracy, and development are more likely to ensue. These reforms have, at times, included changing laws and legal procedures to advance women's rights (Lake, 2014) and especially prosecuting wartime rape in the aftermath of armed conflict (Henry, 2014). Gender in this respect is about promoting women's rights across states in a universalistic way rather than engaging with local or domestic gender justice discussions.

Yet, investments in legal institutions do not guarantee that people will follow the law or turn to the courts. Thus, ROL projects have also supported educating the population about the legal system and reforms that bring it closer to internationally agreed upon legal standards and practices; they invest resources and expertise into the legal system *and* encourage the population to use it (Carothers, 2006; Chandler, 2015; Stromseth et al., 2006). Essentially, this 'human side' of intervention is meant to turn traditional and conflict-affected *people* into modern, liberal ones[15].

Given the dominant ROL beliefs and practices amongst scholars and practitioners, encouraging a ROL culture requires that society recognize and believe in the value of the law and legal system and its efficacy in resolving disputes in a neutral manner (Stromseth et al., 2006, p. 310). Thus, the underlying, although rarely explicit, goal is the construction of liberal legal subjects, *individuals* who understand themselves as rational rights-holders whose rights are upheld through the law (Carlin et al., 1966; Hunt, 1985; Galanter & Trubek, 1974; Merry, 1990). This subjectivity reflects liberal legal consciousness.

Importantly, Stromseth et al. (2006) recognize that reaching the ROL ends—protecting the population from abuses of power, facilitating people's ability to organize their daily lives, resolve disputes, and access redress for harms—does not necessarily entail the types of legal institutions and processes associated with Western legal systems (p. 328). Yet, they argue that in a globalizing world, these institutions are increasingly required; every prosperous, peaceful society has the same liberal legal institutions (Stromseth et al., 2006). Engel and

Engel (2010) note that the theoretical relationship between legal consciousness and globalization is the creation of "new expectations about the place of law, legal norms, and legal institutions in their [ordinary people's] everyday life." These new expectations, if they are indeed created to reflect the dominant international legal norms, reflect *liberal legal consciousness*. They implicitly link the ROL to dominant understandings of modernization and liberal peace, and their implications for the legal system (see Chandler, 2015).

The third phase in this cyclical trend is an assessment of outcomes. Rule of law indicators[16] are often used to judge how closely a country fits with global liberal legal standards (Urueña et al., 2015). Often, through the use of these metrics, scholars assess the results as discouraging, or, at best, ambiguous (Channell, 2006; Haggard & Tiede, 2014; Stromseth et al., 2006; Zürn et al. 2012). Rarely do transitioning countries exhibit complete implementation of the sought-after legal changes. This may be especially true in those contexts that do not have a history of deeply internalized Western-style law. While these ROL assessments are often aggregated concepts measured at the national level, these connect back, directly or indirectly, to whether people follow the law or use courts to resolve harms and disputes.

These assessments and disappointments lead to the final step of the cycle; international actors reaffirm their commitment to peacebuilding and the ROL. The conclusions of reports are generally that more work is needed; more strengthening of the ROL is required. International organizations commit themselves to advancing reforms; they commit more time, resources, and expertise to institution building and awareness raising. And, frequently, the cycle begins again. The UNDP's (2011), *Strengthening the rule of law in crisis-affected and fragile situation: A UNDP global programme for justice and security (Phase II)* is a useful example of a document that reaffirms much of the conventional international ROL 'wisdom' through its programme strategy, which is revisited in this second phase of the UNDP's programme. The emphasis throughout much of the document is on strengthening ROL institutions, such as the police, corrections, and the judiciary. In this sense, this UNDP programme aligns with the conventional, statist ROL approach.

Notably, the UNDP document does mention a role for community-based policing, mediation, and traditional justice. However, these are seen as temporary 'fixes' while state institutions are built and reinforced. In other words, the community-based, traditional justice considerations seem to be understood as more of a 'stop gap' (see Harper, 2011). The complex, interactive nature of legal pluralism is not recognized or engaged with. Thus, as some peacebuilding scholars observe, while the international–local encounters can transform international discourse and practices (eg. Björkdahl & Gusic, 2016; Hellmüller, 2016), the approach to long-term ROL building has remained remarkably stable.

At the same time, this mainstream understanding of the connection between law and peacebuilding has been problematized. Scholars have critiqued various underlying assumptions and themes that perpetuate the cycle, particularly the implicit bias towards Western liberal understandings of the rule of law, ignoring local culture, norms, and practices (Carothers, 2006; Channell, 2006; Grenfell, 2013; Hadfield & Weingast, 2014; Hertogh, 2016; Kleinfeld, 2006; Park, 2010; Peterson, 2010). Further, research has shown that the international community's anticipation of a global turn to liberal legalism has been challenged, even if not directly resisted, by local realities (eg. Engel & Engel, 2010; Godoy, 2006). While these critiques are of fundamental importance, they are not new. Various scholars have made these arguments for over a decade, yet the ROL building cycle largely persists in transitioning contexts.

This leaves open a major question and area of study that my work seeks to address: What are the outcomes of legal encounters in transitioning contexts and why do they take particular forms? How do people engage with ideas and institutions that ROL builders share, advocate, and attempt to implement in relation to other beliefs and practices? If these interventions largely 'fail' on their own terms, do they have other consequences? I explore the effects of legal reforms on shaping legal consciousness and the construction of legality. In particular, instead of looking at traditional or community-led justice practices as a stop gap while the 'real' ROL is constructed, I consider the experiences of the local population to draw out the hybridization of justice and its emergent character. My research recognizes the limitations of international ROL building practice to be rooted in the underlying assumptions that are based in a liberal legal and colonial framework that is committed to a particular type of Western style law and justice to be the goal regardless of context. However, I also argue that there are ideas and practices tied to the liberal legal framework that have been taken up by local actors and contribute to ongoing discussions of what law and justice mean. This book draws on nine months of fieldwork to explore these complexities and how they are playing out in Uvira.

Methods and Ethics

Beyond the theoretical and conceptual contributions of this book, I further aim to add to the growing body of scholarship on methodologies of research in conflict-affected and unstable contexts. My analysis and methodology are intimately entwined. As noted earlier, my research shifted in response to my experiences in the field. I did not go to Uvira with the goal of focusing specifically on women's experiences of gendered harms or disputes. However, these topics emerged as critical to my research, not just because many local harms and disputes had a gendered dimension, but also because the local population *expected* me to be interested in these issues, like other foreigners, funders, and humanitarians. For example, in 2015, I was fortunate to be introduced to a Congolese lawyer, women's rights activist, and NGO director. She shared with me a wealth of information about the socio-legal context and about the experiences of women that she worked with. She even offered to bring me to her NGO near Mboko to introduce me to some of her beneficiaries. Without my prompting, she was certain that I would want to interview rape survivors, some of her key beneficiaries. I made clear that this was not the focus of my research and that I did not feel qualified to conduct such sensitive interviews at that point. I pointed out that I was more interested in 'everyday' harms and disputes, of which sexual violence may be a part, but given the amount of attention on wartime rape, I wanted to bring other aspects of everyday life to the fore of international awareness. We then agreed that she would take me to see the facilities and informally meet whoever was around. The following Tuesday, we convened in the morning at the designated location and hired some *motaris* to take us to Mboko; I was accompanied by my interpreter at the time. We chatted about the poor state of the road and other common topics as we shared the uncomfortable ride behind the '*moto*' driver.

My stomach dropped when we arrived at the site, and I saw a line-up of people. I had a sinking feeling that they were survivors and that they were waiting for me to interview them, which turned out to be the case. Despite my best efforts to avoid this situation, it was hard to compete with the power dynamics that had emerged in recent years incentivizing sharing narratives of sexual violence. I could not fully blame the lawyer for her bait-and-switch. This fits with findings that local women's organizations use the discourse on wartime rape to become visible in international networks and gain access to international funding (Jean-Bouchard, 2014). The presence of foreigners, especially white Westerners, had come to be associated with a rather perverse exchange—aid, and other resources or support in exchange for narratives of sexual violence. This exchange permeated legal aid, psycho-social and medical care, and broader development initiatives. Indeed, some local NGOs have felt pressured to include sexual violence in their mandate to improve their odds of receiving funding from these international organizations.

As I experienced this—my encounters with the local population being shaped by their expectations of me, viewed as a member of the 'saviour economic complex' (Dunn, 2020)— I started to analyse the landscape of encounter alongside and in dialogue with my analysis of legal consciousness and legality. The 'saviour economic complex' refers to "peacebuilders, humanitarian and aid workers, and even the international media and researchers . . . typically (if we are being optimistic) pushed from a moral imperative to help the victims [of sexual violence]" (Dunn, 2020, p. 162). It further refers to the exchanges that are initiated, facilitated, or modified by those foreign actors seeking to 'help' or 'save' the local population. The exchange of rape narrative for support and resources has been recognized as the 'commodification of rape narratives' (Freedman, 2016) and as an element of 'rape tourism' (Baaz & Stern, 2010). The implications of the 'saviour economic complex' further extend to research and the creation of expectations around researchers. The presence of foreigners may elicit expectations of assistance, and it is left to the researcher to mitigate false expectations (Lake, 2014b). Navigating and reflecting on this context became an essential part of my research methodology and analysis.

I started to recognize that the gap in the scholarship was also tied to common methodological approaches of some social science disciplines, where the researcher is viewed as an objective, neutral observer, rather than a politicized, embodied actor. Through iterative, abductive analysis, I had to recognize how my methodology, research question, and the kind of information that was being shared with me through both interviews and observations were all intertwined and inseparable. So, instead of fighting against the expectations people had of me and imagining myself as an unembodied observer, I try to analyse and make sense of these interactions as part of my study. My research methods and ethics thus explicitly recognize the power dynamics of the local legal terrain, specifically defined by the 'saviour economic complex'.

The Research Setting Further Considered

As a result of the interactional dynamics shaped by the saviour economic complex, I constantly had to reflect on the power dynamics of my research's setting in relation to the information I was collecting and how I was analysing it. It was impossible to 'just' be a neutral observer, as my embodied presence, as an educated, white, English- and French-speaking young (unmarried) woman, already signified something to the population, already shaped how they were interpreting me and my goals, based on their own experiences and understandings. I draw on Mutua's (2001) savages–victims–saviours metaphor as a heuristic for making sense of the local power dynamics and where I fit within them.

The Congo, especially the eastern region fits with how Mutua (2001) situates the 'savage' in his metaphor. In recent decades, international actors have employed a discourse that represents the country and the population as 'inherently violent' (Autesserre, 2010, p. 74) and have participated in recycling familiar colonial images of Congo (Baaz & Stern, 2010). For example, Koddenbrock (2012) illustrates how Western policy actors have imagined a backward and lawless Congo and instilled those images in policy papers and international discourse on conflict in the region. In this context, men and Congolese culture have been defined as the savages. Rebels and warlords, corrupt government officials and unrestrained military personnel, and, perhaps most problematically, Congolese culture itself have all been reduced, in the international realm, to the metaphorical and literal savage.

Women, through media and NGO attention, have been portrayed equally reductively as a homogenous group: Victims. This is 'proven' in the international imaginary by the high rates of sexual violence and reinforced through media reporting on the most heinous acts of sexual violence. Baaz and Stern (2010) have labelled the media's approach 'rape tourism'. By contrast, the West or the international community, through their interventions, is represented as the saviours. Saviours have the knowledge, power, and goodwill to intervene and save the victims from the savages (Mutua, 2001). Well-intentioned international actors have interpreted and constructed women's bodies as sites of protection and intervention (Mertens & Myrttinen, 2019) by under-acknowledging women's agency and essentializing their experiences to that of 'victim'. Humanitarian actors, the saviours, must protect women from the 'savage' rapist and the culture that is seen to accept and normalize sexual violence. Thus, interventions take the form of projects and programmes focused on combatting and addressing wartime rape (see D'Errico et al., 2013), including medical, psycho-social, and, notably, legal support. Through the discourse and action aimed at protection and intervention, international actors essentialized gendered violence to wartime sexual violence against women, constructing what Kapur (2002) calls the 'hegemonic victim subject'. This creates a thorny ethical situation, as well as a need for critical reflection in making sense of observations and interviews.

This is not a new phenomenon. The dominant international view that sustains a dual interpretation of Congo as savage and victim finds its roots in the history of colonization. K. Dunn (2003) illustrates how the West has come to 'know' the DRC through earlier Western representations of the country. Women were seen as victims of culture, most specifically because of the ongoing practice of polygamy, which equally framed Congolese men as in need of civilizing (Mertens & Myrttinen, 2019). In other words, the frames through which Europeans imagined Congolese were just as gendered as they were racialized. While King Leopold II's utter pillaging of the country eventually came to be criticized by those in Belgium and Europe more broadly, these critiques removed control of Congo from Leopold and put it into the hands of the Belgian government, only serving to reinforce essentializing encounters and narratives. The new narrative: The poor people of Congo need to be 'saved'. This history, dating to the late 1800s through to the mid-1900s, was a process of creation in the European and Western imaginary about how to make sense of the Congo.

The conflict, the country, and the people have continued to be defined in an essentialized, racialized, and reified manner (Koddenbrock, 2012). "By persistently employing images of the Congo as chaotic, backward, and uncivilized/uncivilizable, external actors . . . have worked to forcefully replace existing sociopolitical practices and systems of knowledge with Western-scripted notions of sovereignty, modernity, and development" (Dunn, 2003, p. 6). Images of Congo as backward are and were a product of political discourse, but also quite literally found in photographic images that were taken and circulated internationally for political purposes. 'Humanitarian crisis images', for example, have characterized international organizations' approach to 'helping' the Congo, from the Congo Reform Associations' work in the early 1900s to the photography created in support of ending wartime rape (Graham, 2014). These visual representations, while useful for initiating human rights activism, also tend to reify one simplistic image of the Congo.

The above sketch of the ways in which international actors engage with the Congo to produce certain narratives and images that are consumable by

Western populations, but not reflective of the complexity of culture and experiences of conflict, provides a glimpse into the fieldwork setting. This setting is clearly fraught with the politics of encounter and the imaginary—stereotypes and fears mixed with the international humanitarian community's desire to 'help' in the face of violence.

How did I conduct research in such a fraught space defined by assumptions, misperceptions, and misunderstandings? Imperfectly, to be sure, but guided by what I think of as the three Rs of ethical research: Reflexivity, re-presentation, and reciprocity. The underlying goal of my methodology and ethics was to challenge any assumptions I had that conformed to the savages–victims–saviours metaphor and to actively seek to complicate and nuance this picture, specifically through my research on legal consciousness. I did this by, first, engaging in reflexivity, meaning frequent critical reflections on my research questions, findings, positionality, and assumptions. My use of the 'savages–victims–saviours' metaphor and the 'saviour economic crisis' concept form the framework of my critical reflections.

Second, I also expose some of the politics of re-presentation that manifest in this context. By re-presentation, I am referring to how I write about people, places, and events. In this book, I actively try not to impose my view of the world on my findings. This is notable in Chapters 5 and 6, which are composed of a deeper exploration of particular harms and disputes. Notably, in Chapter 5, my goal is a deeper understanding of how the local population understands disputes and justice around statutory rape and early marriage. Rather than presenting local norms, beliefs, and practices as inherently wrong or problematic when they do not conform to international standards, I try to do justice to the ideas and stories that were shared with me, and thus hopefully re-present the nuances of people's thoughts and experiences. Similarly, in Chapter 6, I prioritize popular beliefs in witchcraft, rather than framing the analysis from a Western point of view that would hold that witchcraft does not exist.

Finally, in terms of reciprocity, perhaps one of the most difficult ideas to exact in my research setting, I have perhaps fallen short. However, I can offer that I have attempted to share my findings and analyses with some of the local actors who facilitated my research. I did this through a two-day workshop, which I held in 2019. I share some of the details of the event in Chapter 3, specifically around the difficulties of this type of reciprocity in a context where different participants may have different evaluations of what my research means for them and their social position. Thus, while I could by no means change the power dynamics of the setting that I entered into, I took steps to assess those dynamics and avoid blindly repeating or conforming to them.

Conducting research in that space as a white Westerner could not be divorced from the specificities of these recently constructed power dynamics. Thus, as noted early, my findings cannot be divorced from my methodology. By making my methods and reflections transparent throughout the analytical chapters, I hope that this book not only makes a contribution to the socio-legal scholarship but also to methodological scholarship on research in conflict-affected areas.

Chapter Organization

Chapter 2 starts by elaborating the conceptual and theoretical framework and developments of this book. It provides a more detailed and nuanced definition of legal consciousness and outlines its components to elucidate how they can be researched. Further, I develop the two main forms of contradictory legal consciousness, namely a *disconnect in harm naming* and *different logics of justice*, that emerged from my research. These are important building blocks in the construction of legality. I thus provide the argument that contradictory legal consciousness is linked to certain manifestations of *emergent hybrid legality*. In other words, how contradictory legal consciousness manifests will have a direct impact on the way that *emergent hybrid legality* manifests. This is not an argument of direct causation, as there are various factors that play a role, notably, as I discuss in Chapter 4, the local legal complex. However, there is a meaningful relationship between the two that has heretofore largely been ignored.

Chapter 3 provides a detailed account of my methodological approach and fieldwork. In highly politicized and internationalized contexts of transition, a nuanced discussion of methodology serves to enhance understanding of how knowledge is constructed amidst varying power dynamics, especially between the researcher and participants, interlocutors, and the community generally. The interpretive, feminist-informed methods I used in my study begin with the idea that methodology, analysis, and ethics are fundamentally intertwined. I critically reflect on my experience as an embodied researcher engaging in the power dynamics that already existed in my field site and how I navigated them. I further explore the strengths and weaknesses of working with researchers and the three Rs of ethical research: Reflexivity, re-presentation, and reciprocity.

Chapter 4 links contradictory consciousness and *emergent hybrid legality*. In the substantive chapters, 5 and 6, I dive more deeply into a few examples of harms and disputes, but in Chapter 4 I draw on my fieldwork to explore how local organizations shape popular legal consciousness through their daily activities. One important aspect of this is awareness raising, or *sensibilisation*, and efforts to educate the population about the laws and legal reforms. At the same time, local organizations are just as likely to try to dissuade people from turning to the legal system. How do we make sense of these seemingly opposing practices, and how might they play out in people's legal consciousness as they process this disconnect?

Chapters 5 and 6 provide examples of harms/disputes, where we can see the manifestation of contradictory consciousness and the production of *emergent hybrid legality*. Chapter 5 addresses disputes around early marriage and statutory rape, highlighting contradictory legal consciousness. The chapter outlines how the harms of early marriage and statutory rape are defined in the law as categorical, whereas the population largely views them as situational, reflecting the *disconnect in harm naming*. As a corollary, the state and the population understand justice for harms and disputes around these issues differently, with the state focusing on punishment and the population on more restorative measures, reflecting the *different logics of justice*. The combination of these two areas of legal consciousness shape *emergent hybrid legality* through the practices of the local legal complex as well as the population.

Chapter 6 explores the relationship between witchcraft accusations and *emergent hybrid legality*. Notably, in the case of witchcraft accusations, both types of contradictory legal consciousness—*disconnect in harm naming* and *different logics of justice*—shape the outcomes. The *disconnect in harm naming* comes from the tension between the state not recognizing witchcraft as a harm and the population experiencing it as a common and troubling harm for both individuals and the community at large. As a result of this interpretation of the harm, the population often prefers punishment as the justice response. By contrast, the state, which does not recognize acts of witchcraft, obviously does not punish them. The courts may, however, punish someone for making a witchcraft *accusation* that may be legally damaging to the other person. In this context, some people turn to mediation, but there are certain important limitations, such as the lack of punishment and fears on the part of mediators. Thus, in rare cases, people turn to popular justice, vigilantism. This chapter illustrates that *emergent hybrid legality* is not something to be romanticized, as it may include violent action, but it does capture the outcome of tensions that manifest in legal consciousness.

In Chapter 7, the conclusion, I return to the broader theme of ROL building, and liberal legalism, and provide a critical analysis of its role in transitioning contexts. I explore the foundations that link liberal legalism and the ROL and provide a brief assessment of how *emergent hybrid legality* can contribute to our understanding of the ROL in theory and practice.

Notes

1 13 April 2015.
2 *Motaris* are motorbike taxi drivers. They are the dominant means of local transportation alongside *bajajas*, auto rickshaws that were introduced in the early 2010s.
3 Chiefs.
4 Chieftaincy.
5 Wise person.
6 Public prosecutor's office.
7 Wikha Tshibanda (2019) identifies this practice as 'kupiana' and explains it as the marriage between a widow and her deceased husband's brother.
8 Chiefs.
9 Eg. (Falk Moore, 1972; Merry, 1988; Santos, 2006; von Benda-Beckmann, 1984. See also Mamdani, 1996).
10 This became the target of sustained critique about a decade ago. Carothers' (2006) edited volume and Stromseth et al.'s (2006) book engage with many of the problems associated with the ROL orthodoxy. However, the goals of democracy, development, and human rights remain part of the underlying assumptions about why it is necessary to build the ROL in transitioning contexts.

11 Merry (2006) uses the term 'vernacularization' to refer to the process by which international human rights are translated by a diverse set of actors in a way that allows local actors to reframe their grievances in the language of human rights. This can happen more generally with laws or aspects of the legal system.
12 See Felices-Luna (2012) for a critique of how 'corruption' is mobilized by the international community in contexts that they define as 'weak states', such as the DRC.
13 The 'legal complex'—judges and lawyers, legally trained civil society and professionals—attempts to advance liberal legalism through different channels, such as developing legal knowledge and making the courts more accessible to the general population (see Halliday et al., 2007). I use the term 'local legal complex' to refer specifically to elements of the legal complex who are Congolese nationals working directly with the population. In the context of legal pluralism, this can also include mediators and other civil society actors with some training in human rights, conflict resolution, and/or the law.
14 For example, MONUSCO's ROL Section, the EU's REJUSCO programme, Avocats Sans Frontier's PARJ-E programme, and the American Bar Association's Rule of Law Initiative (see also Lincoln, 2011).
15 This is my addition to the argument advanced by numerous scholars that ROL interventions are undertaken to build modern, liberal *states* (eg. Massoud, 2013, Park, 2010, Peterson, 2010).
16 International actors often use popular ROL indicators as a yardstick for measuring the ROL and how countries have progressed. Recently, a body of literature has begun to dissect and critique, from a different perspective, ROL and other governance indicators. Concepts have been poorly operationalized and relied on previously collected data that has been misused (Narduli et al., 2013). There has been a limited reflexivity around the theoretical approaches used by those relying on ROL indicators (Merry et al., 2015).

Bibliography

Autesserre, S. (2010). *The trouble with the Congo: Local violence and the failure of international peacebuilding* (Vol. 115). Cambridge University Press

Autesserre, S. (2012). Dangerous tales: Dominant narratives on the Congo and their unintended consequences. *African Affairs, 111*(443), 202–222.

Baaz, M., & Stern, M. (2010). *The complexity of violence: A critical analysis of sexual violence in the Democratic Republic of Congo (DRC)*. Sida: Nordiska Afrikainstitutet.

Benda-Beckmann, K. V., & Turner, B. (2018). Legal pluralism, social theory, and the state. *The Journal of Legal Pluralism and Unofficial Law, 50*(3), 255–274.

Björkdahl, A., & Gusic, I. (2016). Sites of friction: Governance, identity and space in Mostar. In A. Björkdahl, K. Höglund, G. Millar, J. van der Lijn, & W. Verkoren (Eds.), *Peacebuilding and friction* (pp. 98–116). Routledge.

Carlin, J. E., Howard, J., & Messinger, S. L. (1966). Civil justice and the poor: Issues for sociological research. *Law and Society Review*, 9–89.

Carothers, T. (2006). The rule of law revival. In T. Carothers (Ed.), *Promoting the rule of law abroad: In search of knowledge* (pp. 3–14). Carnegie Endowment for International Peace.

Carothers, T. (Ed.). (2010). *Promoting the rule of law abroad: In search of knowledge*. Brookings Institution Press.

Channell, W. (2006). Lessons not learned about legal reform. In T. Carothers (Ed.), *Promoting the rule of law abroad: In search of knowledge* (pp. 137–160). Carnegie Endowment for International Peace.

Davis, K., Kingsbury, B., & Merry, S. E. (2012). Introduction. In Davis, K., Fisher, A., Kingsbury, B., & Merry, S. E. (Eds.), *Governance by indicators: Global power through classification and rankings*. Oxford University Press.

de Sousa Santos, B. (2006). The heterogeneous state and legal pluralism in Mozambique. *Law & Society Review, 40*(1), 39–76.

Derks, M. (2012). *Improving security and justice through local/non-state actors: The challenges of donor support to local/nonstate security and justice providers.* Netherlands Institute of International Relations 'Clingendael.

D'Errico, N. C., Kalala, T., Nzigire, L. B., Maisha, F., & Malemo Kalisya, L. (2013). 'You say rape, I say hospitals. But whose voice is louder?' Health, aid and decision-making in the Democratic Republic of Congo. *Review of African Political Economy, 40*(135), 51–66.

Donais, T. (2013). Power politics and the rule of law in Post-Dayton Bosnia. *Studies in Social Justice,* 7(2), 189.

Dunn, H. (2020). Research in the land of savages, victims, and saviors. In G. Hoogensen, P. Weitsman & R. Matthew (Eds.), *Women's perspectives on human security: Violence, environment, and sustainability* (pp. 154–182). Ohio University Press.

Dunn, K. (2003). *Imagining the Congo: The international relations of identity.* Palgrave Macmillan.

Engel, D., & Engel, J. S. (2010). Tort, custom, and karma. In *Tort, custom, and karma.* Stanford University Press.

Felices-Luna, M. (2012). Justice in the Democratic Republic of Congo: Practicing corruption, practicing resistance? *Critical Criminology, 20*(2), 197–209.

Freedman, J. (2016). *Gender, violence and politics in the Democratic Republic of Congo.* Routledge.

Fukuyama, F. (2010). Transitions to the rule of law. *Journal of Democracy, 21*(1), 33–44.

Galanter, M., & Trubek, D. M. (1974). Scholars in self-estrangement: Some reflections on the crisis in law and development studies in the United States. *Wisconsin Law Review, 1062.*

Godoy, A. S. (2006). *Popular injustice: Violence, community, and law in Latin America.* Stanford University Press.

Golub, S. (2006). The legal empowerment alternative. In T. Carothers (Ed.), *Promoting the rule of law abroad: In search of knowledge* (pp. 161–187). Carnegie Endowment for International Peace.

Graham, A. (2014). One hundred years of suffering? "Humanitarian crisis photography" and self-representation in the Democratic Republic of the Congo. *Social Dynamics, 40*(1), 140–163.

Hadfield, G. K., & Weingast, B. R. (2014). Microfoundations of the rule of law. *Annual Review of Political Science, 17,* 21–42.

Haggard, S., & Tiede, L. (2014). The rule of law in post-conflict settings: The empirical record. *International Studies Quarterly, 58*(2), 405–417.

Halliday, T., Karpik, L., & Feeley, M. (Eds.), (2007). The legal complex in struggles for political liberalism. In *Fighting for political freedom: Comparative studies of the legal complex and political liberalism* (p. 1). Hart Publishing.

Harper, E. (Ed.). (2011). *Working with customary justice systems: Post-conflict and fragile states.* International Development Law Organization.

Hellmüller, S. A. (2016). Connections for peace: Frictions in peacebuilding encounters in Ituri, Democratic Republic of Congo. In A. Björkdahl, K. Höglund, G. Millar, J. van der Lijn, & W. Verkoren (Eds.), *Peacebuilding and friction* (pp. 172–187). Routledge.

Henry, N. (2014). The fixation on wartime rape: Feminist critique and international criminal law. *Social & Legal Studies, 23,* 93–111.

Hertogh, M. (2016). Your rule of law is not mine: Rethinking empirical approaches to EU rule of law promotion. *Asia Europe Journal, 14*(1), 43–59.

Hilhorst, D., & Douma, N. (2018). Beyond the hype? The response to sexual violence in the Democratic Republic of the Congo in 2011 and 2014. *Disasters, 42,* S79–S98.

Hunt, A. (1985). The ideology of law: Advances and problems in recent applications of the concept of ideology to the analysis of law. *Law & Society Review, 19*, 11.
Jean-Bouchard, É. (2014). The (in) visible subject: Women's normative strategies in eastern Congo. *The Journal of Legal Pluralism and Unofficial Law, 46*(3), 357–373.
Kapur, R. (2002). The tragedy of victimization rhetoric: Resurrecting the "native" subject in international/post-colonial feminist legal politics. *Harvard Human Rights Journal, 15*(1), 1–37.
Kelsall, M. S., & Stepakoff, S. (2007). 'When we wanted to talk about rape': Silencing sexual violence at the Special Court for Sierra Leone. *The International Journal of Transitional Justice, 1*(3), 355–374.
Kirby, P. (2015). Ending sexual violence in conflict: The preventing sexual violence initiative and its critics. *International Affairs, 91*(3), 457–472.
Kleinfeld, R. (2006). Competing definitions of the rule of law. In T. Carothers (Ed.), *Promoting the rule of law abroad: In search of knowledge* (pp. 31–74). Carnegie Endowment for International Peace.
Koddenbrock, K. (2012). Recipes for intervention: Western policy papers imagine the Congo. *International Peacekeeping, 19*(5), 549–564.
Koomen, J. (2013). "Without these women, the tribunal cannot do anything": The politics of witness testimony on sexual violence at the international criminal tribunal for Rwanda. *Signs: Journal of Women in Culture and Society, 38*(2), 253–277.
Lake, M. (2014a). *Building the rule of law in fragile states: The role of external actors in shaping institutional responses to mass violence in the Democratic Republic of Congo and South Africa* (unpublished doctoral dissertation). University of Washington.
Lake, M. (2014b). Organizing hypocrisy: Providing legal accountability for human rights violations in areas of limited statehood. *International Studies Quarterly, 58*(3), 515–526.
Lake, M. (2018). *Strong NGOs and weak states: Pursuing gender justice in the Democratic Republic of Congo and South Africa*. Cambridge University Press.
Lake, M., Muthaka, I., & Walker, G. (2016). Gendering justice in humanitarian spaces: Opportunity and (Dis) empowerment through gender-based legal development outreach in the Eastern Democratic Republic of Congo. *Law & Society Review, 50*(3), 539–574.
Lemarchand, R. (2008). *The dynamics of violence in Central Africa*. University of Pennsylvania.
Mamdani, M. (1996). *Citizen and subject*. Princeton University Press.
Massoud, M. F. (2013). *Law's fragile state: Colonial, authoritarian, and humanitarian legacies in Sudan*. Cambridge University Press.
Merry, S. E. (1988). Legal pluralism. *Law & Society Review, 22*, 869.
Merry, S. E. (1990). *Getting justice and getting even: Legal consciousness among working-class Americans*. University of Chicago Press.
Merry, S. E. (2009). *Human rights and gender violence: Translating international law into local justice*. University of Chicago Press.
Mertens, C., & Myrttinen, H. (2019). 'A real woman waits'—heteronormative respectability, neo-liberal betterment and echoes of coloniality in SGBV programming in Eastern DR Congo. *Journal of Intervention and Statebuilding, 13*(4), 418–439.
Mobekk, E. (2009). Security sector reform and the UN mission in the Democratic Republic of Congo: Protecting civilians in the east. *International Peacekeeping, 16*(2), 273–286.
Moore, S. F. (1972). Law and social change: The semi-autonomous social field as an appropriate subject of study. *Law & Society Review*, 7, 719.
Mutua, M. (2001). Savages, victims, and saviors: The metaphor of human rights. *Harvard International Law Journal, 42*, 201.

Narduli, P. F., Peyton, B., & Bajjalieh, J. (2013). Conceptualizing and measuring rule of law constructs, 1850–2010. *Journal of Law and Courts*, *1*(1), 139–192.

Park, A. S. (2010). Peacebuilding, the rule of law and the problem of culture: Assimilation, multiculturalism, deployment. *Journal of Intervention and Statebuilding*, *4*(4), 413–432.

Peterson, J. H. (2010). 'Rule of Law' initiatives and the liberal peace: The impact of politicized reform in post-conflict states. *Disasters*, *34*(s1), S15–S39.

Prunier, G. (2009a). *Africa's world war: Congo, the Rwandan genocide and the making of a continental catastrophe*. Oxford University Press.

Prunier, G. (2009b). *From genocide to continental war: The 'Congolese' conflict and the crisis of contemporary Africa*. Hurst & Co.

Rajkovic, N. M. (2012). 'Global law' and governmentality: Reconceptualizing the 'rule of law' as rule 'through' law. *European Journal of International Relations*, *18*(1), 29–52.

Raz, J. (2015). The rule of law and its virtue. In R. Cunningham (Ed.), *Liberty and the rule of law* (pp. 3–21). Texas A&M University Press.

Silbey, S. (2008). Legal consciousness. In S. Silbey, P. Cane, & J. Conaghan (Eds.), *New Oxford companion to law*. Oxford University Press.

Stearns, J. (2011). *Dancing in the glory of monsters: The collapse of the Congo and the great war of Africa*. Public Affairs.

Stromseth, J. (2008). Post-conflict rule of law building: The need for a multi-layered, synergistic approach. *William & Mary Law Review*, *49*, 1443.

Stromseth, J., Wippman, D., & Brooks, R. (2006). *Can might make rights? Building the rule of law after military interventions*. Cambridge University Press.

Suarez, C. (2017). 'Living between two lions': Civilian protection strategies during armed violence in the Eastern Democratic Republic of the Congo. *Journal of Peacebuilding & Development*, *12*(3), 54–67.

Tsing, A. L. (2005). *Friction: An ethnography of global connection*. Princeton University Press.

United Nations. (2010, 27 April). Tackling sexual violence must include prevention, ending impunity—UN Official | | UN News. *United Nations*. https://news.un.org/en/story/2010/04/336662.

United Nations. (n.d.). *What is the rule of law—United Nations and the rule of law*. United Nations. www.un.org/ruleoflaw/what-is-the-rule-of-law/

United Nations Development Programme. (2011). *Strengthening the rule of law in crisis-affected and fragile situations*. United Nations Development Programme, Bureau for Crisis Prevention and Recovery. www.undp.org/sites/g/files/zskgke326/files/publications/UNDP_CPR_ROLGlobal ProgrammePhase2August2014.pdf

Urueña, R., Merry, S. E., Davis, K. E., & Kingsbury, B. (2015). Indicators and the law. *The Quiet Power of Indicators: Measuring Governance, Corruption, and Rule of Law, 75*.

von Benda-Beckmann, F. (1984). Law out of context: A comment on the creation of traditional law discussion. *Journal of African Law*, *28*(1–2), 28–33.

Zurn, M., Nollkaemper, A., & Peerenboom, R. (Eds.). (2012). *Rule of law dynamics: In an era of international and transnational governance*. Cambridge University Press.

Chapter 2

Legal Consciousness and the Construction of *Emergent Hybrid Legality*

Given the extensive international and domestic focus on prosecuting SGBV in the eastern DRC, and raising popular awareness about legal developments, one might expect to see a broad shift to popular use of the state legal system. We might anticipate that people's awareness and trust in the state legal system will rise as they see the legal system functioning to address these cases. To a certain extent, that has indeed occurred, and people do sometimes turn to the legal system in a variety of select cases and situations (eg. Rubbers & Gallez, 2012; Lake, 2018). However, the ways in which people engage with the state legal system do not follow a singular pattern, meaning there is not a general, uniform turn to increased usage of the legal system as a result of increased awareness. Instead, popular engagement with the state legal system has developed in unexpected ways, shaped not only by the nature of intervention but also by popular beliefs and practices and the diverse terrain of legality. The developing landscape of legality may fall short of the expectations of liberal legalism, but it certainly is not beyond liberal legalism's influence through ROL building practices. So, how can we understand the developments of this new terrain of legality that is being constructed?

Scholarly efforts to understand popular engagements with legal systems, in conflict-affected contexts and beyond, frequently turn to the concept of legal consciousness. Legal consciousness refers to how people experience, understand, and act in relation to the state legal system (Chua & Engel, 2019). Studies of legal consciousness help illuminate people's common sense or everyday understandings of the law. Thus, this concept is foundational to exploring the context of legality in Uvira, DRC, as it reflects how and why people engage with the law. Importantly, I expand the concept of legal consciousness to include popular engagements with other realms of 'law', such as informal and custom-based practices. In contexts of legal pluralism where there are multiple different sources of law and justice in a single social field (Merry, 1988), people's legal consciousness manifests not only in how they make sense of the state legal system but also how they engage with the variety of other legal-justice institutions, systems, and practices that exist. I use the term 'legal-justice' to denote the inclusion of the breadth of practices and institutions available in

DOI: 10.4324/9781003289715-2

legally plural contexts. The variety of legal-justice systems and practices are explored in more detail in the next chapter, but include dispute resolution via traditional and administrative chiefs, local organizations, wise elders, and family members to name a few. Further, I note here that my research specifically explores everyday harms and disputes for which some form of justice is sought but not always through formal, state channels, making 'legal-justice' an appropriate covering term.

In this chapter, I elaborate the connection between legal consciousness and the terrain of legality that is constructed as popular legal consciousness integrates differing norms, beliefs, and practices of legal-justice that are highlighted in periods of legal flux, such as the conflict-affected contexts and the associated legal reforms and interventions. Legal consciousness is important because it lends insights into how and why people engage with different mechanisms of legal pluralism. Often, legal consciousness is internally contradictory (Ewick & Silbey, 1998), which, I argue, is essential to understanding the complex foundations of the legal-justice outcomes that emerge. I elaborate on different dimensions of legal consciousness—knowledge, perceptions, judgements, worldviews, and ideology—to provide the foundations for understanding the underlying forces of contradictory legal consciousness. From my research in Uvira, I have constructed two major themes of contradictory legal consciousness: *A disconnect in harm naming* and *different logics of justice*. I explain these concepts in this chapter and employ them as part of my analysis in the substantive chapters that follow.

I explore legal consciousness to prioritize the local population's experiences and understandings of the phenomenon of legal reform, rather than employing the conventional top-down analysis of how ROL interventions succeed or fail. Exploring legal consciousness and its contradictions, in turn, lends insights into the terrain of legality, which I label *emergent hybrid legality*. It has become hybridized through legal encounters and their effects on legal consciousness. *Emergent hybrid legality* is open to continuous legal flux but reflects a space of possibility for achieving contextually relevant approaches and outcomes to everyday harms and disputes in the eastern DRC and beyond. Thus, this chapter provides the conceptual and theoretical foundations for Chapters 4, 5, and 6, which explore these concepts in relation to people's experiences of harm and disputes.

Legal Consciousness: Definitions and the Particulars

Legal consciousness is the concept that reflects people's everyday engagements, understandings, and practices with the law and, in my research, other areas of legal-justice. As legal-justice covers the diverse array of legal and alternative justice practices, institutions, and systems, the term reflects the individual components of legal pluralism, recognizing these are already hybrids or palimpsests, given the history of encounters (Santos, 2006). In other words, post-conflict legal reforms and the broader ROL building enterprise do not represent the first encounter with Western or internationalized legal ideology. In much of Africa, including Congo, these encounters extend back to at least the colonial period, when 'customary' justice or law was moulded to fit the needs of the colonizers; through this process, the role of 'customary' chiefs was formalized and became part of the administration (Dembour, 2000; Mamdani, 1996). This was the era when the power of local customary chiefs grew through their partnerships with the colonial administration, and administrative chiefs played a key role in regulating the activities of African populations (Mamdani, 1996). In Congo, the importance of both customary and administrative chiefs is still clear, but in some ways their roles have blurred and depend on context. For example, conflict resolution is not a part of administrative chiefs' official duties, yet people turn to them in a variety of circumstances. This is likely, at least in part, a colonial relic because, as Dembour (2000) highlights, Belgians serving as judges in some of the colonial courts were often officers, administrators, or functionaries, some of whom were swiftly appointed as magistrates. In other words, Belgian judges, who presided over 'native' cases, were often not formally trained legal experts. Meanwhile, the role of customary chiefs in legal-justice is still prevalent but has to a certain extent been supplanted by the vast array of NGOs doing dispute resolution. As I discuss in Chapter 4, all of these roles are fluid and shift in response to local changes in legal consciousness.

Thus, in my exploration of legal consciousness, I take seriously the role of a variety of justice actors, institutions, and mechanisms, rather than focusing solely on the state legal system. This is an important distinction to make, as legal consciousness scholars tend to emphasize the hegemony of the law (see Silbey, 2005) or the idea that 'the law is all over' (Sarat, 1990), but as Hertogh (2018) points out, this assumes the position of state law as the most salient in people's everyday lives and tends to ignore other forms of non-state law. Some studies have gone beyond this tendency (eg. Engel & Engel, 2010; Holzer, 2013; McConnachie, 2014), but a focus on the formal legal system is still the norm in research on legal consciousness. Of course, state law and the legal system remain central to my analysis as I am looking at legal encounters and ROL building, but it is also essential to take seriously the broader terrain of legality in which people are enmeshed.

In order to employ legal consciousness as a concept that applies to legal-justice and not just state law, I break down the concept into components of subjectivity[1], enabling my empirical analysis of why and how people engage with legal-justice and to elucidate the complex effects of legal reform on popular engagements with the legal system. I explore five components—knowledge, perceptions, judgements, ideology, and worldview. Drawing on constituent parts allows us to conceptualize the complexity of legal consciousness by outlining the roots of *contradictory* legal consciousness. The underlying components are the bedrock of my analysis of contradictory legal consciousness—*disconnect in harm naming* and *different logics of justice*—but I will not always refer to these roots in my analyses through the remainder of the chapters, which is why I elucidate their meaning here. Of course, the different aspects are not wholly independent of one another, which, as I will highlight in my analysis, is partly the point. Indeed, one may think of them as constituent parts of a web, where impact in one area of legal consciousness is surely to be felt in some way throughout the rest of the web. Thus, using component parts provides some tangible elements to engage with when exploring an otherwise abstract and complex concept.

The components of subjectivity that I outline are similar to the three elements of subjectivity outlined by Chua and Engel (2019)—worldview, perception, and decision—but with some unique distinctions in order to highlight areas of contradiction within an individual's legal consciousness, as well as socially. The latter is important to consider since legal consciousness is a social phenomenon, even if it is largely explored at the individual level. Legal consciousness is constructed through social interactions, and, in turn, it shapes the terrain of legality through the population's actions, which become routinized into practices and institutions. These aspects of subjectivity manifest in what people say and do and the stories they tell.

The five different areas of subjectivity encompass major individual and social-level aspects of legal consciousness. The individual level shapes the societal level through social relations just as the social level influences individual thought and action in a co-constitutive interaction that is not wholly stable but rather responsive to experience and social life. Throughout my analysis, I frequently consider both experience and action; I see these components as both shaping legal consciousness and being shaped by legal consciousness, respectively. However, I see them as distinct from the elements of subjectivity that make up legal consciousness, even if they play an important role in shaping it. Below I elaborate on the five elements of subjectivity that make up legal consciousness as the scaffolding for my conceptualization of the *disconnect in harm naming*, *different logics of justice*, and *emergent hybrid legality*.

Individual-Level Factors

I label knowledge, perceptions, and judgements 'individual-level' factors. This is partly for methodological reasons; these aspects are usually shared through individual interviews to glean insights into an individual's understandings of legal-justice. At the same time, while articulated at the individual level, they are also relational or social phenomena. Chua and Engel (2019) raise this point in their overview of the legal consciousness scholarship. They state that, "it is often impossible to disentangle the consciousness of any one person from those of her family members, fellow villagers, or other intimate associates" (Chua & Engel, 2019, p. 345). These relational considerations often shape individual-level factors and are clearly a component of people's worldviews and ideological influences. Indeed, much of what shapes legal consciousness at the individual level are the stories that circulate between neighbours, family members, church attendees, and others about the law and other justice practices. Yet, even if that is so, they are expressed in an individual's words and actions. Thus, I continue to consider these as individual-level factors, often shaped by relationships with others, worldview, and ideology.

I separate knowledge, perceptions, and judgements in contrast to Chua and Engel's single category 'perception'. In part, this draws on Gallagher's (2006) research that shows how knowledge and perceptions, as components of legal consciousness, can move in different directions, meaning as knowledge of the law and legal system increase, perceptions may become more negative. Gallagher's (2006) work in conceptualizing legal consciousness in China is important for the first two components of legal consciousness: Knowledge and perceptions. She points out that scholars have often conflated legal knowledge/awareness and court usage with legal consciousness. Gallagher (2006) clarifies that legal consciousness is reflected in two different areas that can shift in opposite directions. The first is indeed knowledge of the law, which is reflected in individual feelings of competency vis-à-vis the law. The second is perceptions/evaluations of how the legal system works; is it fair and effective? When the former rises and the latter diminishes, Gallagher (2006) conceptualizes that phenomenon as *informed disenchantment*, a concept that easily travels to the eastern DRC and reflects one area of contradictory consciousness, although not the area of focus of this book. While Gallagher (2006) conceptualizes perception and evaluation together in her analysis, I disaggregate these concepts into perceptions and *judgements*, as these may also develop in contradictory ways within individuals and society, and they represent different elements of subjectivity.

Thus, first, *knowledge* means an accurate understanding of the state laws and how the system works and an accurate understanding of the various legal-justice options available and their different functioning logics. I define knowledge in this way to distinguish it from the tacit, practical, implicit, or taken-for-granted knowledge that defines legal consciousness more broadly. It is identifiable in statements about legal-justice that reflect how things are *supposed* to work. For example, in Uvira, knowledge would be reflected in the understanding that a land title gives you legal right to your land, the legal age of marriage is 18, and NGO-run mediation offices cannot sentence people to prison. These are examples of knowledge of how things are *supposed* to work, or the law in the books and legal procedures.

Second, *perceptions* reflect what people *believe they know* about the functioning of legal-justice. This element is about what people perceive about legal-justice, which may or may not accurately reflect the written law or legal procedures. An example may be the perception that the law punishes people, while *chefs* reconcile people. This may be more or less true in practice; however, in reality, some court cases are dismissed and in other cases payment of fines may be similar to compensation required by *chefs* in a mediation process. The point of creating a distinction between knowledge and perceptions is *not* to suggest that knowledge reflects facts, while perceptions reflect *mis*perceptions of legal-justice. Instead, this distinction provides the nuance to think through the difference between people's knowledge of law in the books and ideas and understandings that circulate about law in practice. This may be a thornier distinction in the realm of mediation and other justice sources given that they tend not to be written, so there is no law on the book *per se*. However, there can be distinctions between what, for example, *chefs* or mediators say they do and what people perceive them to do.

Third, *judgements* are the value-laden assessments of the legal-justice. In other words, it refers to people's assessments about the rightness, goodness, fairness, and worth of the different legal-justice options. For example, one might judge that the state legal system is 'unfair' because of the *perception* that it favours the wealthy, or 'good' because of the *perception* that it treats people equally. Other socio-legal scholarship on *judgements* highlights the role of fairness in how people make sense of the legal system. For example, one may view the process to be fair even when they do not view the outcome as fair (Ewick & Silbey, 1998). These types of judgements can apply to all legal-justice systems and practices.

To add one more layer of nuance to these individual-level dimensions, when taken together, *perceptions* and *judgements* can be conceptualized as *wisdom*. In contrast to *knowledge*, which is based on how things *should* technically work, *wisdom* encompasses the more *practical knowledge* of how things do work in practice and associated assessments. I include *wisdom* to counter the idea that people lack understanding of legal-justice when their legal consciousness reflects a more-practical-than-technical understanding of these systems. For some people, *wisdom* may be the more prominent aspect of subjectivity, but that far from suggests a lack of understanding.

Social-Level Factors

While the aforementioned aspects of subjectivity lend insight into legal consciousness, they do not explicitly or sufficiently address the social side of legal consciousness. *Worldview* and *ideology* are two further aspects of subjectivity that help us understand legal consciousness. These represent important elements of the social context that are influential in how people understand the world around them, including legal-justice. They include the frames and schemas people use to make sense of individual experiences and information. Studying legal consciousness cannot simply focus on individual-level components, but the nexus between these and socio-cultural constructs that shape common sense interpretations and engagements with legal-justice. Thus, disaggregating aspects of the social-level from individual-level components helps clarify the unique and unexpected ways that they can be in conflict, even as they constantly impact each other. The social and individual levels are mutually constitutive, but they are not static. Separating them helps identify directions and areas of shifting subjectivity and social change. I thus draw on two fairly broad, yet powerful, social-level concepts that shape how people interpret and make sense of the law and legal pluralism—*worldview* and *ideology*.

Worldview is crucial to understanding legal consciousness and is entangled with cultural context. It refers to the way people define and interpret the world around them; it is the lens through which they see the world. Methodologically, this makes worldview accessible not only through interviews with individuals, but through observations and group interviews in order to develop an understanding of the cultural milieu. Furthermore, worldview also encompasses how individuals then situate themselves within that socio-cultural setting. Worldview shapes people's understanding of their place in the social world and thus influences relationality—how they see themselves situated in relation to others (Chua & Engel, 2019). At the same time, worldview also shapes their understanding of the world more broadly. Building on the brief example provided previously, why would someone judge reconciliation to be 'good' and punishment to be 'bad'? These sorts of judgements are largely, although not solely, shaped by worldview and reflect what has been socially constructed as normal and, for example, ethical or appropriate. Thus, locales, such as Uvira, with a long-standing emphasis on community and its importance in everyday life might tend to prioritize reconciliation, as they understand it to promote harmony in the community. This is not to suggest that worldviews are monolithic, but there is some stability and shared understandings that exist in large sections of the population, such that they are more or less taken for granted.

This component of subjectivity provides important insights into understanding popular approaches to justice for harms and disputes that may actually be defined in the state law but are not predominantly framed as legal matter by the local population, such as early marriage, which has been commonly accepted and practiced by teenage girls and their families. Additionally, it lends insight into the contrasting phenomenon of harms that are not defined in law but to which the population would like to see an official (and punitive) response, such as witchcraft. Analysing these disconnects illuminates previously unacknowledged accounts of the perceived localized failures of the legal reforms advanced by ROL projects. In contrast to simply blaming the local culture, legal consciousness, including worldviews, allows one to explore the complexities and contradictions of these perceived failures in a more nuanced way.

It is worth briefly mentioning the further relevance of worldview when exploring legal consciousness in the context of post-conflict internationalized legal reforms, or ROL building. We can see the importance of worldview, and its roots in culture, to socio-legal scholarship in the analysis of legal 'fit' and 'transfers'. The scholarship on legal 'fit' and 'transfers' suggests that the laws and the legal system should 'fit' with domestic cultural practices and worldviews (eg. Holterhus, 2018; Nelken, 2003). This point is explored in some of the socio-legal studies literature that takes into consideration the possibilities of transferring laws or legal institutions from one context to another; post-conflict ROL building is one specific area (eg. Grant, 2021). The risk in these instances is that if the laws and legal system do not fit with popular understandings of the world, then people will not follow them or will ignore them; thus, *worldview* and culture need to be considered. At the same time, counter-arguments have been made that laws should be forward-looking, not simply adhere to the cultural status quo. This has been especially noted in the realm of gender justice, where the post-conflict context might be seen as a window of opportunity to revisit and challenge inequalities, such as those based on gender (Reilly, 2009). In other words, some would argue that it is sometimes better to implement laws that do not fit with the domestic culture but provide guidance for positive cultural change, such as around gender equality. But, again, this may create a situation where people ignore or subvert the written law, creating a sense that the law is not for them.

For the aspect of ideology, I am specifically interested in liberal legal ideology, which, as I outlined in the Introduction, is very much linked with the ROL concept and practice. As Hunt (1985) argues, I see ideology "as a constituent of the unconscious in which social relations are lived" (p. 16). Worldviews tap into the local population's socio-cultural realm, while liberal legal ideology reflects the beliefs and practices associated with the ROL interventions and the internationally influenced legal reforms. I argue that liberal legal ideology is being advanced, both explicitly and implicitly, in the eastern DRC through legal reforms and ROL building projects that include components aimed at reshaping socio-legal relations, or how people understand their relationships to each other in legalistic terms. Here, liberal legal ideology is seen in the taken-for-granted assumptions of reformers that normalize and prioritize a particular way of 'doing law'. However, as I will make clear in the following chapters, reformers are trying to recast the population's legal consciousness in line with liberal legalism through their awareness-raising activities.

Following Hunter (2016), I understand liberal legalism to refer to specific understandings of the individual and the law based in classical liberalism, combined with the norms and institutions associated with the legal systems of, typically Western, liberal states. Beyond that, as a component of legal consciousness, I am interested in how interveners assume these understanding but also try to normalize them for the broader population. Expanding on the meaning of liberal legalism, it, first, includes the assumption that the individual is the fundamental unit of society, existing prior to social organization, and that the individual is rational[2] and self-interested (Scales, 2006). Second, "Liberal legalism posits law as an essentially benign, neutral and autonomous institution" (Hunter, 2016, p. 19). The liberal legal subject is essentially stripped of all differentiated and embodied characteristics and exists simply as a decontextualized, rational, autonomous entity (Grear, 2011). Thus, formal equality—equality before the law—is often viewed as the way to promote substantive equality, such as gender equality, an idea that has been persistently critiqued and supported (Phillips, 2001). Regardless of where one falls on this debate, the point I want to make here is that the underlying assumptions about the individual are not universally held, at times bringing them into tension with worldviews.

Third, and relatedly, liberal legalism is the legal ideology of most Western states and the general source of globalized legal norms (Engel & Engel, 2010). In recent decades, international and domestic actors have sought to transplant these legal systems, which have come to be associated with democracy and development. This practice reflects the pervasiveness of liberal ideology in internationally funded ROL building projects, which, as others have argued, are deeply tied to a globalizing liberal project (Engel & Engel, 2010). Liberal legal ideology is often linked with certain ROL precepts, including that law be general, public, prospective, coherent, clear, stable, and practicable (Fuller, 1964). The precepts have come to define Western-style legal systems. Further, "liberal legalism . . . includes some commitment to rule of law practices and institutions, individual rights, free markets, and democratic government. . . . Liberal legal regimes provide a universal discourse that defines obligations, relationships and actors" (Engel & Engel, 2010, p.). In sum, liberal legalism is the legal ideology that interveners and their domestic partners seek to advance through post-conflict legal reforms. This is often disconnected from local worldviews and lived experiences but also becomes integrated into legal consciousness.

Returning to the importance of studying legal consciousness, what can it tell us about legality? Outlining the different aspects of subjectivity that make up legal consciousness provides the scaffolding for elucidating contradictory legal consciousness and the production of *emergent hybrid legality*. Here, through engagement with the concepts of *friction* and *hybridity*, I move away from Western, top-down interpretations of legality to theorise the outcome in transitioning contexts: *Emergent hybrid legality*. This form of legality emerges from contradictory legal consciousness.

Manifestations of Contradictory Legal Consciousness

Building on the above conceptualization of legal consciousness, there are two main themes of contradictory consciousness that I explore in this book. The first is what I call a *disconnect in harm naming* and the second I label *different logics of justice*. The key to understanding these themes is recognizing that they are not meant to suggest a hard binary between two opposing elements of legal consciousness. Rather, they reflect complex interactions between different elements of legal consciousness that do not suggest one simple, uniform, coherent understanding of legal-justice. Instead, individuals and their social realms are constantly engaging in multiple understandings of legal-justice and thus enacting different forms of legality. Indeed, the concept *emergent hybrid legality* recognizes that legality is heterogenous in both origin and outcome, meaning, not only is there a mixing of practices but also of the ideas and beliefs that undergird them. Before elaborating on the concept *emergent hybrid legality*, I first provide an overview of the two main themes of contradictory legal consciousness.

First, the *disconnect in harm naming* is characterised by a situation where the state law defines an act as a harm (ie. a crime), but the population does not experience it as such. The crime does not map onto their lived realities, specifically in terms of beliefs and practices tied to worldviews. The exact opposite may also be true of a *disconnect in harm naming*, where the population understands a particular act as a harm, but the state does not define it as such. I develop this concept by building on the feminist transitional justice scholarship that recognizes a hierarchy of harms and that women's experiences of gendered violence during war do not always map onto the dominant transitional justice understandings of harm, namely the focus on sexual violence (Buss, 2009; Henry, 2014; Kirby, 2015; Ni Aoláin, 2009). These dynamics have played out in eastern DRC, with a very visible externally defined hierarchy of harms with rape and wartime sexual violence at the top (Dunn, 2020). But, the problem of legal definitions of 'harms' is not limited to gendered harms, nor to the hierarchical positioning of 'harms' by foreign actors in the realm of transitional justice, but also in the realm of *everyday* harms and legal-justice.

Part of the problem with hierarchies of harm is that harm may be understood in a top-down or decontextualized way, with outsiders placing value on different types of harms than those experiencing them might. In other words, different groups may interpret and prioritize harms differently. But, perhaps even more fundamental is the question of who gets to name the harms to begin with. Ni Aoláin et al. (2011) state,

> One firm conclusion for us as we reflect on the density of the relationship between gender and war is that extensive empirical work is needed to measure more accurately women's experiences of conflict violence and to measure the gap between existing legal categories and what women "name" as harms experienced by them in conflict and post-conflict situations.
> (p. 48)

The question of who defines, not just what a harm is but also what is *not* a harm, is crucial and relevant beyond wartime considerations. Naming is a process of first identifying then labelling or categorizing. Harm naming is thus a question of who defines a harm and then what label it is given. State law and local populations have differing ideas about this, but they do not exist wholly independent of each other. Thus, local understandings of harm shift over time through processes of contradictory consciousness, integrating different understandings in unique and sometimes unexpected ways, while, at times, also maintaining stark differences in definitions. As noted earlier, I am not focusing on the harms associated with transitional justice practices but rather 'everyday' or 'ordinary' harms. This decision reflects a first step in listening to those who were part of my research project to hear the problems they identified as harms[3].

The *disconnect in harm naming* reflects a theme in legal consciousness as people process different ideas about what constitutes harm, ideas from their family and local community and those that are defined in state law, often with international influence, and form a part of broader efforts at *sensibilisation* about the formal legal system. I understand this area of *friction*—"the awkward, unequal, unstable, and creative qualities of interconnection across difference" (Tsing, 2005, p. 4)—not as oppositional or irreconcilable but as disconnected; they do not quite relate in an expected or consistent way, leading to unexpected legal-justice outcomes. The reality of contradictory consciousness is that differing ideas and understandings of harm are incorporated into legal consciousness. This situation creates what Tsing (2005) calls 'emergent cultural forms'—that do not solely reflect the tenets of liberal legalism, nor the relevant aspects of local worldviews.

Disconnects in harm naming occur around a variety of issues but are particularly salient around women's rights, given the recent history of international focus on SGBV in the region. An example of the theme of *disconnect in harm naming* is the gap between the legal definition and popular understandings of early marriage. The DRC has updated its laws to align with international standards and has set the legal age for marriage at 18 years old. Thus, marriage before that age is categorically defined as a harm, illegal. However, in practice, many people, especially girls, get married before that age. While the local population sometimes understands early marriage to be a harm, for example if the family views the girl as *too* young, this understanding is flexible and situational. Thus, a *disconnect in harm naming* is a frequent aspect of everyday life.

The second theme of contradictory legal consciousness is *different logics of justice*, which reflects a situation where different ideas about justice manifest in people's legal consciousness, influencing how they understand and engage with their justice options. Exploring different justice options is not a new idea in research on legal pluralism, but my approach is also distinct. The *different logics of justice* theme, as a form of contradictory consciousness, is about how people understand and make sense of the different justice options available to them; this incorporates the five elements of legal consciousness—knowledge, perceptions, judgements, worldviews, and ideology. By contrast, some legal pluralism scholarship understands people to prefer customary justice (eg. Isser 2011) or legal-justice, for different reasons, or to focus on strategic forum shopping (see Benda-Beckmann & Turner, 2018). While each of these lends insight into how and why people pursue different justice options, understanding how their consciousness is shaped through various sources can add nuance to these ideas. Specifically, it helps clarify puzzles, such as why people might think that laws are good but not want to pursue legal remedies. Or, why mediators cite the law but avoid recommending legal options to disputants. Or, why people turn to the courts even when they perceive corruption.

The *different logics of justice* theme of contradictory legal consciousness builds on Engel & Engel's (2010) understanding that globalization interacts with more localized justice norms and procedures, which, I would argue, reflects an example of Tsing's (2005) concept *friction*. In their work in Thailand, Engel and Engel (2010) consider how globalized flows of information provoke the local population to cultivate new ideas and questions about justice and what it means to achieve it. These flows of information, in the context of eastern DRC, often come through *sensibilisation* campaigns meant to raise popular awareness of the state approach to legal-justice and shape people's legal consciousness to normalize these approaches. Yet, the main result is *different logics of justice*, which means the population engages with varied ideas about justice, but legal understandings do not replace other understandings. This creates a complex set of options, evaluations, and preferences for people to work through as they seek to determine what justice looks like for particular harms. As some scholars have noted, legal consciousness is about taken-for-granted common-sense understandings (eg. Merry, 1990), but what is taken for granted can be in flux or challenged by different ideas, or the increased permeation of particular ideas, which is what my research captures with the two themes of contradictory consciousness.

I thus explore how people engage with various justice ideas and practices. Specifically, I consider the friction between *different logics of justice* associated with liberal legalism—such as scientific rationality, individual guilt, and punishment—and those associated with localized, long-standing ideas and practices—often based on local worldviews, which tend to emphasize reconciliation, non-scientific forms of rationality, and may understand both guilt and victimhood as not solely individual. *Different logics of justice*, as it manifests in Uvira, is often reflected in popular knowledge of the options for more restorative and more retributive forms of justice for everyday harms. Generally, people see the legal system as more punitive and other approaches as more restorative, and preferred in most cases. However, in some instances, the lack of punishment through formal legal channels is contradictory to the moral understandings of the population. Specifically, harms of witchcraft and repeat offenders are deemed offensive and threatening enough to the moral order and stability to warrant punishment. Yet, these are areas where the state is seen as failing to deliver, leading some to turn to violent acts of popular justice.

I engage with and elaborate on these two themes of contradictory consciousness throughout the book while exploring how contradictory legal consciousness shapes the legal landscape and produces *emergent hybrid legality*. To be clear, I am not suggesting that these are the only possible themes to emerge when exploring contradictions in legal consciousness, but they are two that frequently stood out in the context of Uvira. I also elaborate on these specific themes because they touch at a core issue of legality: What constitutes a harm and what constitutes justice for a harm. As will become clear in the second section of the book, the particulars of these areas of contradictory consciousness can be gendered, as they are shaped by the specific context of legal reform and international influence.

Emergent Hybrid Legality and Its Themes in Practice

The above outlined disaggregation of legal consciousness allows us, when trying to interpret people's thoughts, actions, words, and stories, to understand why and how contradictions in legal consciousness play out in practice. What are the trends in contradictions? From these analyses of contradictory legal consciousness, and the themes of *disconnect in harm naming* and *different logics of justice*, the contours and innovations of (inter)legality become discernible. One way of thinking about legality is as "the meanings, sources of authority, and cultural practices that are commonly recognized as legal, *regardless of who employs them or for what ends*" (Ewick & Silbey, 1998, p. 22, *emphasis added*). In other words, norms and practices that do not emanate from the state can still constitute legality. Further, as Santos (1987) has argued, there are various spheres of law and legality that people engage with, but it is more important to think about the changing relationships between these orders rather than simply identifying them. He refers to this way of thinking about the various spheres of law and legality as interlegality. I use the term legality to capture these shifting and hybridized relationships to normalize the diverse sources of law and how they interact with each other to produce an emergent legal landscape; thus, my use of the term legality readily maps onto Santos's term interlegality.

Legality is a structural component of society produced through legal consciousness. Meanings and understandings circulate in social relations and become repetitive, patterned, and stabilized (Silbey, 2005). This definition makes clear that in the production of legality, there is much more at play than top-down, state law; legality links legal consciousness, both as an individual and a group phenomenon with the social structures of society, not only those structures that work to constrain the possibilities of legal consciousness but those produced through it. The specific addition that needs to be made to this understanding is to transport this conceptualization to a different context, one where state law is not hegemonic[4]. Thus, the study of the production of legality through legal consciousness in eastern DRC needs to actively explore: 1) The implications of profound and entrenched legal pluralism, and 2) the penetrative role of global influence in localized contexts. Through these developments in the study of legal consciousness and legality, I develop the concept *emergent hybrid legality* to reflect these considerations.

Contradictory consciousness, and its implications for legality in the context of transition, can be understood through the lens of *friction* (Tsing, 2005). *Friction* is a conceptual tool to make sense of outcomes of the encounter between global liberal legalism and local, plural justice beliefs and practices; it helps conceptualize both the *emergent* and *hybrid* aspects of legality that I refer to. The study of legal consciousness in a transitioning context is firmly rooted in the encounter between global liberal legal norms, some of which are prioritized by interveners (Lake, 2018), and local justice beliefs and practices. Global liberal legal norms are implemented through the state legal system; due to the fragility of the state, international actors have played an extensive role in defining its legal priorities and funding them (Lake, 2018). At the same time, aspects of the legal system reflect popular beliefs and practices, many, for example, are laid out in the Family Code. Additionally, global liberal legal norms also filter through local organizations and localized actors in the legal complex. Thus, the current realms of *friction* are multifaceted and build on previous eras of *friction*. There is not just a single moment of contact or negotiation between the global and the local. "Much that is new co-exists with and modifies the old rather than replacing it entirely" (Falk Moore, 1972, p. 742). This means that there is an ongoing layering of different hybrid justice beliefs and practices, a palimpsest (Santos, 2006; see also Chanock, 1985; Sieder, 2013).

Often, scholars focus on the clash of norms or the imposition of external norms. However, local norms do not just clash with liberal universalisms but also produce emergent cultural forms through encounters (Tsing, 2005). "Emergent cultural forms . . . are persistent but *unpredictable* effects of global encounters across difference" (Tsing, 2005, p. 3, *emphasis added*). Unpredictability is key to making sense of the outcomes of interventions. Encounters will never create a localized reproduction of global norms; this is certainly true in the case of legal encounters. While scholars have recognized this in the postcolonial settings (eg. Engel & Engel, 2010; Falk Moore, 1972; de Sousa Santos, 2006), the unanticipated outcomes of legal reforms and ROL interventions are rarely explored through this lens. And yet, unpredictability is clearly observable in the outcomes that fail to adhere to interveners' expectations and standards. "The specificity of global connections is an ever-present reminder that universal claims do not actually make everything everywhere the same" (Tsing, 2005, p. 1). My argument is that friction plays out in legal consciousness, producing emergent cultural forms in the realm of law and justice. But, the specifics of these outcomes cannot be predicted *a priori*, as they are dependent on the conditions of the local context; they may even manifest differently within a single state as a result of local dynamics.

Thus, in *emergent hybrid legality*, 'emergent' denotes the ever-changing, fluid, unpredictable nature of hybridity, in contrast to the development of ideas about engineering hybridity. The unpredictability of *friction* clarifies the kind of hybridity I am referring to, one that cannot be instrumentalized because its emergent form cannot be predicted. In the realm of law and justice, those emergent cultural forms could also be understood as hybrids, but they cannot be designed to look and perform a certain way as with, for example, hybrid courts of transitioning contexts, such as the International Criminal Tribunal for Rwanda. Such design goals would remove the organic, shifting, and local nature of emergent hybridity, which are actually some its strengths in post-conflict contexts.

Manifestations of Emergent Hybrid Legality

As I have argued in this chapter, the outcome of legal reforms and ROL building is not the widespread, complete normalization of state legality based on the globalized norms that interveners aim for. Instead, the outcome is legal hybridity. There are four clear phenomena that reflect *emergent hybrid legality* in Uvira. Some of these hybridized outcomes are likely not unique to the DRC, while others appear to be shaped more by the local context.

First is the combination of written law and informal mediation. In this particular hybridization of legal-justice, systems and practices that might be categorized as informal or non-state forms of justice incorporate the law into their mediation or dispute resolution processes. This often occurs in NGO-run mediation offices, where mediation is done by local actors who are knowledgeable about the context—worldviews and culture—but also the law, at least certain aspects of it, which reflects liberal legal ideology. These actors thus use mediation as a space to inform and educate the population about the law, while performing their primary function—peacefully addressing disputes—outside the legal system and in line with local practices focused on restorative justice and reconciliation. Interestingly, some other actors, such as local traditional *chefs*, have begun to do this as well. This space of legality both enhances knowledge of the law and also facilitates access to contextually relevant dispute resolution. Further, mediators allow many voices to be heard, facilitating mini public discussions about the intersection of globalized and local legal-justice norms, beliefs, and practices. This is certainly the case around women's rights and experiences of gendered harm. These spaces integrate laws that reflect internationalized standards around women's rights with localized worldviews and experiences of what it means to be a woman and how harm is understood. This creates microcosms of broader debates and discussions about what women's rights mean in a particular context—in the Congo, and Uvira more specifically.

Second, and related to the previous example of *emergent hybrid legality*, law can be used strategically as a threat. If one party to a dispute is reluctant to cooperate or outright hostile to the process, mediators use awareness raising about the law and legal process to encourage participation in mediation. Typically, disputants are informed about the cost of state courts—both time and money, the possibility of jail or a larger fine, and that the NGO will represent the party who was willing to do the mediation. Many NGOs perform both legal aid and mediation, and thus have lawyers on retainer. While they encourage many disputes to be resolved through mediation, in some instances, they will be willing to provide legal representation for a party to a dispute or for what they define as serious cases, for example many types of SGBV. Again, this provides various channels for women to consider in their attempts to achieve justice for everyday gendered harms.

Third, the role of community leaders and authorities has shifted in response to localized needs and emergent practices. One notable example is that the role of local administrative *chefs* in resolving disputes has shifted and been entrenched. Many of these *chefs* do not have mediation or dispute resolution as a formal part of their job description, but they play a crucial role in addressing harms and disputes. This practice has historical roots in colonialism, as noted earlier, but in the era of developing liberal legalism, one would expect these authorities to refer people to the legal system rather than taking on the additional burden of mediation. Yet, this practice has become a deeply accepted and practical way of accessing justice. The role of traditional leaders, *chefs*, in addressing local conflicts also persists, usually as the first point of contact, but in some areas their power is less solidified due to the variety of options available. These first three manifestations of *emergent hybrid legality* are discussed generally in Chapter 4 and more specifically in Chapter 5.

Fourth, and finally, popular justice is one last manifestation of *emergent hybrid legality*. Now, popular justice, as a form of vigilantism, sits awkwardly with the above manifestations that are focused on peacefully addressing harms and disputes, but I argue it is still a manifestation of *emergent hybrid legality*. Notably, as with other aspects of EHL, this is part of a complex history and layering of legal-justice realities. Popular justice is primarily used against two groups of people—witches and repeat offenders. People are aware that serious offenders, such as armed robbers, should be prosecuted in court and receive jail time. This awareness creates a deepened sense of disappointment and fear when the technicalities, with which people are less familiar, of the state legal system allow offenders to be released without serving any or much prison time. In these cases, popular justice is sometimes used as a last resort.

In the other situation, popular justice against witches, people are very aware that cases of witchcraft are not heard in state courts and that making a witchcraft accusation is a prosecutable offense. At the same time, the accessibility of the *mwami*, who historically played an important role in regulating witchcraft, has been reduced. This has left the population, who have deeply held beliefs in witchcraft, in a situation of fear and uncertainty about how these will be dealt with. While there is a diversity of responses to this situation, popular justice is one of them that is used, not regularly, but frequently enough to recognize it is an important manifestation of *emergent hybrid legality*. Popular justice is explored in more detail in Chapter 6.

Clearly, then, I am not suggesting that *emergent hybrid legality* has provided a perfect or idealized system of legality, but rather that there are notable opportunities to be found within it, such as an increased awareness of the law, access to legal-justice, and constructive, although not necessarily explicit, social dialogue about what contextualized women's rights and gender justice should like. These points challenge the idea that a Western-style legal system is the only way to advance justice goals for harms. They also raise serious questions about the possibilities of building one standard form of ROL; it will invariably be modified and challenged. Yet, liberal legal norms can be a source of power or inspiration for local actors.

Conclusion

Bringing legal consciousness into our research on ROL building and transitional legal reforms lends new insights into the dynamics on the ground and possibilities and limitations of such interventions. The various aspects of legal consciousness, knowledge, perceptions, judgements, worldviews, and ideology provide insights into how the population processes legal encounters, often experiencing an integration of contradictory elements into their legal consciousness. This contradictory legal consciousness plays an important role in shaping the terrain of legality. It is clear that globalized legal norms and practices will always encounter alternative norms, beliefs, and practices. This chapter highlights how globalized legal norms and practices do not override local ones but encounter them and through this meeting produce an emergent and hybridized legal realm. This provides a new way to think about legal encounters and outcomes. However, to fully grasp how I came to make these arguments, a better understanding of the research context is required. The limitations of the ROL building practice are also linked to how research on the ROL is done. Again, my research challenges the idea that the best way to assess the legal terrain is by measuring it against a number of ROL (read: Western, liberal) standards. My bottom-up approach to making sense of legality requires a nuanced engagement with the research setting, a way of thinking about my interactions with the population, and the strengths and limitations of what I learned through the co-generation of data with participants and interlocutors.

Notes

1 This approach to identifying elements of subjectivity follows the work of Chua and Engel (2019) in their review and analysis of the state of legal consciousness scholarship.
2 Imbued with a post-Enlightenment, scientific rationality.
3 Ni Aolain et al. (2011) write:

> the current focus on gender crime prosecutions assumes that both "extraordinary" and sex-based violence are a priority even though other types of violence may be more keenly felt by women in situ. If asked and consulted, they might ascribe different priorities in the substance, timing, and structure of accountability.
>
> (p. 19)

This is not to suggest that sex-based crimes and wartime rape not be taken seriously, but it is an important reminder to scholars as well as practitioners to listen to local voices, especially women, whose voices may be marginalized as foreigner actors presume to know their needs. During my first field trip, a variety of everyday harms were explained and shared with me while I was trying to ask people about their experiences of conflict-related harms. Their responses led me to reconsider my research direction, framework, and goals.

4 Ewick and Silbey's work on legal consciousness is based in the USA and explores the hegemony of the law; Chua and Engel (2019) call this the hegemony school. However, not all contexts are defined by legal hegemony, but legal consciousness is still necessary for understanding legality.

Bibliography

Benda-Beckmann, K. V., & Turner, B. (2018). Legal pluralism, social theory, and the state. *The Journal of Legal Pluralism and Unofficial Law, 50*(3), 255–274.

Buss, D. E. (2009). Rethinking 'rape as a weapon of war'. *Feminist Legal Studies, 17*(2), 145–163.

Chanock, M. (1985). *Law, custom and social order: The colonial experience in Malawi and Zambia.* Cambridge University Press.

Chua, L. J., & Engel, D. M. (2019). Legal consciousness reconsidered. *Annual Review of Law and Social Science, 15*, 335–353.

Dembour, M. B. (2000). *Recalling the Belgian Congo: Conversations and introspection* (Vol. 9). Berghahn Books.

Dunn, H. (2020). Research in the Land of Savages, Victims, and Saviors. In G. Hoogensen, P. Weitsman & R. Matthew (Eds.), *Women's perspectives on human security: Violence, environment, and sustainability* (pp. 154–182). Ohio University Press.

Engel, D., & Engel, J. S. (2010). Tort, custom, and karma. In *Tort, custom, and karma*. Stanford University Press.

Ewick, P., & Silbey, S. S. (1998). *The common place of law: Stories from everyday life.* University of Chicago Press.

Falk Moore, S. (1972). Law and social change: The semi-autonomous social field as an appropriate subject of study. *Law & Society Review*, 7, 719.

Fuller, L. L. (1964). *The morality of law.* Yale University Press.

Gallagher, M. E. (2006). Mobilizing the law in China: "Informed disenchantment" and the development of legal consciousness. *Law & Society Review, 40*(4), 783–816.

Goodale, M. (2008). *Dilemmas of modernity: Bolivian encounters with law and liberalism.* Stanford University Press.

Grant, H. B. (2021). The cultural ingredient to rule of law promotion. In *Building a culture of lawfulness* (pp. 1–9). Springer.

Grear, A. (2011). 'Sexing the matrix': Embodiment, disembodiment and the law—towards the re-gendering of legal rationality. In *Gender, sexualities and law* (pp. 48–61). Routledge.

Henry, N. (2014). The fixation on wartime rape: Feminist critique and international criminal law. *Social & Legal Studies, 23*, 93–111.

Hertogh, M. (2018). *Nobody's law: Legal consciousness and legal alienation in everyday life.* Springer.

Holterhus, T. P. (2018). A theoretical introduction and legal perspective on rule of law transfers. *Goettingen Journal of International Law, 9*, 7.

Holzer, E. (2013). What happens to law in a refugee camp? *Law & Society Review, 47*(4), 837–872.

Hunt, A. (1985). The ideology of law: Advances and problems in recent applications of the concept of ideology to the analysis of law. *Law & Society Review, 19*, 11.

Hunter, R. (2016). Contesting the dominant paradigm: Feminist critiques of liberal legalism. In V. E. Munro (Ed.), *The Ashgate research companion to feminist legal theory* (pp. 25–42). Routledge.

Kirby, P. (2015). Ending sexual violence in conflict: The preventing sexual violence initiative and its critics. *International Affairs, 91*(3), 457–472.
Lake, M. (2018). *Strong NGOs and weak states: Pursuing gender justice in the Democratic Republic of Congo and South Africa*. Cambridge University Press.
Mamdani, M. (1996). *Citizen and subject*. Princeton University Press.
McConnachie, K. (2014). *Governing refugees: Justice, order and legal pluralism*. Routledge.
Merry, S. E. (1988). Legal pluralism. *Law & Society Review, 22*, 869.
Merry, S. E. (1990). *Getting justice and getting even: Legal consciousness among working-class Americans*. University of Chicago Press.
Nelken, D. (2003). Comparatists and transferability. In P. Legrand & R. Munday (Eds.), *Comparative legal studies: Traditions and transitions* (pp. 437–466). Cambridge: Cambridge University Press.
Ni Aoláin, F. (2009). Women, security, and the patriarchy of internationalized transitional justice. *Human Rights Quarterly, 31*, 1055.
Ni Aolain, F., Haynes, D. F., Cahn, N., & Fionnuala, N. (2011). *On the frontlines: Gender, war, and the post-conflict process*. Oxford University Press.
Phillips, A. (2001). Feminism and liberalism revisited: Has Martha Nussbaum got it right? *Constellations, 8*(2), 249–266.
Reilly, N. (2009). *Women's human rights*. Polity.
Rubbers, B., & Gallez, E. (2012). Why do Congolese people go to court? A qualitative study of litigants' experiences in two Justice of the Peace courts in Lubumbashi. *The Journal of Legal Pluralism and Unofficial Law, 44*(66), 79–108.
Santos, B. de Sousa. (1987). Law: A map of misreading. Toward a postmodern conception of law. *Journal of Law and Society*, 279–302.
Santos, B. de Sousa. (2006). The heterogeneous state and legal pluralism in Mozambique. *Law & Society Review, 40*(1), 39–76.
Sarat, A. (1990). The law is all over: Power, resistance and the legal consciousness of the welfare poor. *Yale JL & Human, 2*, 343.
Scales, A. (2006). *Legal feminism: Activism, lawyering, and legal theory*. NYU Press.
Sieder, R. (2013). Subaltern cosmopolitan legalities and the challenges of engaged ethnography. *Universitas Humanística, 75*, 221–249.
Silbey, S. S. (2005). After legal consciousness. *Annual Review of Law and Social Science, 1*, 323–368.

Chapter 3

Fraught Fieldwork

Embodied Experiences and Imagined Spaces

On one of my initial visits to Makobola in 2015, I was with two of my research partners, and we were going to meet the *chef de village*[1] to discuss with him my intention to do research in the area. While we were walking and joking about my Kiswahili errors (like 'talking on my feet'), we encountered the *chef de commune*[2] who joined us in our search for the *chef de village*. We walked up some of the hills and shared with the *chef de commune* my research plans. In our discussions, this *chef* said, "Often, when white people come, we expect something from them. It is important to clarify that you are just a student, and you are just there to collect important information." This was my second trip to Uvira, so his remarks did not surprise me. I was already starting to grasp how all of my interactions with interlocutors, interviewees, and the population more broadly would be shaped by the white people who came before me. This was only one of the many dynamics that I had to reflect on during my nine months of fieldwork in Uvira.

Indeed, every field site is fraught with entanglements that reflect both recent and older histories of interaction, including the attendant power dynamics, assumptions, and expectations. Uvira is no exception and exemplifies some of the trends of interaction between the DRC and the broader international community. The effects these entanglements have on the research project are complex and can change over time, as the researcher gains deeper understandings of the context and the nature of her relationships to participants[3], interlocutors, and the broader local population shift. This requires flexibility and reflexivity to further the goals of the research endeavour without being limited to predefined categories and assumptions that have been constructed, both on the side of international actors and interveners and on the side of the Congolese population. My research, based on nine months of immersive fieldwork over four different trips, allowed me to develop a contextualized, although still limited, understanding of the research site and some of the pre-existing dynamics that were shaping my interactions with people. Thus, knowledge created through this research project cannot be understood separate from my embodied experiences in Uvira and my methodological and ethical approach. In this chapter, I outline my methodology to provide the context for readers to understand the

DOI: 10.4324/9781003289715-3

contributions of this book, and I reflect on it in conversation with background on the conflict in the DRC and the role of the international community in shaping the context. To elaborate my interpretive approach, I address typical methodological issues, such as who was interviewed and where I did participant observation, but I also tackle methodological issues at the intersection of methods and ethics to elucidate the strengths and limitations of my research for understanding legal consciousness, everyday harms and disputes, and the development of *emergent hybrid legality*.

First, I provide a few introductory thoughts on my research questions to set the stage for elucidating my methodology. When I first began my research in 2011, I had some concerns that the primary topic of extant research and media attention in the eastern DRC was wartime rape and prosecuting these acts in the eastern provinces. There was a dearth of scholarship that prioritized popular understandings of, or reflections on, transitional justice for these and other rights abuses (a notable exception is Vinck & Pham, 2008). Additionally, I found the media portrayals of the most depraved wartime rape accounts to reflect a single narrative of the conflict[4]. When I started my research, I had two main goals: I wanted to conduct research on local transitional justice initiatives, and I did *not* want to focus on wartime SGBV. In a sense, I failed at both goals, but through the iterative and adaptive processes of interpretive research (Schwartz-Shea & Yanow, 2013), my initial field experience guided how I rethought my research. First, in response to initial interviews and participant observation, I moved away from a transitional justice framework and started to explore the legal terrain more broadly, engaging with the scholarship on legal pluralism and ROL building.

Thus, my topic shifted from an interest in transitional justice and war-related harms to 'everyday' harms and disputes, those that occurred regularly since the end of the wars and even prior to and throughout the times of armed conflict. I explained the importance of this choice in Chapter 2. I use the term 'harm' to denote a situation where one person wronged another; this may have a physical dimension, such as assault or rape, but may also include other non-physical transgressions, such as destruction of property. By contrast, a dispute is where two or more people may be laying claim to something, such as child support, land boundaries, or debt repayment. However, there is not always a clear-cut binary between a harm and a dispute; this can depend on people's interpretation of events. Additionally, these two categories loosely map onto crimes and civil disputes, respectively, but I avoid the language of law because I have generated areas of harm and dispute from the local population's understandings of these issues rather than the definitions outlined in laws. As will be clear throughout the book, local understandings often do not map onto legal definitions; statutory rape and witchcraft are two examples that are addressed in subsequent chapters.

Second, I experienced some notable difficulties in my attempts to *avoid* SGBV as a research topic. The local landscape was already painted with expectations about which issues foreigners were interested in. Notably, being a white woman from a US university shaped how interlocutors imagined me—who I wanted to meet, the stories that I wanted to hear, as well as my expected role as benefactor. Of course, these understandings were not universally held, but I encountered them repeatedly over my multiple trips to Uvira, and they significantly shaped my research. Further, and in reflection of my commitment to transparency, I would point out that the higher number of female participants and interlocutors in my research is at least partially a function of the dynamics of my field site rather than an intentional methodological goal. I could have 'fought' the tendency of local actors to ascribe certain expectations to me, such as the expectation that I was interested in researching SGBV, and at times I did, but I also quickly realized that these dynamics help inform my understanding of the encounter between local and international actors that shape legal consciousness and the terrain of legal pluralism. They were also surprisingly entrenched. I develop these points in this chapter and reflect on them throughout the book.

The remainder of this chapter begins with a discussion of the research site and how I selected it, as well as a critical analysis of the power dynamics that shaped my research in this setting. I thus provide more specific information about the context of Uvira. In terms of methodology, I elaborate on my immersive, interpretive approach to fieldwork. Within this elaboration, I also highlight the opportunities and risks associated with working with interpreters in this particular context and how that shaped my analyses. Finally, I turn to a brief consideration of the three Rs of ethics that guided my fieldwork, analysis, and writing: Reflexivity, reciprocity, and re-presentation.

Research Locale and Fieldwork Contingencies

My research was conducted in the territory of Uvira, specifically in Kiliba, Makobola, and Uvira City[5], where I lived mostly with a host family. I wanted to avoid being in the capitals of Goma in North Kivu or Bukavu in South Kivu because they appeared to already be the base for numerous scholars and reporters. I was interested in incorporating a perspective from a different locale, but one where there was momentum in the realm of post-conflict justice, broadly understood. Uvira reflected those goals. Another reason I chose Uvira as my primary research cite was that there was extensive international humanitarian involvement, including with the legal system, although much of this was done through partnerships with local organizations. Fewer international organizations maintained an ongoing presence with expatriate staff at the time of my research, but there were many local–international partnerships. This allowed me to focus on building relationships with members of the local populations and getting their views on the law and different approaches to justice, while reducing the sense that anything they shared with me was likely to get back to their funders. In other words, I was able to maintain some distance from the broader humanitarian complex, which I hoped could reduce the assumptions that I was a part of that group, although in practice I believe my ability to reshape these assumptions was limited. Additionally, my first field trip taught me that expats 'hang out' together, especially in post-conflict contexts where security protocols may be very strict. For future research endeavours, I sought to avoid being viewed as a part of the expat in-group in the hopes of developing more meaningful connections with local interlocutors. I further pursued this approach by living with a local Congolese family in all but my first trip to Uvira.

Beyond the factors just described, there were other methodological reasons for choosing Uvira as home base. Uvira City is the administrative capital of the territory of Uvira and the seat of the three official state courts for the province of South Kivu (excluding the provincial capital, Bukavu, which is independently administered). The three courts are: The Tribunal de Paix ('Tripaix' Peace Court/Magistrates court), which hears cases punishable by less than five years prison time and/or a fine, as well as addressing delinquent children[6]; the Tribunal de Grande Instance (High Court), for crimes warranting over five years prison, the death penalty, or forced labour, as well as appeal from the Tripaix[7]; and the Tribunal Militaire (Military Court), which hears cases involving military offences, all offences committed by soldiers and punishable by the Penal Code, and, in the case of hostilities, offenses committed by nationals, agents in service of the administration, and agents in service of enemy interests[8]. Thus, outside Bukavu, this is a location where one would expect to see more of the impact of legal reforms and ROL building, in contrast to those areas where the courts are highly inaccessible.

All three courts are in the 'Zone Parquet', an area on the road that branches off from the main National Rt. 5 at the monument (see Map 4: Monument and 'Zone Parquet'). This road was being rebuilt with Chinese investments in 2017. The Tripaix is somewhat off the street, behind the Bureau de Territoire[9]. The Military Tribunal was also under construction in 2017, funded by MONUSCO. Most cases in all courts are public, but the Military Tribunal is the only one that holds hearings outside on the front stoop, attracting passersby. There is also a Tripaix in the fenced in area of the Prison Centrale in Mulongwe, which hears the cases of those who are held in pre-trial detention.

I received conflicting information regarding when the Tripaix was established in Uvira. One legal official[10] at the Tripaix said that, officially, they were created by state ordinance in 1989[11], but the one in Uvira was only established in 2007. The director of MEK[12], a legal aid NGO, by contrast, said that the Tripaix had been in Uvira since around 2010 but had only become functional in the past year. It makes sense that the Tripaix might be interpreted as only functional since 2015–2016 because, as one of its legal officials[13] pointed out, it only got its own *parquet* in 2015. The *parquet*, or *ministère public*[14], decides whether to prosecute a case and is meant to apply the law and represent the interests of society. The official[15] added that the Tripaix existed in Uvira as early

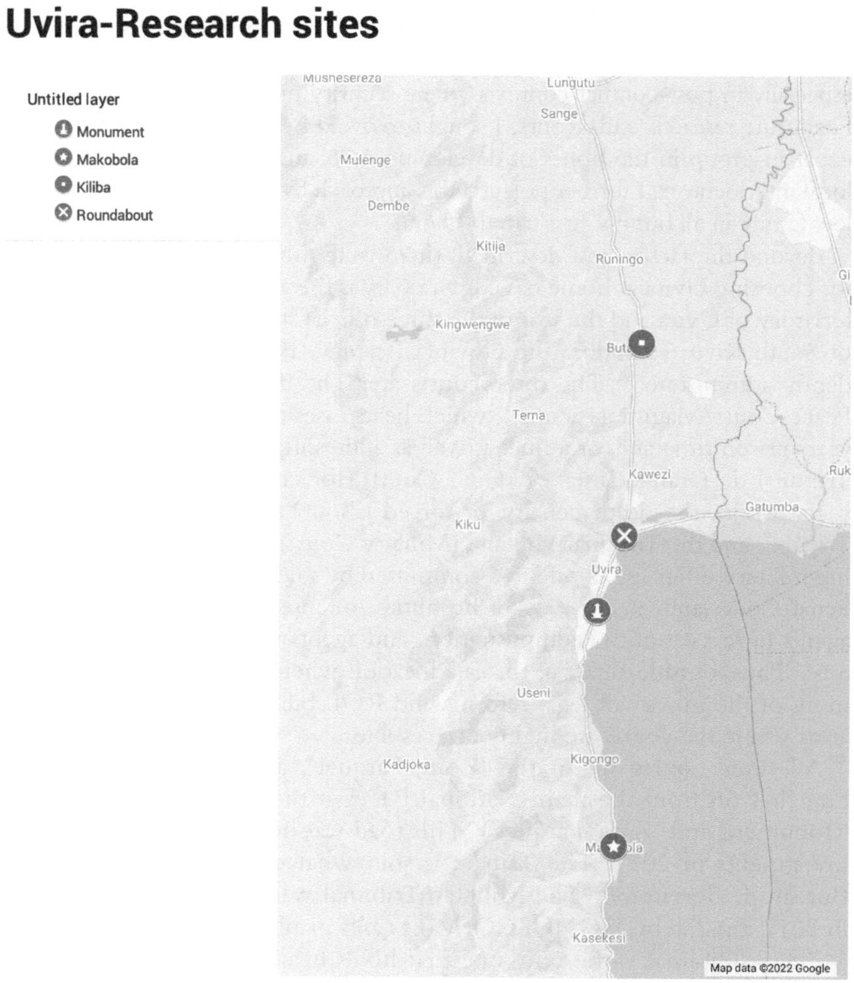

Map 3 Research Sites

as 2008, but it was at the *chefferie*[16] Bavira's office. By contrast, the Director of CIRESKI[17] said that the Tripaix was created in 2006. Thus, from interviews, it is ambiguous when the Tripaix was really established in Uvira City, when it started functioning, and when the population became aware it, but my best assessment is that by the time of doing fieldwork in 2015, people in Uvira were generally aware that it was operative, while those in Kiliba and Makobola made less reference to it, likely because it is less accessible to them.

Access to courts is just the beginning of the differences between my research sites. I began my research with an interest in looking at the variation between the three locations and was thinking about my research through a positivist

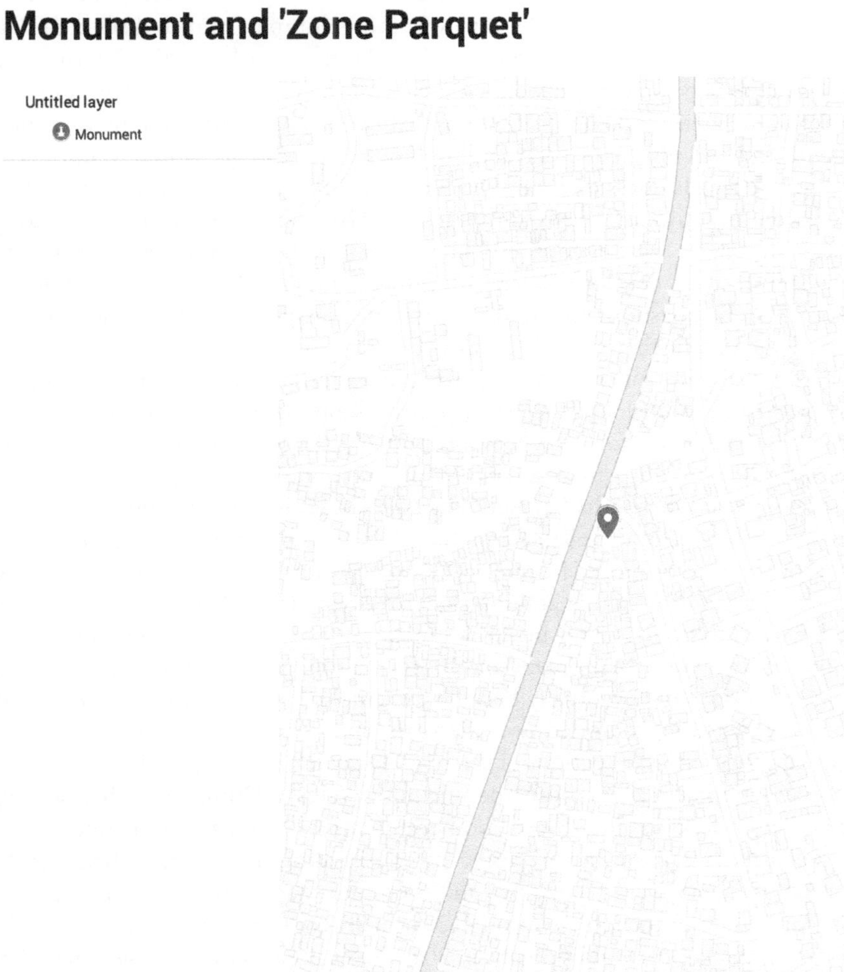

Map 4 Monument and 'Zone Parquet'

lens. Makobola is a rural town approximately 20 kilometres south of Uvira along the National Route 5 (Map 3: Research Sites). It is still largely governed as a chieftaincy. Kiliba is also more or less rural. It was once the home of a large sugar factory that employed many people in town but now stands empty. Kiliba lies about 15 kilometres north of Uvira along National Route 5, and an additional five or ten kilometres off National Route 5 is where I was conducting research, Kiliba ONDS (Map 3: Research Sites). My aim was to explore the variation in approaches to justice for everyday harms and disputes across the more rural, 'traditional' Makobola to the more urban, 'modernized' Uvira, with Kiliba falling somewhere in between. However, encountering the realities of fieldwork, the terrain of legality was more complex and multifaceted than fit with my research design. Knowledge construction lay at the interstices of the complicated ways that people understand themselves, harms, and justice in relation to their worldviews. This context of legal encounter led me to rethink my design and pivot to understanding how people engage with law and justice in their everyday lives and why that did not conform to either liberal ROL or so-called 'traditional' norms and practices. How was popular legal consciousness affected by legal encounters? How did new and unexpected hybrid legal-justice practices develop? What could this context tell us about building the ROL? These questions emerged from my initial experience with fieldwork and were pursued further in subsequent trips.

As I was reformulating my research questions, I was also rethinking my choice of research locales. I narrowed the scope of my research to focus on the Uvira City area for a few reasons. Notably, the logic of the three-site comparison was no longer necessitated by my methodological approach. But, why not continue where I had already started to build research relationships? First, I was unable to find a reliable and safe place to stay for an extended period in the other two locations. I came to this conclusion through numerous discussions with my host family and interlocutors. Second, daily travel by taxi motor bike was physically tiring in 2011 but became worse with each subsequent bout of fieldwork. Main roads and bridges through Uvira were either washed out or eroded, and eventually became extremely dusty. The route to Makobola became increasingly eroded over the years, and the dirt road in Kiliba required walking around large sections of the road. Daily travel for research was exhausting and impractical for both me and interpreters. Third, in both instances, travel after dark was ill-advised and became more of an issue over time.

Security became a further topic of conversation after Papa Félicien and a group of friends were robbed by bandits on their way home from a soccer game in Baraka, along the same section of National Route 5 that I travelled in order to get to Makobola. Additionally, in 2015, I developed concerns over the safety of one of my key interlocutors in Kiliba. Those concerns stemmed directly from his known association with me and the possibility that local authorities suspected he was sharing information about certain corrupt and violent practices[18]. Thus, over time, I reduced my fieldwork to Uvira for the outlined reasons, but I draw on the insights gleaned from the three locales. Indeed, some of the local power dynamics in Kiliba[19] relate directly to *emergent hybrid legality*, as I have written about elsewhere (Dunn, 2020).

Finally, focusing on Uvira was also feasible because it is rich in various justice systems and practices, typically understood to exist outside the state. Thus, I did participant observation in court proceedings, NGO mediation, and other custom-informed justice processes. For many everyday harms and disputes, people first attempt *arrangements à l'amiable*[20]. These are understood as informal arrangements that 'bring people together' to come up with a solution. These settlements are often organized and mediated by family members, especially elders. If this is not possible, or the issue is not resolved, the conflict will often be brought to an alternative mediator. In a sense, the amicable settlement becomes more formalized as it shifts to different sources of mediation, such as a local traditional *chef*, a wise person in the community, a *mwami*, or an NGO-run dispute resolution office, or even administrative *chef*. While these more formalized approaches may be 'amicable', the expression *arrangement à l'amiable* typically refers to the least formalized process within and between families, and actors associated with more formalized approaches, such as NGO mediators and state legal actors, often view it as highly problematic. The problem they see is that the law is completely ignored in these situations.

NGOs may situate themselves in the legal-justice terrain as an improvement or a step above family or community-based *arrangements à l'amiable*. Local and international NGOs have drawn upon state law, international norms, and customary practices to create mediation offices. Thus, many, although by no means all, view *arrangements à l'amiable* as problematic or a barrier to 'real' justice. These NGO mediation projects are often supported by international donors who have some influence in shaping the goals and missions of the organization. For example, one local organization explained how they had to change the name of the project multiple times to respond to changing donor demands[21]. These varying forms of mediation—*arrangements à l'amiable*, *chef* mediators, local NGOs—have varied relationships with the state legal system and local authorities; these can be complementary, overlapping, or contentious.

Finally, when researching everyday harms and disputes, I learned that the topic of popular justice was almost unavoidable. Popular justice can be conceptualized as a type of vigilante justice with its own unique set of logics; it is retributive in aim, typically defined by ad hoc violence or exile, and is perpetrated against an individual for a wrong or harm that members of the local population understand them to have committed. Throughout Uvira, I came to understand that popular justice is on the rise and is most clearly organized around cases of witchcraft (see also Verweijen, 2015), but it is also used against repeat offenders who are released from prison[22]. This form of justice is more difficult to get information about, as it is secretive and anonymous. Although I did not observe such phenomena, I spoke with numerous interlocutors, often from local NGOs who had first-hand experience with several cases, as well as participants who were familiar with cases in their neighbourhoods.

In exploring the array of everyday harms and disputes that arise in Uvira, I was able to map out the various approaches to justice described earlier. They will be addressed in more detail in the ensuing chapters, but here I have provided an outline for beginning to understand the layout of the different legal-justice mechanisms; these can be understood as the practice-based roots of *emergent hybrid legality* that are further shaped and nuanced by contradictory legal consciousness. Having laid out the research locale and provided a basic description of the associated concepts and legal-justice practices, I turn to an overview of the remainder of my methodology, including specific methods.

Interpretations and Translations in Fieldwork

Accounts of why the ROL is difficult to build often come from the perspectives and analyses of the domestic and international actors who are attempting to build it, rather than the population affected by it. More recently, some ROL scholarship has pivoted to the study of popular perceptions of state legitimacy and capacity and how these shape behaviours associated with legal norms and institutions (Hilbink & Gallagher, 2019). My research aligns with and advances these aims by exploring the popular side of ROL interventions through immersive, interpretive fieldwork. This methodological approach helps highlight the situated knowledge and perspectives of different interlocutors (see Schatz, 2013). Through immersive fieldwork, I sought to build trust and relationships with members of the local population to learn about their experiences of harms and how they make sense of, and engage with, the law and different co-existing systems of rules.

For me, immersion suggests a high degree of direct participation in day-to-day life to build networks of contacts and interlocutors. Immersion in daily life is necessary to address my research questions by facilitating *access* to 'everyday' comments, stories, and jokes (Ewick & Silbey, 2000). This meant participating in community activities. For example, I attended a protest in 2011 that shut down the main bridge connecting the southern region of the province to Bukavu and Bujumbura, the capital of Burundi. The demonstration was in response to the lack of official reaction to numerous rape–robberies that had occurred in the area in recent months. In 2017, I marched with community members on International Women's Day. Over the span of multiple fieldwork trips, I attended numerous weddings. Immersion is further about the more banal aspects of everyday life, buying toilet paper and *unités*[23] at the corner stand, talking to kids and neighbours while walking around, taking a *moto*[24] and chatting with the *motaris*[25], going to the local dress-maker, and eating *beignets*[26] and drinking Fanta in 'restaurants' not bigger than a walk-in closet. These were the places and spaces where I was able to observe and be a part of the everyday activities that provide the cultural scaffolding for my interpretations and analyses of more specific issues related to conflicts and legal-justice.

Interpretation and Translation: Field to Book

Over the course of my fieldwork, I did 94 semi-formal interviews[27] with a variety of actors, including lawyers, disputants, mediators, and *chefs*; 10 group interviews with particular segments of the population; and had regular informal discussions with people on a daily basis. Much of this was done with the help of interpreters. Scholars who do fieldwork, especially ethnographic fieldwork, generally argue that being able to communicate with people in a shared language is foundational to developing rapport and building contextual knowledge. While I support the idea of shared language, my research experience provides for some nuance to this argument, which is supported by the work of others, such as Fujii (2013). There are many languages spoken in Uvira, but Kiswahili is the *lingua franca*. French is also a commonly spoken language amongst educated sections of the population. Prior to my first field trip, several expat sources had informed me that French was widely spoken. As I am fluent in French, I believed that this would be sufficient language skills. Once I arrived in Uvira, I found that to be a tremendous overstatement regarding the population I was working with.

In subsequent trips, I studied with my host family and a tutor in Uvira to learn Kiswahili, but I did not progress to anywhere near proficiency, let alone other spoken languages, such as Kibembe and Kifulero. Contributing to my limited language development was the fact that I was trying to learn the language at the same time as doing fieldwork in my second language, French. By the time I arrived to my end-of-day lessons, I was often mentally and physically fatigued. Yet, the lessons were useful, and I developed enough skills to have basic exchanges with people. Additionally, in some interviews and observation situations, I was able to glean more than what I was being told. For example, I observed one military magistrate in Uvira interrogating a presumed rebel, and I was able to determine that they did not fully understand each other after the magistrate mistranslated several of the suspect's statements. I was confused, but it was not the appropriate time for me to ask questions. Afterward, in an interview with the magistrate, I discovered that he was from Kinshasa and was fluent in Lingala and French, but not Kiswahili. In other instances, I was able to follow up on some points that were not fully translated during interviews. Thus, the development of basic language skills was useful, even if insufficient for completing my research without an interpreter.

I worked with different interpreters through the various phases of the research. The first interpreter I worked with was a woman about my age, mid-20s at the time, who was based in Bujumbura but would come and work with me for several days at a time. She was recommended to me for her ability to translate from Kiswahili to English. I quickly learned that she was not a good fit. This individual only wanted to translate interviews and would not debrief afterward. Frankly, she also seemed uncomfortable with the low-income, low-education population that I was interviewing and did not seem sufficiently interested in their stories. I made the decision to change interpreters and worked with a man I had met in Uvira. The work went much smoother, as he had a real interest in the research. However, when I returned for fieldwork in 2015, he was no longer in Uvira. I ended up working with two interpreters, a man and a woman about my age. Both were interested in the research and would spend time debriefing with me after interviews. As Fujii (2013) notes, interpreters can also become key informants and provide crucial local knowledge; this was true of these interpreters. However, they also both moved on, one to do his PhD and the other received asylum in Europe after a series of threats, which I confirmed were unrelated to her role as an interpreter. In the following, I provide more information on the interpreter I worked with during the final phase of fieldwork, Jeanne, a woman in her late 50s to early 60s. Working with Jeanne allowed me to experience very fully the benefits of working with an interpreter who had a wealth of knowledge, connections, and interest in research, even if there were still some limitations.

Language interpreters can double as cultural interpreters (see also Fujii, 2013); for me, they became trusted research partners who were interested in debriefing, clarifying, and building rapport with interlocutors. Most of the interpreters I worked with helped with cultural interpretation in ways that sometimes directly influenced the shape and texture of the interviews. First, I cannot sufficiently emphasize the important role Jeanne played in facilitating access to participants and providing insights into interview questions. She had a recent history of working with several local NGOs, so she would reach out to make initial contact with them. She often made first contact, from which we were able to get further interviews with their beneficiaries and continue to snowball from there. Jeanne already had established trust, relationships, and rapport with these organizations, and I was often accepted as a result; I was likely seen as 'vetted' by Jeanne. Of course, this process and method for accessing interviewees influenced the types of people I interviewed. For example, working with Jeanne in 2017 led to more interviews with women in this round of fieldwork. Arguably, Jeanne performed the role of gatekeeper, facilitating access to some people and not others, whether intentionally or as a by-product of her positionality, or a combination of the two. Interestingly, in the context of my research site, most interlocutors were also gatekeepers. At least with Jeanne, the gatekeeping was somewhat more transparent.

Second, Jeanne very directly helped me improve my interviewing process and questions. She had already done research and interviews for local NGOs, so she suggested ways to develop a better understanding of people's socio-economic realities and everyday lives based on her previous research experience. For example, asking an interviewee their salary or monthly income may be a standard demographic or introductory question for some research in a Western context, but in a context largely defined by subsistence farming and small commerce, the question was met with odd looks and unexpected answers. Instead, asking questions about everyday living standards, such as electricity, sleeping arrangements, and meat consumption, led to greater insights. Additionally, Jeanne and earlier female interpreters made it clear that the topic of sex was not off limits. In trying to understand what 'dating' and married life were like, especially for women, sex is an important aspect of ascertaining the power dynamics in the home. While I felt uncertain about how to ask these questions in an appropriate way cross-culturally, amongst 'us women' there was never a sense that these questions were unexpected, inappropriate, or taboo, once Jeanne encouraged me to ask them when relevant. This sits in stark contrast to the taboo around rape and the stigma still sometimes attached to it (Aroussi, 2018), but in these private interviews, women would sometimes share their experiences of sexual violence without being prompted. However, this did not become a key interview topic; my awareness of the 'hype' and 'commodification' of rape narratives still made me hesitant to broach this subject.

Finally, working with interpreters can be important for safety reasons within the context of immersion in areas where acts of armed violence and an underpaid security sector coexist (Fujii, 2013). International humanitarian organizations often view immersion with local populations in DRC as too dangerous (Autesserre, 2014). The highly publicized rates of rape and sexual violence mean these organizations see the DRC as particularly unsafe for women, including foreign women. Researchers affiliated with international organizations may rely on them for safety and protection due to their status, but this also has the potential to reduce the level of immersion possible if the researcher adapts aid organizations' security protocol, keeping them distant from the population (see Autesserre, 2014). For example, when I attended a wedding in Bukavu—home to numerous international organizations and researchers—my presence was met with some surprise. As one guest said, "whites do not usually get close to us. It is like they're scared of us." My understanding is that this distance is an outcome of security protocols rather than a generalized fear of the population; however, the void created is a space open for interpretation by members of the local populations, at least some of whom seem dismayed by this segregated living.

Thus, in order to avoid falling into the security-based distance trap, I formed strong connections with certain well-informed local actors. I relied on my relationships with local partners, interlocutors, and interpreters for their in-depth, insider knowledge of 'how things work' to safely conduct research[28]. Notably, it was my experience that state security officials were increasingly suspicious of researchers. One key informant[29] told me that they create problems for "those of us working on human rights because they don't want there to be rights." This has been reaffirmed by several other researchers who have had difficulty obtaining visas (personal communications), as well as researchers having visas revoked or being expelled (CRG, 9 April 2016; HRW, 9 August 2016). I also did not receive a visa in 2016. Although I was not officially denied a visa, it seems as though they stalled (for months) until after my departure date, after which I simply requested that the embassy return my passport and received it shortly thereafter. I thus believe that the type of research that I am doing may not be possible without working closely with local partners. Although this does not mean I required an interpreter specifically for safety reasons, it is an important double-role that deserves to be recognized.

At the same time, local interlocutors and friends may not always fully understand the risk to foreign researchers if they do not have prior experience working with them. For example, when I was hesitant to take a picture in a marketplace, one interlocutor encouraged me to do so, saying that it would not be a problem. However, after taking only two pictures, I was stopped by a police officer and threatened with prison time for spying. I had to go through a lengthy and extremely stressful 'discussion'[30] with him in order to get his permission to leave the market. Reminders to 'trust your gut' may seem trite, but they can serve the researcher well, in addition to dialoguing with local contacts.

For me, working with interpreters also meant certain drawbacks in terms of the research methodology. The most fundamental concern, especially for interpretive research, is, of course, interpretation. The interpreter translates, in this case, Kiswahili to French, in real time. As with any language, there are some expressions, words, and references that do not easily translate to another language (see also Fujii, 2013). The interpreter must either provide a literal translation, which may not best reflect the meaning of the phrase. Or, she can try to explain the meaning of the phrase, which can in turn take time and disrupt the flow of the interview. I tried to address this by debriefing with my interpreters after interviews. Additionally, when permitted, I recorded interviews and requested that transcribers include anything that was said by the interviewee that the interpreter did not translate in real time. While I think these are positive steps, there is a deeper problem: It is very difficult to build rapport with someone when working through an interpreter. I tried to start all interviews with some of the basic Swahili I had learned, to at least get a laugh and alleviate some nervousness or tension the participant might feel about being interviewed.

Thus, while working with interpreters can be problematic and difficult for a variety of reasons, from individual personalities to the extra layer of interpretation that is added to research, they can also be invaluable colleagues that facilitate the researcher's understanding of the local context. Further, interpreters can help access participants as well as keep the researcher informed of shifting security contexts.

Ethical Considerations

An ethnographic sensibility, an awareness I incorporate into my research, is "an approach that cares—with all the possible emotional engagement that implies—to glean the meanings that people under study attribute to their social and political reality" (Schatz, 2013, loc. 240). I conceptualize this form of caring as considering and prioritizing the humanity of those who have shared their time, stories, and resources to contribute to my research. My research and writing are thus guided by ethical concerns outlined with the three Rs: *Reflexivity*, *reciprocity*, and *representation*.

Analytic Reflexivity and Transparency

Reflexivity is about analysing one's positionality and how it may influence the information collected. To practice reflexivity, the researcher must "constantly locate and relocate themselves within their work, and to remain in dialogue with research practice, participants and methodologies" (Bott, 2010, p. 160). Positionality—the researcher's social position and power vis-à-vis participants—is based on different aspects of one's identity, such as age, gender, race, ethnicity, and sexual orientation, combined with one's personal biography (Berger, 2015; England, 1994). But, beyond that, reflexivity is also a part of qualitative research transparency and 'internal validity'[31] that can be done in a way that again emphasizes the human side of research.

Knowledge, and knowledge construction, is enmeshed in power relations (Schwartz-Shea & Yanow, 2013; Wedeen, 2013), which reflexivity helps us understand. These relations are between interlocutors or participants and the researcher but also more broadly between interveners of all sorts and the local population. Specifically, in my research site, I was acutely aware of how participants perceived me as a type of intervener, and how their assumptions about interveners shaped my access to information, people, and places as a result (see Dunn, 2020; also, Thomson et al., 2013). During my time in Uvira, it appeared that most foreigners fit the 'saviour economic complex' (Dunn, 2020), which essentially commodifies rape narratives—share a rape narrative and get access to resources (Baaz & Stern, 2010; Dunn, 2020; Freedman, 2016). Peacebuilders, humanitarian and aid workers, and even international media and researchers can fit in this category. My seeming identification with the saviour economic complex shaped how some interlocutors and participants interacted with me based on assumptions about the kind of information I wanted and the possible resources I could provide.

To illustrate, conducting fieldwork in an environment where I was at times perceived by community members and participants as belonging to the saviour category led to some interactions being guided by interlocutors' expectations about what I was doing and what I was interested in. For example, many people assumed that I was researching sexual violence. As I pointed out in Chapter 1, this even led to a situation where I was brought to meet NGO beneficiaries under false pretenses. Others assumed that I would want to follow similar security protocols as international organizations and were surprised that I would ride with a *motari*. Still others believed that I would impose my Western understandings of law to negatively judge other arrangements (see Dunn, 2021). These beliefs were shaped by how people read my embodied presence in their space. Thus, based on their own understandings of what international actors are looking for, and their strategies for engaging with international actors, interlocutors shaped my research agenda and findings. Without immersion and reflexivity, I would risk blindness to these dynamics and reproducing some misguided data. I thus practice reflexivity to think critically about my interpretations of the information and interactions that I experienced.

It is also necessary to be transparent about the assumptions and power dynamics of my interactions with participants to assess my findings. Interpretive scholars are aware of the implications of the researcher's presence in the field site and acknowledge the importance of transparency (Schwartz-Shea & Yanow, 2013).

Reflections on my presence were noted earlier in the chapter in terms of the expectations the population had about my role as a beneficiary. Additionally, I had to reflect on the power relationship between myself and participants or interlocutors regarding potentially dangerous situations, as well as the possibility of retraumatization. In other words, at times I was in situations where I thought the participation of interlocutors, interviewees, or even interpreters may pose some risk to them, from the physical risk of travelling to certain areas with a white person to retraumatization through narrating experiences of violence or other traumas. I cannot say that I applied a uniform approach to these questions. At times, I made the final decision, such as the decision not to conduct research in Fizi even though my interpreter said that she was comfortable doing so. At other times, I provided individuals with as much information as possible but left them to make the final decision, such as interviewing the survivors of rape that had been arranged for me by an interlocutor. I cannot document each and every decision here, but I believe it is worth noting that these were ongoing reflections, deliberations, and discussions throughout my fieldwork that speak to the value I place on deep ethics, even if I could only imperfectly enact them.

Beyond considering the implications of my *presence* and decisions about the agency of participants, I also want to be transparent about my actions. In certain situations that I was observing, I played a consciously active role that changed events. For example, at an NGO-run mediation proceeding, the disputants were a married couple, and the woman was seeking a separation. During the process, Jeanne interpreted for me. The wife was accompanied by her older sister, while the husband had an uncle and another male family member with him. I learned that the wife did not have an older male family member to represent her, which is why her sister escorted her. During the proceedings, mediators asked the husband's male relative to provide information and contribute to the discussion, but the wife's sister was not given the same space. When the mediators sent all parties out of the room so they could discuss and deliberate, I asked why the wife's older sister was never allowed to speak, even though she attempted to multiple times. When I raised the question, the mediators quickly discussed in Kiswahili and then asked the sister to return and share her thoughts. I had very actively influenced the process.

I influenced the process as a reflection of my broader ethical commitments to provide space for the voices of people who have been marginalized, but clearly this also has implications for the co-creation of data. Throughout the book, I am clear about when and how I actively participated in events and how that might have shaped outcomes. In other situations, my influence was more passive, simply an outcome of my presence. I reflect on both types of occasions to provide a more transparent and profound account of my research, so readers may have a firm footing on which to consider questions of validity.

While analytic reflexivity certainly has important implications for research ethics as well as knowledge creation, the intersection of methods and ethics is not limited to critical reflection on positionality and power dynamics. Questions of reciprocity and member-checking reflect another area of intersection.

Reciprocity and Member-Checking

In my research, member-checking (Schwartz-Shea & Yanow, 2013) and reciprocity were attempted through the same channel, a two-day workshop that I hosted in Uvira in 2019. A common complaint voiced by local NGOs, activists, and civil society is that researchers have come seeking information and data but have not shared their results and recommendations, leaving under-resourced organizations at a loss for strategies to improve their services. I understand their complaints to reflect both practical and ethical concerns related to reciprocity in academic fieldwork. During the workshop, I shared my data, analyses, and recommendations; in turn, these were discussed and critiqued by the numerous local organizations and authorities that have provided information, assistance, and access to beneficiaries for my doctoral research.

This workshop thus provided the opportunity to correct, enhance, re-evaluate, and modify my analyses and recommendations in response to discussions facilitated by the workshop, a form of 'member-checking' (Schwartz-Shea & Yanow, 2013). Misinterpretation is always a possibility, so sharing my analyses and recommendations was an occasion to improve how my research represents people's lived experiences of justice and injustice. Although many of the people who participated in my research were not part of the workshop, as this would have been logistically impossible and may have created tensions between various participants, the local organizations who did participate were the ones working directly on legal-justice issues. The workshop provided them with valuable information, resources, and linkages. Local organizations and actors have been working on these issues for years, and my research highlights a number of common problems and difficulties beyond the obvious lack of stable funding.

Notably, however, the workshop was also a politicized compromise. I had to attend to local political power dynamics in order to hold this event, which meant that the space created was not one that could enable a completely free and open dialogue. The presence of certain actors, such as members of local government, limited the possibilities of critique, yet the inclusion of these actors was necessary for the event to take place. Although there were some in the local administration who were open to critique, I did not want to jeopardize the possibility of doing future research or of the success of any of the local organizations that participated.

I was reminded of the political nature of the event when the organization I partnered with made it clear that we would have to send out letters of information to all local government offices to get their support, identify which officials would have to be invited, and bring the invitations to their offices. To further emphasize this point, an official from the Agence Nationale de

Renseignements (ANR, the government intelligence agency) showed up at my partner organization's office accusing them of not following proper protocol because they had not received a letter of information but had heard about the event from another government office. Fortunately, and further reinforcing the clear benefits I received from working closely with local partners, they *had* brought the letter and had ensured that the ANR official who received them had documented it. The misunderstanding was resolved, but it was a strong reminder that I had to navigate local power structures carefully, as well as reflect on how to represent my research to this politically diverse group of participants.

I also viewed the workshop as contributing to reciprocity, giving something back to the community. Paraphrasing a Sierra Leonean professor[32], "Western researchers get your PhDs off our backs and then disappear." Doing research requires participation from individuals and community members; it requires relationships, give and take. These relationships have two sides, the expectations of the researcher and those of participants, which may correspond but can also be misaligned despite how explicitly either side communicates their expectations.

In contexts of humanitarian intervention, as in the eastern DRC, the presence of foreigners may elicit expectations of assistance, and it is left to the researcher to mitigate these false expectations (Lake, 2014a). I found navigating these hopes to be confounding; they persisted after I had explained that there is no compensation for the research. This may well be due to different understandings of 'compensation', but also from the unspoken norms that took me some time to learn. I discovered there was a norm for NGOs to secure participation in events by paying the *transport*. This was not locally understood as a type of compensation *per se* but appears to have become an unspoken, taken-for-granted practice, even when the participant had not travelled, or travelled only a short distance by foot. This tacit knowledge made it difficult to assess whether individuals were participating because they expected this tacitly recognized exchange.

While recognizing problems of not wanting to influence participants by creating expectations of exchange, as in the commodification of rape narratives, I also recognized that some of these individual interviews were with people I might not see again but from whom I would greatly benefit. I became more flexible with these expectations over time, from strictly avoiding any form of compensation to paying elevated transportation costs or providing another small sum of money for people's time.

Re-Presentation in Research and Writing

Finally, my research is designed to develop a contextually informed understanding of harms and justice practices. Yet, the nature of academic research is such that it puts the researcher, me, in a position to speak authoritatively on harms and justice using the narratives collected as *I* choose. My underlying ethical concern is to avoid contributing to the racialized and essentialized portrayals of the Congo outlined in the previous chapters of this book. Instead, my goal is to offer a rich account of legal-justice that helps us better understand the complexity of the law and justice in people's everyday lives and is willing to look critically at both international ROL building assumptions and practices, as well as local beliefs and practices.

How I write and talk about my research require critical reflection informed by the politics of speaking for others and re-presentation, which highlight the power of the researcher. Reflexivity in the use of narratives is crucial in order to reduce the risk of fetishizing, romanticizing, and essentializing the experiences of others. Women in the DRC have already been subjected to these reductionist tendencies, where the focus on wartime rape has tended to eroticize victimhood and create voyeuristic spaces and interactions (Baaz & Stern, 2010; Henry, 2014; see also Graham, 2014). I do not conceive of research ethics as being limited to the field. Research ethics can also be about writing in ways that challenge the power dynamics of knowledge production that prioritize certain ways of knowing. The privilege of 'getting close' lends an authoritative voice to the author who is re-narrating the experiences of others who are often 'othered'. I attempt to prioritize contextually relevant and often experiential knowledge about justice and legality. This does not mean that all voices are represented or that this analysis signifies *the* truth about justice in Uvira because my presence and questions of course shape the types of information to which I have access, as discussed previously. There is no way to disentangle research methods, data, and analyses from power relations. Rather, my point is that I recognize these entanglements, and I also try to prioritize people's own understandings of their lives and the systems of justice and injustice that surround them, while at the same time speaking to the broader research community in their language as well.

The goal for me is to draw on the complexities that immersion allows me to observe and experience in order to complicate simplistic and essentializing narratives and the de-humanizing but also problematic data that they encompass (see also Dunn, 2020).

Conclusion

As researchers, our findings, analyses, and conclusions are profoundly wrapped up in the methodological approach of the researcher and the context in which the research is being conducted. Often, the focus is on methods. How many interviews were conducted? With whom? What was the sampling technique? In this chapter, I put the emphasis on the interaction between myself, the researcher, the population, and the context of encounter. In the eastern DRC, I had the challenge of trying to make sense of my experiences as an embodied researcher and situating them within the international, racialized politics that are firmly rooted in a colonial history and recent interventions. Had I chosen not to recognize, reflect on, and engage with these dynamics, I may have had access to different information and drawn different conclusions that may have more thoroughly affirmed dominant, international understandings of the context and its problems. This is not to say my approach is perfectly devoid of these dynamics, but I used this chapter to be transparent about my methodology for dealing with these realities and to highlight where I focused my reflections and critiques, as well as highlighting the decisions that went into my choice of research locale.

Choosing a research site can be based on different logics. While I started my research trying to focus on varying my specific sites according to different authorities, access to courts, and rural–urban divides, I encountered practical barriers to completing extensive research in two of the sites—Makobola and Kiliba. In rethinking my research design and questions, I was still able to use some of the information that was shared with me in those sites, but I focused on areas within Uvira city. Uvira was also an important site because it is home to three different courts—the Tripaix, Tribunal de Grande Instance, and Military Tribunal. This meant that it was the place within Uvira territory where physical access to the courts was most likely. This occurred alongside the use of a variety of other justice mechanisms and practices. So, even as my research question changed, Uvira remained a good choice as research locale.

Notably, as a result of what I was learning in the field during my first research trip, I chose to reformulate my research question and framework. This meant frequent forays back to theory and literature to develop understandings of everyday harms, legal reforms, and ROL building rather than my original focus on exceptional harms and transitional justice. Of course, there are limitations to my methodological approach, such as working with interpreters and gatekeepers, which I have attempted to address but still recognize, especially the difficulty in developing rapport when working with an interpreter and the multiple layers of interpretation that go into the analysis. Another possible limitation of working with interpreters as gatekeepers is that they may be selective in choosing who to introduce to you. That being said, these limitations are taken into consideration in the analysis, which I recognize as part of the interpretive construction of knowledge; participants, interlocutors, hosts, partners, and community members have agency and a certain amount of power to decide on my level of access to people and information. We may look at this as a limitation to research, but it is also a part of being human. This is important to recognize for transparency reasons but also ethical reasons. The ethical considerations that I briefly addressed were reflexivity, reciprocity, and re-presentation. Each of the Rs is meant to reduce the potential exploitative nature of research, even if only imperfectly. This chapter establishes my approach to research and the relevance of how interveners have shaped the local landscape. In the next chapter, I begin to explore how interveners and international–local partnerships shape legal consciousness and the terrain of legality.

Notes

1 Village chief.
2 Commune chief. Makobola is made up of three communes, each with its own chief. The village chief presides over all of them.
3 There are different levels and intensities of relationships developed during fieldwork. In my research, I use the term 'interlocutor' to refer to people I have repeated contact with and have developed a deeper relationship, primarily around the research project. 'Participants' and 'interviewees' refer to people I have interviewed but have not been a larger part of the research project. 'Friends' and 'interlocutors' sometimes overlap, but when I refer to friends, I am referring to people with whom my relationship extends substantially beyond the research project. Finally, 'community members' are people in the communities where I have done research who I may not have interviewed but who may contribute to the research through informal conversations and participant observation.
4 Around that time, "The trouble with the Congo: Local violence and the failure of international peacebuilding" (Autesserre, 2010) outlined this narrative and provided a framework of critique. The simple narrative included the idea that the cause of the conflict were minerals, the consequence was wartime rape, and the required response was international intervention and peacebuilding.
5 When I arrived in Uvira in 2019, people were excited to inform me that Uvira had recently been officially designated a city.
6 Ordonnance-Loi 82–020 portant Code de l'organisation et de la compétence judiciaires (ORDER-LAW 82–020 on the Code of Judicial Organization and Jurisdiction), Chapter 1, Section 1, from 31 Mars 1982.
7 Ordonnance-Loi 82–020 portant Code de l'organisation et de la compétence judiciaires (ORDER-LAW 82–020 on the Code of Judicial Organization and Jurisdiction), Chapter 1, Section 2, from 31 Mars 1982.
8 Loi N°023/2002 du 18 Novembre 2002 Portant Code Judiciaire Militaire (Law N°023/2002 Enacting the Military Judicial Code), Book 2, Chapter 2.
9 Office of the Territory.
10 Interview, 22 April 2015.
11 The earliest official record of the tribunaux de paix that I can find is in ORDONNANCE-LOI 82–020 portant Code de l'organisation et de la compétence judiciaires (ORDER-LAW 82–020 on the Code of Judicial Organization and Jurisdiction), from 31 Mars 1982.
12 Interview, 16 April 2015.
13 Interview, 11 February 2017.
14 Public prosecutor.
15 Interview, 11 February 2017.
16 Chieftaincy.
17 Interview, 6 February 2017.
18 I came to this conclusion when we were meeting one day and he was giving me several updates, including some sensitive information about local police. He seemed excited to share but also a little agitated. He asked me several times not to mention his name or ask about the case in Uvira because it might become known to the police that he was sharing information. At the same time, I felt like our meetings were not at all private, and people in the area saw us meeting regularly, meaning this information could get back to the police regardless of what I did or did not say.
19 While I used a pseudonym, Amikali, in the published article, I believe sufficient time has passed that transparency about location will not pose a threat to my interlocutors or others.
20 Amicable settlements.
21 Fieldnotes, 2017.

22 Rush-Smith (2015) argues that in South Africa, vigilantism is linked with the rise of individual rights and procedural justice associated with the transition to liberal democracy. This is viewed by some as a threat in the sense that people who are perceived as criminals are given too many rights and are not punished severely enough. I would argue that there is a parallel phenomenon happening in Congo, where the population views legal punishment to be too light in some cases and do not support some of the procedural aspects of legal-justice, such as interim or pre-trial release (Interview, lawyer, 30 January 2017).
23 Phone credit.
24 Dirt bike.
25 Dirt bike taxi drivers.
26 Fried dough balls.
27 For additional information on my interview methodology, see Appendix A.
28 Of course, this has its own set of security concerns for partners and interpreters, which I was in continuous dialogue with them about.
29 8 April 2015.
30 The officer attempted to exhort a bribe from my friend by asking for *unités* for his phone. When she refused, he asked me for *unités*, and I offered to let him use my phone. This was not what he expected; while not paying the bribe was risky, he eventually let up and actually started joking around with us.
31 Positivist understandings of validity do not fit well with interpretive work given the researcher's presence in the field site and role in the construction of 'data' and knowledge, as well as the privileging of local knowledge (Schwartz-Shea & Yanow, 2013). Reflexivity is one tool that interpretive researchers have as a 'check' on the trustworthiness of their research (Schwartz-Shea & Yanow, 2013).
32 Sexual and gender-based violence workshop. 2013. Burundi, Bujumbura.

Bibliography

Aroussi, S. (2018). Perceptions of justice and hierarchies of rape: Rethinking approaches to sexual violence in Eastern Congo from the ground up. *International Journal of Transitional Justice, 12*(2), 277–295.

Autesserre, S. (2010). *The trouble with the Congo: Local violence and the failure of international peacebuilding* (Vol. 115). Cambridge University Press

Autesserre, S. (2014). *Peaceland: Conflict resolution and the everyday politics of international intervention.* Cambridge University Press.

Baaz, M., & Stern, M. (2010). *The complexity of violence: A critical analysis of sexual violence in the Democratic Republic of Congo (DRC).* Sida: Nordiska Afrikainstitutet.

Berger, R. (2015). Now I see it, now I don't: Researcher's position and reflexivity in qualitative research. *Qualitative Research, 15*(2), 219–234.

Bott, E. (2010). Favourites and others: Reflexivity and the shaping of subjectivities and data in qualitative research. *Qualitative Research, 10*(2), 159–173.

CRG. (2016, 9 April). Press statement regarding the expulsion of Jason Stearns from the DR Congo. *Congo Research Group, Groupe D'Etude Sur Le Congo.* congoresearchgroup.org/press-statement-regarding-the-expulsion-of-jason-stearns-from-the-dr-congo/.

Dunn, H. (2020). Research in the land of savages, victims, and saviors. In G. Hoogensen, P. Weitsman & R. Matthew (Eds.), *Women's perspectives on human security: Violence, environment, and sustainability* (pp. 154–182). Ohio University Press.

Dunn, H. (2021). Emergent hybrid legality: A study of legal encounters in the DRC. *Journal of Intervention and Statebuilding, 15*(2), 201–220.

England, K. V. (1994). Getting personal: Reflexivity, positionality, and feminist research. *The Professional Geographer, 46*(1), 80–89.

Ewick, P., & Silbey, S. S. (2000). No laughing matter: Humor and contradiction in stories of law. *DePaul Law Review, 50*, 559.

Freedman, J. (2016). *Gender, violence and politics in the Democratic Republic of Congo*. Routledge.

Fujii, L. A. (2013). Working with interpreters. In L. Mosley (Ed.), *Interview research in political science* (pp. 144–157). Cornell University Press.

Graham, A. (2014). One hundred years of suffering? "Humanitarian crisis photography" and self-representation in the Democratic Republic of the Congo. *Social Dynamics, 40*(1), 140–163.

Henry, N. (2014). The fixation on wartime rape: Feminist critique and international criminal law. *Social & Legal Studies, 23*, 93–111.

Hilbink, L., & Gallagher, J. (2019). The state and law: A critical assessment. In K. Ansolabehere & R. Sieder (Eds.), *Handbook of law and society in Latin America*. Routledge.

HRW. (2016, 9 August). DR Congo: Human rights watch researcher barred. *Human Rights Watch*. www.hrw.org/news/2016/08/09/dr-congo-human-rights-watch-researcher-barred.

Lake, M. (2014a). *Building the rule of law in fragile states: The role of external actors in shaping institutional responses to mass violence in the Democratic Republic of Congo and South Africa* (unpublished doctoral dissertation). University of Washington.

Schatz, E. (Ed.). (2013). Introduction: Ethnographic immersion and the study of politics. In *Political ethnography: What immersion contributes to the study of power*. University of Chicago Press.

Schwartz-Shea, P., & Yanow, D. (2013). *Interpretive research design: Concepts and processes*. Routledge.

Thomson, S., Ansoms, A., & Murison, J. (2013). Introduction: Why stories behind the findings? In *Emotional and ethical challenges for field research in Africa* (pp. 1–11). Palgrave Macmillan.

Verweijen, J. (2015). The disconcerting popularity of popular in/justice in the Fizi/Uvira region, eastern Democratic Republic of the Congo. *International Journal on Minority and Group Rights, 22*(3), 335–359.

Vinck, P., & Pham, P. (2008). Ownership and participation in transitional justice mechanisms: A sustainable human development perspective from eastern DRC. *The International Journal of Transitional Justice, 2*(3), 398–411.

Wedeen, L. (2013). Ethnography as interpretive enterprise. In Edward Schatz (Ed.), *Political ethnography: What immersion contributes to the study of power* (pp. 75–93). University of Chicago Press.

Chapter 4

Top-Down Approaches to Shaping Legal Consciousness

In Uvira, the buzzword on the lips of local NGOs was *sensibilisation*. Nearly every local NGO I interviewed or spoke to informally explained how they do *sensibilisation* and how more *sensibilisation* is needed. By common definition[1], *sensibiliser* means to make someone, a vulnerable group, receptive to something in which they had previously lacked interest. Local organizations have infused this concept with a lot of power by arguing its importance for building community knowledge of the law. *Sensibilisation* can apply to just about any social or development issue. For example, an employee at the Bureau de Cadastre explained, "People just as often do not get [land] titles because they have not experienced sensibilisation, rather than the cost [of the title]"[2]. However, the local legal complex has clearly put the spotlight on *sensibilisation* in women's rights and gender equality work. I was interested in how it was used in Uvira to shape people's legal consciousness, whether intentionally, through explicit use of *sensibilisation* practices or through implicit means of shaping legal consciousness. The important distinction between *sensibilisation* and various English translations, such as 'awareness raising' and 'educating', is that it suggests reframing or changing people's interests, not simply providing additional information. Since *sensibilisation* was the buzzword of various organizations and other actors, it suggests that they interpret part of the struggle as making the general population interested in the law and legal system, not just in providing information.

The way I understand this undertaking of *sensibilisation* in Uvira is thus twofold. First, it is a way to raise people's awareness of the law and legal system. Second, it is also a way to influence popular interest in law or to shape people's legal consciousness so that law becomes the dominant frame through which people understand certain harms or disputes, shifting subjectivity towards liberal legalism. This has most clearly occurred around the issue of sexual violence. Through my interviews, people seemed to interpret most harms and disputes through a variety of frames, not necessarily identifying them as legal issues. By contrast, most people put stranger rape in a category of harm that should be dealt with by the state legal system, an issue that has been subjected to years of *sensibilisation* and legal mobilization. This chapter thus explores how

DOI: 10.4324/9781003289715-4

sensibilisation activities are reshaping people's legal consciousness, but this does not mean a comprehensive shift to liberal legalism and state legality.

Active attempts to shape legal consciousness are often undertaken by the local legal complex. These actors may be formally trained, like lawyers; however, they frequently comprise those civil society actors who have received some form of training on rights, law, and law-based mediation. These individuals play an important role in building popular knowledge of the legal system and introducing the population to some of the tenets of liberal legalism. At the same time, they also play a role in shaping people's perceptions and judgements of the various systems and practices of legal-justice. Thus, the local legal complex plays an influential role in actively shaping legal consciousness, which is the scaffolding of *emergent hybrid legality*. At the same time, legal consciousness is also affected by everyday experiences and interactions, a more passive shaping of legal consciousness that forms part of my analysis in Chapters 5 and 6. Here, I focus on the role of top-down shaping of legal consciousness through the legal complex. This chapter begins to lend insight into contradictory legal consciousness, the themes of the *disconnect in harm naming* and *different logics of justice*.

Internationalized Legal Reforms and Shaping Legal Consciousness

In the wake of multiple wars, certain areas of eastern DRC, notably the provincial capitals of Bukavu and Goma, became the focus of a variety of international actors and internationally funded post-conflict programming. Much of this programming was focused on post-conflict reconstruction, namely state-building and peacebuilding, incorporating a variety of components, such as 'disarmament, demobilization and reintegration'; conflict resolution; access to justice; and various approaches to ending SGBV (Autesserre, 2010; Baaz & Stern, 2010; Lake, 2018). The legal-justice components of these interventions often fall under the broader umbrella of ROL building. This includes writing new laws and building legal infrastructure and institutions, as well as educating people about the state laws and legal system (Lake, 2014b; Lincoln, 2011). The former is the topic of much ROL scholarship, while the latter component is what I explore in relation to the influence of internationalized legal norms and practices in popular legal consciousness.

Big Players and the State-Centric Approach to Legal Reform

The international influence in the eastern DRC is distinguished by its extensive presence—DRC has become home to the largest UN mission, the UN Organization Stabilization Mission in the Democratic Republic of Congo (MONUSCO) (previously, MONUC) (Koddenbrock, 2012). It has also hosted numerous peacebuilding activities implemented by foreign government agencies, foreign and international NGOs, and other entities (Arnould & Vlassenroot, 2016; Koddenbrock, 2012). An overview of these projects suggests that when it comes to the ROL, these organizations are largely interested in state-level institutions. For example, USAID's Country Development Cooperation Strategy for DRC (2014–2019) lists as its stakeholders: The government of DRC, US government interests, and donors. Their goals include developing effectiveness of national-level institutions by enhancing the state capacity to create and implement laws. At the local level, they are interested in strengthening service delivery institutions. The population's input is noticeably lacking in this strategic outline.

As another example, the EU has taken a noticeably active role in peacebuilding and security in DRC, also with an emphasis on building formal state institutions and rehabilitating the justice sector (Arnould & Vlassenroot, 2016). While this may have contributed to some of the successes in gender-based violence prosecutions noted by Lake (2014b) and in making the law the dominant frame through which people understand rape, its broader impact is limited. For example, Restauration de la justice en l'est du Congo (REJUSCO), which received 15 million Euros to restore the legal system in the east of Congo, predominantly focused on infrastructure, leaving out access to justice and corruption, as well as cost and length of trials (Arnould & Vlassenroot, 2016). Incidentally, the people I interviewed frequently criticized these problems with the state legal system. Additionally, the EU policy documents include little to no mention of incorporating the population in the process of legal reform, nor do they seem interested in considering local norms and practices, or informal justice institutions[3].

As a final example, the DRC is one of the United Nations Development Programme's (UNDP) focus countries for their ROL programming. In UNDP document, "Strengthening the Rule of Law in Crisis-Affected and Fragile Situations: A UNDP global programme for justice and security (Phase II) 2012–2015", they state that the report "represents a framework for UNDP's renewed contribution to strengthening the UN to work together in this important area." In reviewing the document, it clearly reflects mainstream, international approaches to ROL building. Three[4] of its main 'outputs' are focused on very conventional statist approaches to ROL building. One output states: "It provides technical, operational and financial support to UNDP Country Offices to implement comprehensive rule of law, justice and security programmes in countries affected by conflict, disaster, violence and fragility" (p. 2). Another output is: "Increase rapid deployment of rule of law expertise" (p. 2). Finally: "Foster UN-wide policy development and coordination on rule of law" (p. 2). Notably, their outlined understanding of the ROL is aligned with the statist paradigm. 'Customary law' is mentioned a few times in passing but is not integrated into any of the outputs[5]. The report does at times reference awareness raising/sensitisation; thus, it has certain goals directed at the population through educating people about the laws and courts, in line with what one would expect from mainstream ROL building that recognizes education as a necessary component.

Notably, the dominant aspects of these projects not only ignore popular norms, beliefs, practices, and contributions; they also largely overlook the alternative justice and regulatory systems that shape and govern people's everyday lives. In Autesserre's (2014) research on peacebuilding, she found that, "In Congo, many programs also failed to achieve their intended objectives because they tried to reform formal institutions but had no effect on the people who actually controlled the situation, or because they focused on formulating new legislation while *the population would usually rather obey customary laws and a series of semi-formal rules*" (*emphasis added*, loc 4836). This is the practice reflected in some of the major international ROL interventions in eastern DRC. This overview is brief but highlights some of the ROL critiques outlined in the Introduction, notably that major international actors tend to focus narrowly on state legal institutions, actors, and law.

One area of ROL building that has received significant international attention is prosecuting extraordinary crimes, such as wartime rape. This is incorporated into ROL activities because international interveners believe that resources and expertise that are invested in rape trials, including the provision of legal aid, enhance public awareness of the possibilities of prosecution for such harms and have created a space for victims to come forward and find support, at least in the capitals of Goma and Bukavu (Lake, 2014b). Thus, international actors are not organizing direct awareness-raising activities in these cases, yet they are participating in raising awareness through the demonstration effect of holding effective trials. In other words, by showing that trials are happening according to the ROL, some believe that they play a role in enhancing trust and awareness of the state legal system. More broadly, however, the role of major international organizations and actors in Uvira is one of a partnership with the local legal complex who actually execute the programmes and activities.

Local–International Partnerships and Funding

The local legal complex has its own protagonists and practices, but it is internationalized in two clear ways. First, international actors guide the legal reform agenda, identifying and influencing laws and legal procedures that they believe need to be changed to bring the country closer to international standards, as described earlier. Second, international actors play a major role in shaping and directing the types of projects that local organizations decide to undertake. Knowledge of the law cannot be taken for granted anywhere, but especially not in a context where access to the internet and television is limited for the average person. Thus, some of these partnerships between international actors and local actors have emphasized *sensibilisation* activities, as well as access to justice projects.

International and local NGOs frequently partner to raise awareness about Congolese law and provide legal assistance to victims of SGBV (Lake et al., 2016). More broadly, the internationalized legal complex has undertaken some initiatives to inform the population of the law and functioning of courts. As one local NGO leader[6] stated, "International [actors] woke us up through sensibilisation. Now our laws are very good, but they are just put in cabinets." She noted both the increased awareness about the law but also alluded to its limits in terms of access and practice. Recent legal reforms, largely shaped by interventions from external actors[7] (see Lake, 2014b), have gone hand in hand with popular promulgation of laws and changes to the legal system—both written laws and procedural aspects—in areas such as torture[8] (in Uvira), rights of the child[9], and gender equality[10]. In other words, international partners are especially interested in raising awareness about particular areas of law. Local partners, in turn, often respond to these preferences in order to secure funding.

Indeed, international donor preferences can be fundamental to how the local organizations develop, propose, and manage their projects. Referring to their international donors, MEK, an NGO that does advocacy work and legal assistance, stated that:

> The finances they give as support go where *they* want according to *their* priorities. . . . Maybe they agree to finance a certain number of cases, for example, sexual violence cases. Since I have been here, the ABA[11] [their primary donor] has only focused on sexual violence cases. . . . Our funders expect certain results, and we target people based on that[12].

This point was also noted by someone[13] who works at the Tribunal de Grande Instance, who noted that the court also gets financial support from donors, but that it must be used to support their priorities. He stated, "For example, since I have been here, the ABA has only focused on sexual violence cases." Unsurprisingly, funders of legal projects may prioritize sexual violence cases, even if those were not what their domestic partners would recommend based on their experiences with the local population.

A pertinent discussion on the topic of international assistance developed during a conference I helped organize that was held on 27 April 2015. The topic was civil society mobilization, and it was attended by numerous local organizations. One participant raised the question of whether Western funders and organizations define or impose the projects that local NGOs pursue. He specifically cited international focus on sexual violence as the first example of this phenomenon. One of the panelists, a local professor, denied that funders impose projects, saying, "You are entering their space and world by choice, so you are *choosing* to adapt your project that way"[14]. Many agreed with the professor that if you were requesting money you are *choosing* to modify your project to have a better chance at obtaining funding. In other words, projects come to be shaped by donors, not only, or not primarily, by the local population's stated needs.

However, participants' agreement with the professor surprised me. Throughout my fieldwork, numerous interlocutors had complained about NGOs having to tailor their projects to donors' preferences rather than local needs. One possible way to make sense of the conference dynamics is by reference to the saviour economic complex. Given the gendered and racialized assumptions and expectations surrounding my presence, it would fit that the Professor's argument, and participants' agreement, was linked with perceptions that I was a possible source of funding and thus a less critical tone was warranted. Whereas in more personal meetings with NGOs, I had more time and space to address and mitigate these expectations, and it was in these closer encounters that I heard NGO staff voice their annoyances with international funders.

Whether or not local organizations feel that donors impose or too strongly shape projects, the local stories that circulate suggest that it is common knowledge that some NGOs 'take advantage' of their funders. Civil society actors spoke of some of the perverse dynamics of NGO–donor relationships. One participant said,

> The one who has power can do whatever they want. . . . Many people have gotten rich here. For example, organizations don't actually help; they just say they are going to in order to get money from funders and then find ways to keep it. For example, it is common for them to take pictures of something like a bridge and say that they built it when it was a bridge that already existed somewhere else[15].

This interview suggests that civil society actors are aware that some amongst them are manipulating their relationships with donors. In a workshop[16] I attended on UN Resolution 1325, someone framed a problem as NGOs getting funds but not using them as expected. For example, they might receive donor visitors in an office that is not actually their own. These dynamics are unsurprising given NGO–donor dynamics where donors have expectations of certain results and a very limited understanding of how things actually work on the ground. Indeed, some informants pointed out that international donors should come visit more often to see the functioning and impact of the projects that they are funding. Thus, while there are some actors in the local legal complex who are willing to tailor their projects in order to get funding, unsurprisingly, in a context of scarce resources, others seek to personally benefit from donor arrangements.

This section only begins to shed light on some of the unanticipated dynamics that structure how local organizations navigate and manipulate international pressures and associated power dynamics. And, while they are not the focus of my research, it is worth keeping in mind as I illustrate how the local legal complex functions to raise popular awareness of the legal system. These dynamics are in some ways influenced by perverse donor–recipient incentives. In the following section, I outline the areas where the local legal complex engages in spaces of *friction* and plays a role in shaping contradictory consciousness, and hence the terrain of *emergent hybrid legality*.

Local NGOs and Sensibilisation

Local NGOs, working independently and through partnerships with international organizations and foreign governments, have endeavoured to raise popular awareness of the law and legal systems as part of broader legal reform efforts. These awareness-raising activities are a clearly identifiable intervention in the continuous construction and reconstruction of legal consciousness, whereby understandings of the law are being created, sustained, reproduced, challenged, and changed through day-to-day activities. Thus, in this section, I focus on elucidating the actors and processes of *sensibilisation*, while in later chapters, I explore the manifestations of popular legal consciousness, the *disconnect in harm naming*, and *different logics of justice*. In other words, here I am looking at the local legal complex's processes of shaping legal consciousness. Specifically, I examine *which* local actors are doing *what* to try to educate people about the state law and legal system. Additionally, these actors often combine different aspects of legal pluralism in unique and accessible ways for the local population, both shaping contradictory legal consciousness and building *emergent hybrid legality*.

Training Leaders

Local NGOs, some who partner with state offices, work to educate and raise awareness about the laws and legal system through training programmes. However, accessing large swaths of the population for meaningful training is difficult. Driving or walking through town with loudspeakers, one method of publicizing laws and legal functions, provides limited time and space for *engagement* with the population. In other words, the level of popular comprehension is unclear, limiting the viability of this approach. So, some organizations concentrate their resources on educating community *chefs* and other local leaders, such as teachers, religious figures, wise elders, and local organizations, who are then expected to disseminate information more broadly about the law. I label this vertical *sensibilisation*, where the process is from those with more information, education, training, and resources to people with (generally) less. MEK undertakes this form of awareness raising:

> We cannot do everything, but at least we contribute to building legal access. We do activities of *sensibilisation* and training of community leaders. We did a 3-day workshop where we taught community leaders by bringing them together with lawyers to talk about all sorts of conflicts, including

> over land. We used a lawyer as the host. We try to address the concrete problems in the community. We make a list of all the forms of sexual violence, for example, and then they tell us which are the most important types in their area[17].

This quote illustrates one approach used by local organizations: They share their knowledge of the law with community leaders who, through regular interactions with the population, can disseminate it to them more frequently. Many trainings include or are specifically directed at local and traditional *chefs*, as they are the ones who tend to be the first stop for addressing disputes. People frequently turn to their *chef d'avenue* or other local *chefs* to help resolve disputes or even harms that may arise.

In an interview with one of these local *chefs*, a *chef d'avenue* who had had some legal training, she explained that when mediating a dispute or problem, she would frequently refer to the laws relevant to the dispute to share the law and strengthen her own ability to address the problem because she was guided by the laws of the country. I asked, "Do you find that referring to the law can actually change people's behaviour?" She responded,

> Yes, because some people don't know the law, but when we can make them understand what the law is, they will be afraid of doing something wrong. For example, a person was bickering with her neighbours, and she took the megaphone as if she were advertising, shouting that the other person has AIDS. I was with the *chef de cellule*; I sent him to go listen to what they were screaming on the megaphone, and he heard how that *maman* made public her friend's status. "Do you know there is a law that protects people living with HIV?" He asked me. In Congo, the law is respected. The one whose status was made public went to the Tripaix to complain. Now, our presence and testimony were required. We testified that it was the truth because we have a law that protects the people living with HIV–AIDS. This *maman* was convicted and she paid the fines. Now, when this person goes out, she will understand that there is a law that protects people living with HIV–AIDS[18].

In this example, we see how, through this ad hoc interaction, the *chef d'avenue* learned about elements of the law from the *chef de cellule*. Further, for the actors involved, understanding the law was further reinforced when the case was brought to the Tripaix. The *chef d'avenue* herself noted how the people who were involved in the conflict now know the law, at least on this issue. A further step in the analysis is to explore what people do with the information they learn about the law and their experiences with the local legal complex. This is explored in the next chapter.

Targeting community leaders, including, for example, *chefs*, is one technique for broadening the reach of sensibilisation activities. Ideally, there is continued dissemination within the community after leaders receive training. While this may not always work as well in practice, sometimes the reach is indeed expanded. When I met with Olive[19], she explained that she, and other women who had received trainings, had taught others what they had learned. She explained that there was a time when there were a lot of break-ins; people's goods were stolen, and sometimes family members were attacked or raped. An organization distributed whistles so that community members could alert each other of these incidents. She said, "There was a time when we heard that people were robbing a neighbour because they would scream and blow on the whistle, and everyone was alerted. They would get scared and flee." Around this time, she also started doing trainings with the organization that helped distribute the whistles.

> We women [who participated in the trainings] were really the *sensibilisatrices* of others. And, if once they saw us because of a problem, they started to fear us. Hé! . . . Anyway, for the moment, women are in the spotlight . . . we don't really ignore women's rights anymore.

She explained that this shift came from the *sensibilisation* activities of a particular organization that held workshops and brought people together from a number of different communities. It was explained to them that they all had to return to their communities and bring the training to them. In particular, she explained that she shares information about human rights and that women are allowed to tell their husbands they do not want to have sex; any use of force is rape.

Indeed, it is not surprising that SGBV has been a focus of some *sensibilisation* activities. As mentioned previously, the international emphasis on addressing wartime rape and women's rights has influenced the local legal complex and the activities that they undertake. Some have argued that there have been noticeable changes as a result of awareness raising. For example, in one interview with a local NGO director[20], she said, "Custom says women are inferior, but over time, through information and sensibilisation [on women's rights], women are breaking the silence and denouncing this. They are claiming their rights." The leader of a different NGO[21] said, "Through mediation with the family and community she [a rape survivor] can easily be accepted. For those without sensibilisation, it is difficult for the woman to be accepted." They both highlight the effects that *sensibilisation* can and has had on the community, in general, and survivors, in particular. Of course, these shifts in awareness of SGBV have been imperfect, but they certainly deserve recognition.

Returning to my interview with Olive, she explained how *sensibilisation* done with a relatively small group of people can spread to the broader community when individuals, such as herself, take an active role in dissemination. Olive[22] went to her church and announced that she would share her training and meet with those who were interested. Of course, this also requires a certain amount of access to resources, connections, and time. Thus, it is not something that is feasible for everyone who gets some training.

It also bears mentioning that when *sensibilisation* is directed at women and their rights, there can be negative repercussions. This is a point that has been observed in research on development that finds both positive and negative impacts of women's economic and social empowerment (eg. Chant, 2006; Haile et al., 2012; Heath, 2014). The implications of the trainings are situated within the wider social context; the focus on women can disrupt both social norms and expectations in the home. For example, Soleil had done training sessions with 'Women for Women International', a humanitarian NGO working with female survivors of war. In these sessions, they covered positive relationships, including marital relations, an important area of women's rights in the region. This training gave her the courage to start sharing advice with others in the neighbourhood, a more limited form of local dissemination. Interestingly, she added, "You see, here, most Bafuleru women don't like to go to the trainings, believing that they will do nothing for them. But, those of us who know the importance of these trainings, we take advantage[23]. At the same time, as a result of participating in this training, she experienced problems with her husband. She used to walk to and from the trainings in the evening, sometimes arriving home late. Some people started gossiping and saying that she was out on 'adventures' with the husbands of other women. "My husband denied this, but at the same time he started bringing me and picking me up on the bike because he wanted to be certain that is where I was going"[24]. Soleil was *allowed* to continue participating but only under his surveillance.

Additionally, at times, there may be some animosity directed at women's access to resources through *sensibilisation* projects. For example, in 2015, when I went to register with the office of the Directeur Général de Migration[25], I had barely taken my seat before he enthusiastically began to rant about the unfairness of the focus on women's rights and needs. He said, "All the organizations are only working on women's issues. Men are being discriminated against!" In another instance, I interviewed a group of wise (male) elders in Makobola; they talked about how women are being educated about agriculture through Women for Women's programmes. One of these elders[26] stated, "They give them soap, but there is nothing for men." Although participants did not readily state feelings of unfairness or dissatisfaction, it was at least hinted at by the fact that they brought up that 'there is nothing for men'. This also fits with the broader popular discourse that was hesitantly critical of the focus of international and local NGOs on women and women's rights. This critique was emerging, certainly not monolithic, and was reflected in passing comments about how NGOs only focus on or support women. These perceptions of unfairness may limit some women's participation in trainings, as do perceptions of the trainings as either useless or problematic for challenging gender norms, both directly and indirectly.

Thus, discrepancies between who has access to *sensibilisation* is part of the local landscape. Some of these differences in access are intentional, such as focusing on women, while others are simply the outcome of the practical reality that NGOs cannot access or accommodate the needs of everyone. Still, at times, these differences can create negative perceptions of trainings and who is privileged. By contrast, some other mechanisms of awareness raising are more universally available, such as radios.

Sensibilisation through Radio and Theatre

While many of the people I interviewed did not have access to televisions or online content, only a few were lacking a radio. Radios remain one of the most common and affordable sources of information and entertainment. On advisement from Jeanne, my interpreter, I even began asking interviewees if they owned a radio as a means of gauging their socio-economic situation. Additionally, some people I interviewed explicitly recognized learning about the law on the radio. Others stated that they listened to radio stations, such as le Messager du Peuple and Radio Okapi, which is a UN-sponsored radio station. Both have programming that disseminates information about dispute resolution, the law, and the legal system. Even if some people did not actively recognize it, they may have passively been receiving messages about legal-justice. Also, a few local organizations informed me that both do *sensibilisation* through radio programmes[27].

Importantly, a number of people I spoke with mentioned getting their news and information from the radio. For example, Claude[28] explained that he listened to a radio programme that provided information about "conflicts and the violation of certain rights . . . so people learn certain articles [of the legal codes]." He added that some of what he heard was repetitive, "so people remember and understand the laws." Henriette[29] explained that she learned about women's rights on the radio. She said: "I have some notion about women's rights, like the right to food and clothing"[30]. However, in terms of realizing these rights, she was aware of the limitations. She added: "One day we [Henriette and her husband] were joking and he said, 'I know it's your right, but I can't go steal for you!'" Henriette's husband was noting the tension between local understandings of women's rights and the local reality of poverty that acts as a barrier to certain rights, even if the will is there. Claude also noted that, "There is someone on the radio in Sange who does *sensibilisation* . . . on conflicts and the violation of some laws. This is what we try to teach so that people learn some of the articles [laws]." These are just a few examples of what people shared about learning from radio programmes.

Notably, radio shows do not only focus on legal rights or processes. Other forms of legal-justice have also made their way to radio programming. For example, AA told us that they had raised awareness about mediation services through radio programming[31]. Given the preceding statements from people who learned about the law through the radio, it is likely that some of what they learned may have come from shows talking about the AA's mediation services as well. While they do mediation, they are also one of the organizations that cite the law and reflect the characteristics of *emergent hybrid legality*. Thus, information about the law and non-state mediation can be rolled out together, reinforcing the practice of hybridity.

Other people were less precise in identifying a link between radio programming and their legal consciousness, but they frequently stated that the radio is where they got their news and advice on how they should live peaceably with their families and neighbours. Thus, given the programming on the popular radio stations, it is likely that, through their listening practices, people are passively developing knowledge of the law and legal system. While radios are common, still some people do not have them. Naima[32] and Mireille[33], for example, did not have radios. Agathe[34] had one, but she could rarely afford batteries. So, the radio is a popular channel for information, but it is also a limited one.

Another local approach to *sensibilisation* is 'narrative theatre' performances. Narrative theatre is a community activity, where actors perform skits in response to concerns voiced by community members who are present for the performance. It is provided free to the public, and everyone is welcome. I was able to attend three performances in Kiliba, which were organized by a local NGO; two were independently organized and one was a part of a larger social gathering organized by CEEDECO and their local partners.

The theatre performances rely on a flexible and adaptable improvisation cast and a very animated session leader. The local community is invited to gather at a neighbourhood location where wooden benches and plastic chairs have been arranged in a circle, or in front of a stage for a larger event. The session leader begins by asking people who have gathered to provide examples of problems that have arisen in their community that need to be addressed; they do not specify that these must be legal issues or violent conflicts but anything that the community wants to address. Those who have gathered can then call out any number of issues until the animator picks up on one to organize the performance around. Issues that were repeatedly mentioned in the sessions I attended included suspicions and gossip, robbery, sexual violence, witchcraft, poisoning, and early marriage.

At the first performance, the concerns highlighted by the audience as the most pernicious were distrust and gossip. Next, the audience was asked to describe stories where this was the central theme; they could be based on real life but could not include actual names or places. Three stories were shared, and the one that was chosen by the animators focused on a man with three wives whom he treated unequally. Incidentally, my fieldwork finds that polygamous relationships are a common source of dispute (Dunn, 2018) and a *disconnect in harm naming*. A corrupt official and witchcraft were important aspects of the story as well. After approximately five minutes of discussion, the actors were ready to perform, and they put on quite a show! The audience a decent percentage of whom were children, laughed and obviously enjoyed the entertainment of the fabricated drama.

When the first skit ended, the animator returned to the centre of the group to mediate a discussion of the behaviours of the characters. Many in the audience, old and young, participated to point out the poor behaviour and flaws that the characters portrayed. The audience redefined how the skit should be acted to address the problems in a positive way. A briefer version of the skit followed. A key highlight was the 'exteriorization' that occurred at the end of the second skit. The husband was covered in a large scarf, and the 'bad-behaviour spirit' was extracted from his writhing form. The spirit was caught in a bag by the leader, and the opportunity was given to the audience to interrogate this bad spirit. Who are its parents? Why is it here in Kiliba? What does it enjoy? Can we make it leave Kiliba? The grand finale was the spirit being chased away from Kiliba because community members have agreed that they would prefer to be supportive of each other than have the spirit present.

These performances had three notable strengths. First, they created space for the local community to define the problems that they found most consequential and to discuss ways to address them through legal-justice channels or otherwise. This reflects the lived experience that localized harms and disputes do not always map onto legal categories but can still cause problems. Second, they created a framework to help the community let go of the negative stories of the past. Third, they provided free and accessible entertainment and much-needed comic relief. The laughter and the smiles on people's faces suggest that it was a welcome distraction from the difficulties present in a context of high unemployment and poverty in a town that was once the site of a thriving sugar factory, which now sits empty.

A couple of additional points bear mentioning. First, while narrative theatre appeared to play a role in *sensibilisation*, animators were not overly focused on the laws or legal system but were more interested in improving behaviour and relationships. Still, this fits with *sensibilisation* given that the content reflects several local, everyday conflicts and information about how to address them according to the broader terrain of legality. Second, I maintain some scepticism about the integral role of narrative theatre in local legal consciousness because performances appeared to be organized around my visits. That is not to say that they were *only* organized in response to my visits. Indeed, the local population appeared familiar with these events, but it did not seem like they were a regular occurrence. This may be a phenomenon that was also shaped by the saviour economic complex, meaning these events were organized around my visits in the hopes of eliciting additional resources or funding from me or my assumed connection.

Notably, not all interviewees recalled having experienced any form of *sensibilisation*, yet many were still familiar with some aspects of the law, such as the fact that witchcraft is not recognized by the state, land titles are required to prove ownership, civil marriage ensures certain legal entitlements, and rape and other forms of sexual violence are illegal—some of which I explore further in the next two chapters. This suggests, then, that information about the law *also* circulates informally and horizontally through shared stories, experiences, and rumours. Mireille[35], for example, had a phone, but no access to internet. When, towards the end of our interview, I asked Mireille if she was aware of any of the laws, she said: "I know nothing about the laws of the country. . . . It is important, but I don't know them because I don't have the law book." In the same interview, however, she had recognized her responsibility to pay taxes at the market, and that if someone stole her goods and refused to give them back, she might eventually report the person to the police but only after attempting mediation. Mireille's statements illustrate that sometimes people do not believe they know the law because they have not received formal training, but aspects of it still permeate their everyday lives. Notably, people think about the law and courts in relation to other justice practices, such as mediation, as explored later in this chapter.

In addition to training local leaders and using the radio and narrative theatre, local NGOs disseminate legal information in other ways as well, such as through their NGO mediation services. Actors in the local legal complex may disseminate information about legal-justice through their mediation and legal aid processes. This is an additional element of *sensibilisation* that can be more or less intentional on the part of the provider but can still have important effects on legal consciousness. Given the institutionalized nature of the mediation legal services of NGOs, I explore these for their role in producing *emergent hybrid legality*.

Local NGOs and the Production of *Emergent Hybrid Legality*

The outlined approaches to *sensibilisation* educate the population and raise awareness predominantly about the state legal system. At the same time, given that the local legal complex often shares the same worldview as the population, their influence is not purely as legal actors but as local legal interlocutors. Indeed, they are in a unique position to, not just *vernacularize* (Merry, 2009) the law but also to produce, in conjunction with the local population, legality in novel ways that incorporate both internationalized legal norms and local justice expectations and worldviews. I label the outcomes of encounters between international legal norms and practices and local ones *emergent hybrid legality*. Here, I consider the role of local NGOs in the production of *emergent hybrid legality* through their practices beyond direct awareness-raising.

NGOs, the Law, and Mediation

One of the most prominent manifestations of *emergent hybrid legality* is when local actors combine written law with informal mediation. More specifically, this is exemplified by NGO mediators who use the discourse of the law outside of the legal system as either a source of important and meaningful information to combine with mediation or as a coercive tool to 'encourage' people to accept mediated resolutions.

In Uvira, years of violence, forced migration, and instability weakened customary systems and structures[36], resulting in the flourishing of justice alternatives that were less structured or regulated by traditional authorities. These newer, non-state spaces have developed to combine aspects of law and customary justice in NGO-run offices. For example, many NGOs that work on dispute resolution rely on mediators who help the parties come to an agreement or settlement. Those mediators may be chosen because the community or local organization views them as trustworthy and wise, but they also tend to have some human rights or dispute resolution training, often sponsored by international organizations. They engage with norms associated with amicable settlements—which are conventionally performed within the family or by wise, local elders—but they also cite the law to strengthen and add force to their settlements and educate the population. In that sense, mediators vernacularize[37], meaning translate or appropriate (Merry, 2009), the state laws for more localized contexts. At the same time, they actively engage with and retain more localized approaches to justice, namely the focus on reconciliation. The resultant legal-justice outcomes form a part of *emergent hybrid legality* and provide a unique opportunity to facilitate access to justice and a space for discussing localized understandings of women's rights but can also construct a legal terrain, where people can justify acts of popular justice. These are further explored in later chapters.

Amongst various NGOs, and the population more generally, there is a sentiment that while the written laws of the countries are, for the most part, good, they are not properly implemented. Therefore, during mediation sessions, mediators often refer to state laws, while informally resolving a dispute and advancing goals of reconciliation and restorative justice. The lawyer who directs MEK made this point. She[38] said, "The Congo has good legal texts, but the laws are not put into practice because of corruption, lack of political will, and lack of monitoring in the field." This point was echoed by a variety of other organizations in different ways. For instance, local civil society organizations[39] said,

> With conflicts over fields and agriculture[40], we can reconcile people. It helps to know the law so we can explain what we are basing our ideas for reconciliation on, but it is still better to reconcile. . . . But with witchcraft you cannot bring the people together. Also, with sexual violence and killing you must go straight to the *parquet*.

They continued with another example, "With inheritance . . . we bring the two together to show who is wrong. We draw on the law, but we don't read the law. We just say how they should live." These statements show the local legal complex's understanding of the different justice needs of the population and that they can be unique across issue areas, as well as areas where state involvement is expected and, for the most part accepted, such as sexual violence and murder.

In Uvira, given the history of legal pluralism and a recent past of violence that has hampered the legal system's functioning, the local outcomes of *friction* include mediators' support for, and promulgation of, several written laws but also an emphasis on reconciliation. NGO actors are a part of, and play a role in, *emergent hybrid legality*, integrating the formal law with informal arbiters and processes to resolve disputes in a way that resonates with the population. These mixed messages play a role in shaping popular legal consciousness, as well as hybridizing the delivery of justice and therefore the terrain of legality as I show in later chapters.

It is clear, then, that local organizations provide space to educate the population on state laws, but it is also notable that the justice processes that they utilize have long-standing relevance to the local population, in contrast to the court system. We can understand these processes as culturally relevant forms of justice that reflect popular worldviews rather than emphasizing liberal legalism. Some interlocutors even defined reconciliation as 'Congolese or African justice' and emphasized that white foreigners do not understand this form of justice. For example, after a lengthy community-based justice process, one military commander who was leading the procedure said, "Africans are more able to resolve *à l'amiable*[41] than whites"[42]. In another example, members of BB, a local NGO, stated,

> There is a type of Congolese justice that foreigners may not be used to . . . ways of managing conflicts. Not everyone can access *la justice*[43], and not all cases should go to *la justice* anyway. Some should be resolved in the family, by the police, some amicably in the community, like the CMCs do . . . no winners and no losers, just advice linked with justice. If the two parties come to an understanding, it's done. If not, they go to the police or *parquet*. For certain things, like sexual violence, murder and popular justice, there must be a criminal file opened[44].

The CMCs, Committées de Médiation et Conciliation, mentioned in the quote are organized and managed by BB to help resolve everyday disputes. I observed their procedures several times during my fieldwork. BB's office is in a decent-sized cement building with a dusty courtyard. Disputants are given a written invitation[45] to come to a CMC meeting to resolve their dispute. Benches and chairs are set up on BB's back deck. Mediators are both men and women who listen to the different sides to an interpersonal dispute while recording the information on sheet paper.

In the CMCs and other mediation processes, I often heard mediators draw on, and explain elements of the laws around rape, civil marriage, alimony, witchcraft, land tenure, and beyond. Their knowledge of these laws might be used to educate participants, but at other times they would refer to state laws as a starting point to explain how the case would be ruled in court. Notably, they would emphasize the punitive or popular 'winner–loser' understanding of the state legal proceedings. Mediators explained that, by contrast, both parties see themselves as winning with the CMC process. As mediators educate participants about the legal system, they are also integrating their own understandings and preferences into that education. This can function as a subtly coercive tactic to encourage people to resolve their disputes and continue to turn to mediation, reinforcing the need for their presence, and thus further funding. It also reflects the *emergent hybrid legality* produced with the help of the local legal complex.

Additionally, mediators highlight to disputants the time and money required to go to court. They explain how the case would proceed in the courts. As an example, in a case I observed at a local dispute resolution office, one member from a cooperative had not repaid a loan he had received. The other members were reasonably upset and had come to the office to seek repayment. The dispute had escalated, but mediators tried to prevent it from ending up in court. At one point, a mediator said,

> Let's wait three or four days to find a solution before going to the *parquet*. Also, remind your brother that he has two sons who will carry the debt if he dies or does not pay it. You can also let him know this: We will go to Bukavu to try to work out a solution and reduce the interest. . . . But, if the case goes to the *parquet*, he will miss a lot more work having to deal with it then. It is also possible that he will lose his job if he is arrested[46].

As these comments illustrate, mediators use information about laws and the legal system's procedures to buttress alternative justice systems and approaches. In other words, mediators educate the population about laws, normalizing their relevance and importance in everyday life. At the same time, mediators use the law as a form of soft coercion, employing the legal system as a threat and drawing on more localized practices, to advance reconciliation or restorative measures. This reinforces the legitimacy, convenience, and appropriateness of mediation in relation to people's beliefs, needs, and practices, and it again highlights the local legal complex's role in the construction of *emergent hybrid legality*.

At the same time, distinctions of local NGOs between educating people about the law and supporting alternatives to the state legal system are not uniform. In an interview with a group of local church leaders, they made a different point: "The problem is that the NGOs think that if people go to *la justice* they will apply the law, but they actually just want money. If I go to meet police officers, as an individual, they won't follow through. But, if I go with an NGO they will"[47]. This statement reflects a few different ideas. First, this group argued that NGOs think that people *should* use the legal system. Second, they highlighted differential treatment in the legal system for an individual versus an individual with the support of a local NGO. These ideas fit with the complexity of the *emergent hybrid legality*. While some NGOs prioritize mediation, there are certainly others that put the emphasis on utilizing the state legal system. These differences are, at least in part, likely shaped by how their funding is designated. There is such a diverse array of actors, including a diversity of NGOs, and various perceptions and misperceptions about what they do for work, that there will necessarily be contradictions.

The church leaders' remarks also direct us to the next point, which is that some organizations, even those that perform mediation, also provide legal aid for those who wish to use the formal legal system or as a last resort when mediation fails. I briefly situate this common practice within the realm of *emergent hybrid legality*.

Going to Court and NGO Support

Some local organizations provide legal support, primarily if the mediation does not work or in specific types of cases, such as rape. Legal aid, here, typically includes free legal counsel and the payment of some or all the court fees. Even with organizations that identify themselves as 'legal aid', initiating court proceedings is often a last resort, especially in cases that do not involve sexual violence or other major crimes. The local legal complex, and much of the population, typically understands sexual violence and other violent harms as solely the purview of the state legal system. For example, the director of MEK, a legal aid clinic, said,

> For those cases that can be resolved amicably, we do mediation in our offices, but we also reference rights. When it is necessary to go to *la justice*, we pay for their lawyer but only until the level of the judgement. We are not able to follow up after that. We need a solution for compensation because this is why *arrangements à l'amiable* continue. . . . People will continue to offend if they have not suffered the punishment and severity of the law[48].

This statement speaks to the production of *emergent hybrid legality* through the local legal complex. The legal aid organization does mediation, which includes rights education, similar to the work of CMCs, described earlier. As long as the mediation resolves the dispute, the courts are avoided. Support to go to *la justice* is only provided in cases where mediation is unsuccessful. At the same time, this interview highlights the types of mediation that the local legal complex views as acceptable, those performed by one of them, versus the types of mediation that are unacceptable—*arrangements à l'amiable*. When NGO actors use the term *arrangements à l'amiable*, they are not referring to amicable settlements through *chefs* or NGO mediation but to cases settled informally between families, maybe with the help of elders or wise people, as described earlier. When I interviewed the Interim *Procureur de Magistrats*[49], he also made this distinction. He said:

> [People] often do *arrangements à l'amiable*. They often go to customary or administrative authorities. . . . It is a practice we are trying to discourage because the ruling might be arbitrary . . . because the cases are not decided by a legal specialist.

By contrast, when I asked about mediation he said,

> It is good because not everyone can access *la justice*, or they are discouraged by the length of time cases take. There is a piece of wisdom that says: 'Better a bad settlement than a good trial'[50] . . . NGOs do better [than *arrangements à l'amiable*] because at least they [disputants] get some legal advice.

Thus, *arrangements à l'amiable* rarely refer to the law and are often seen by those within the local legal complex as problematic or inferior, even as they are long-standing practices. Meanwhile, mediation done by NGOs garners a certain amount of respect amongst the legal complex *because* of its engagement with the law, even if that is not what makes their processes legible to the population. In other words, mediation in some ways satisfies both the population and legal experts, as it is situated within both local worldviews and includes aspects of liberal legal ideology.

In another example, CRV, an organization working primarily on issues of forced and early marriage[51], usually does awareness raising directed at *chefs de quartier*. However, when a case of early marriage or a related issue is brought to them by a community member, they listen to the details, then take a field trip to interview the victim and other witnesses. If the victim wants, "We can do mediation, or we can go to *la justice*, but this causes more problems[52]. We have a lawyer for these cases"[53]. "What are the hardest cases to resolve?" I asked.

> When one person is not willing to accept the mediation recommendations because of selfishness, they just want to go to the *parquet* or Tripaix. But, if they resolve it here, the problem will end. Going to *la justice*, you will pay, and the problems will continue. So, if there are two people—one with financial means and one without—the one with money can just give it [to the courts/officials] and will likely win, so they prefer to resolve it there. We take the file of the one without money and go to the *parquet* and become witnesses, testifying that that person has no money. And, if they need a lawyer, we will support that person[54].

The work of CRV illustrates the local legal complex's paradoxical relationship with the law. The NGO relies on the legal definition of marriage and statutory rape as a basis for the work they do, yet they try to resolve early marriage disputes through mediation. This practice reflects broader local consensus that going to court only continues to create problems—as it creates 'winners and losers'—rather than ending them. And, as I make clear in the next chapter, people often expect an early marriage to persist even if the man (who is typically the older party) is prosecuted; thus, the animosity created through court proceedings is seen as a barrier to the success of the marriage. Additionally, the legal process is understood to unfairly privilege those with money[55] (see also Jacobs, 2018; Rubbers & Gallez, 2012). Thus, part of the NGO's service is to provide legal assistance if the case does go to court.

The local legal complex's engagement with the law and legal system is clear. Yet, it is also clear that many local organizations, even legal aid clinics, combine the law, reconciliation, and dispute resolution in ways that are meaningful and accessible to the local population in an attempt to address their needs. While providing both mediation and legal services may not be the most innovative example of *emergent hybrid legality*, these organizations are agentic actors in the construction and navigation of the legal-justice terrain and defining and redefining distinctions between the formal and informal realms when it fits with local needs and does not pose a specific problem for funding, yet frequently integrating aspects of law and non-state justice practices.

To this point, I have primarily focused on the role of NGOs as representatives of the local legal complex. However, they are not the only actors doing some form of direct *sensibilisation*. State agencies have also taken on education and awareness-raising activities. Notably, as I detail as follows, the territorial branch of the state Gender Office also plays a role, albeit one that has been critiqued by local actors.

State Actors and Sensibilisation

As this chapter has made clear, local NGOs and a few other local actors do much of the active work of *sensibilisation*, both directly and indirectly. Those who work in the courts, such as judges, prosecutors, and clerks, do not usually do this work, except insofar as their hearings are public and this may raise awareness. I asked one legal official, Jacques[56], if he or any of his colleagues at the Tripaix made any efforts to promulgate laws. He replied,

> How can we? That would be outside what we are paid to do, and we already work so much. Once the law is published, it is at everyone's door [figuratively]. According to the law, once it is published everyone has access and there is no excuse for not following it, or for violating it. That is *in theory*. In reality, it is hard for people outside the cities to access the texts, but even inside the cities it is hard. Not everyone can read and even if they read, the text is written in French. And, even if it were in Swahili, again, not everyone can read.

This legal official explicitly recognized that state authorities expect people to follow the law once it is published, but even as a state official himself, he is aware of the near impossibility of raising popular knowledge based solely on publication. He acknowledged that the high level of illiteracy is a major barrier to widespread knowledge of published law unless it is transmitted to the population via different media. This is why alternative methods of awareness raising have been so fundamental to making the law known publicly.

Yet, some other local government entities take an active role in *sensibilisation* efforts in Uvira. While official state legal actors rarely participate in *sensibilisation*, other state offices have taken on this role. For example, the local office of the Ministère du Genre, de la Famille et de L'Enfant (Ministry of Gender, Family and Children; henceforth, 'Gender Office'), a state agency, works to protect women and children and advance human rights. The Director of the Gender Office explained, "We do sensibilisation about gender equality and Resolution 1325 in the villages; we have trainings for the population"[57]. This office is funded by international partner organizations rather than receiving the necessary operating funds from the government. They are *meant* to be state funded, but they informed me that money from the national fund rarely, if ever, makes it to Uvira[58]. Some suspect that the office in Bukavu is the likely end point for these funds.

In March 2017, the Gender Office was organizing a march for International Women's Day, mostly focused on raising awareness about the elections that were expected to be forthcoming at the time. In the end, the march was organized to start at the bridge in Kavimvira, where dozens of entities, from local organizations to classes from different schools, lined up and marched through the city to the Bureau de Territoire d'Uvira[59] in order to honour women. In the end, the educational component was limited; the representative of the Gender Office said nothing, and I could hear the disappointment murmured throughout the crowd. It had taken hours for all the participants to march approximately 6 kilometres under the glaring sun and for each of them to pass before the Territory's officials who sat outside their office building watching and then barely contributing.

While the Women's Day march was largely perceived by the crowd to have fizzled, this office also undertakes trainings about women's rights and gender equality in villages throughout the Territory. Women's organizations also invite representatives of the Gender Office to participate in and enhance their trainings[60]. One of the Gender Office's interns explained that the Gender Office had partnered with United Nations High Commissioner for Refugees, United Nations Office for the Coordination of Humanitarian Affairs, local organizations, MONUSCO, and others. He had helped organize a 'caravan' from the Bureau de Territoire to 'the roundabout' where a megaphone was used to spread messages about 'women's rights. His message was for women to dress properly to prevent sexual violence and for men to send both their sons and daughters to school to get an education. This message is one that most Western countries would label dated and problematic. However, in an area where the status of women, women's rights, and gender justice are in a moment of flux and renegotiation, this was not a surprising message. It seemed aimed at targeting sexual violence without an analysis of the broader implications of such statements.

I asked what the intern thought were the outcomes of the caravan? He said, "the problem is the lack of funds necessary to do the evaluations and follow-up. They should, but cannot, call and check with people and see how they are receiving the message"[61]. He added that those who experienced the caravan "seemed to understand." This state office voiced one of the concerns experienced by many other local organizations, the limited funds. Despite this, they still undertook campaigns to educate women about their rights. The state Gender Office's participation in International Women's Day is one example of how they contribute to shaping legal consciousness via rights awareness, but much of the coordinated effort is undertaken by local organizations.

Conclusion

This chapter begins to explore the relationship between legal consciousness and *emergent hybrid legality* by looking at *sensibilisation* and how the local legal complex shapes legal consciousness and *emergent hybrid legality*. I developed three main interconnected points. First, international organizations participate in legal reform efforts in line with international standards, and thus largely direct their efforts at state capacity building through ROL programming. Where international organizations do play a role in shaping legal consciousness is through sensibilisation, although they rarely do this directly in Uvira. In other words, most of the visible impact of international actors on popular legal consciousness or legality is through providing information, resources, and trainings for the formal state legal system, as well as funding local NGOs.

The second major point is that the local legal complex plays an important role in shaping popular legal consciousness. The local legal complex includes both state legal actors and civil society actors focused on the legal-justice nexus. Often, the local legal complex is working in partnership with international organizations or actors, and are thus navigating the expectations and responsibilities defined by those actors, including the state laws, with their knowledge of the local context and justice needs and expectations of the population. They also shape legal consciousness through the radio and theatre, as well as *sensibilisation* programmes that often target certain individuals who should further promulgate their training. The other way the local legal complex shapes legal consciousness is through direct interaction with people who have experienced a harm or dispute for which they are seeking support, typically mediation, but sometimes legal aid.

This leads to the third point of the chapter, which is that the local legal complex is not only shaping popular legal consciousness but also playing a role in the production of *emergent hybrid legality* through its interactions with the population when providing legal aid or mediation services. They are sending the population mixed messages about the relevance and importance of the state legal system by repeatedly referencing the law while also advocating avoiding the legal system. In this way, they are both normalizing the written laws of the country *and* the mediation practices associated with historical approaches to dealing with harms and disputes through reconciliation and restorative aims. This hybridizes legal-justice and is emergent in that it is building on the local, contextual realities, or *friction*, of interactions between international norms, practices, and expectations and local worldviews and historical practices. The relationship between popular legal consciousness and *emergent hybrid legality* is further explored in the next chapter through my examination of early marriage and statutory rape, as well as in Chapter 6 through my analysis of the relationship between witchcraft and popular justice.

Notes

1 Rendre quelqu'un, un groupe sensible, réceptif à quelque chose pour lequel il ne manifestait pas d'intérêt (www.larousse.fr/dictionnaires/francais/sensibiliser/72106).
2 Interview, 21 March 2017.
3 For example, in Davis's (2015) analysis of EU's role in peacebuilding in the DRC, there is no mention of informal/traditional law or justice. She writes, "The Strategic Framework [2013] defines the EU's objectives as security and development, including conflict prevention and peacebuilding." (p. 4). Further elaboration of these points makes clear that they align with conventional top-down, statist approaches to peacebuilding.
4 The other outputs are: "Support a preventative approach to conflict and violence in fragile contexts," "Strengthen UN-wide joint programming and approaches," "Strengthen monitoring and evaluation capacities."
5 The most thoughtful mention is: "Finally, based on UNDP's accumulated experience, more consistent and better informed engagement with non-state justice and security providers will be sought, since customary and/or religious based justice providers are often the first port of call for many people living in crisis countries" (pp. 31–32). However, there is no further elaboration on how this could be achieved.
6 Interview, Director of SOFIBEF, 31 January 2017.
7 Legislative modernization has not been solely a project of transition or of international actors. The legal system in DRC itself is largely the product of the colonial era (Dembour, 2000; Prinsloo, 1993) and modernization has occurred at various intervals since independence. However, international actors have continued to play a role in shaping legal changes in DRC, both directly (Lake, 2014b) and through activism.
8 http://reliefweb.int/report/democratic-republic-congo/rdc-le-bcnudh-appuie-la-journ-e-de-sensibilisation-sur-la-loi
9 www.adiac-congo.com/content/pointe-noire-debut-de-la-campagne-de-sensibilisation-sur-la-loi-portant-protection-de
10 www.radiookapi.net/2016/03/26/actualite/en-bref/uvira-long-sofad-sensibilise-les-femmes-sur-la-loi-relative-la-parite; http://reliefweb.int/report/democratic-republic-congo/rd-congo-aru-lancement-dune-campagne-de-sensibilisation-contre-les; www.acordinternational.org/acord/fr/acord/fr/nos-actions/a/zones/rdc/
11 American Bar Association.
12 Interview, 3 February 2017.
13 Interview, 17 May 2015.
14 27 April 2017.

15 Group interview, 14 April 2015.
16 "Atelier dea Organizations de Societe Civils Feminines pour l'Orientation sur l'Accord Cadre pour le Paix, Securite, et Cooperation st la Resolution 1325," 21 February 2017.
17 Interview, MEK director, 3 February 2017.
18 Interview, 3 February 2017.
19 Interview, 18 February 2017.
20 Interview, 31 January 2017.
21 Interview, HAM, 1 February 2017.
22 Interview, 18 February 2017.
23 Interview, 12 April 2017.
24 Interview, 12 April 2017.
25 Director General of Migration.
26 Group interview, wise elders, 15 April 2015.
27 Interview, GAD, 10 February 2017. Interview, AA, 16 April 2015.
28 Interview, 24 March 2017.
29 Interview, 11 February 2017.
30 In many interviews with both women and men in Uvira, women's rights were understood in a very particular way that reflects local manifestations of rights discourse and practice. Women's rights were often understood within the context of their marital relations, such as the right to food and clothing, which is expected to be provided for by their husbands. There was also to be some push back, from both men and women, against the idea that men should be participating in 'women's' duties, such as cooking, cleaning, and childcare.
31 Interview, 16 April 2015.
32 Interview, 14 March 2017.
33 Interview, 20 February 2017.
34 Interview, 24 March 2017.
35 Interview, 20 February 2017.
36 The 'formal' traditional or customary system of turning to *mwamis* and other traditional ethnic *chefs* persists but is not necessarily dominant, especially in the cities. See also Verweijen (2015).
37 The idea of vernacularization may have been primarily developed with the international human rights regime in mind (see Merry, 2006), but it bears mentioning that many of the changes to the Congolese legal code have been shaped by the international community, international legal norms and practices, and the international human rights regimes (Lake, 2018).
38 Interview, legal aid NGO, 2015.
39 Group interview, 24 April 2015.
40 Conflicts in the fields and agriculture disputes typically refer to conflicts between herders and agriculturalists for use of land, as well as the boundaries of the land being cultivated.
41 Amicably.
42 Fieldnotes, 2015. See also (Dunn, 2021).
43 The courts or state legal system.
44 Group interview, 30 January 2017.
45 This may seem like a problematic approach given the high illiteracy rates (just over 20% in 2015 according to the World Bank); however, there are people, including the person who is delivering the invitation and the *chef d'avenue* who could read it. Of course, this raises a question about privacy, but limited detail is included in the invitations.
46 It is fairly common knowledge that people cannot be arrested for failing to repay a debt. However, there could have been other reasons related to the case that would lead to his arrest.
47 Group interview, church leaders, Kiliba, 23 April 2015.

48 Interview, 3 February 2017.
49 Interview, 15 May 2015.
50 "Un mauvais arrangement vaut mieux qu'un bon procès." Generally attributed to Honoré de Balzac.
51 The law that specifically defines 18 as the legal marriage age was only adopted in 2016 (Law N° 16/008, 2016). However, the 2006 rape law defined anyone under the age of 18 as a child with regard to sexual activity; thus, activists and NGO workers were able to mobilize this law to advance their projects around ending early marriage as well.
52 At this point, everyone looks at each other knowingly and laughs. The general difficulties and problems of the legal system are a common sense, running joke in the realm of the local legal complex.
53 Interview, Director of CRV, 7 February 2017.
54 Interview, Director of CRV, 7 February 2017.
55 The belief that the legal system favours those with money—either because of corruption or because of the cost of going to court—was frequently mentioned during my fieldwork. At the same time, those with personal experiences with the system did not necessarily experience these issues.
56 Interview, 11 February 2017.
57 Interview, 28 January 2017.
58 Director of le Ministère du Genre, de la Famille et de L'Enfant, Interview, 2017.
59 Office of the Territory of Uvira.
60 Director of le Ministère du Genre, de la Famille et de L'Enfant, Interview, 28 January 2017.
61 Intern at le Ministère du Genre, de la Famille et de L'Enfant, Interview, 28 January 2017.

Bibliography

Arnould, V., & Vlassenroot, K. (2016). EU policies in the Democratic Republic of Congo: Try and fail? In *Security in transition*. SiT/WP/06/16. Paper commissioned by the Human Security Study Group. Friedrich Ebert Stiftung, ERC, LSE International Development.

Autesserre, S. (2010). *The trouble with the Congo: Local violence and the failure of international peacebuilding* (Vol. 115). Cambridge University Press.

Autesserre, S. (2014). *Peaceland: Conflict resolution and the everyday politics of international intervention*. Cambridge University Press.

Baaz, M., & Stern, M. (2010). *The complexity of violence: A critical analysis of sexual violence in the Democratic Republic of Congo (DRC)*. Sida: Nordiska Afrikainstitutet.

Chant, S. (2006). Re-thinking the "feminization of poverty" in relation to aggregate gender indices. *Journal of Human Development*, 7(2), 201–220.

Davis, L. (2015). *The EU and peacebuilding in the Democratic Republic of Congo*. Civil Society Dialogue Network Discussion Paper No. 9. European Peacebuilding Liaison Office.

Dembour, M. B. (2000). *Recalling the Belgian Congo: Conversations and introspection* (Vol. 9). Berghahn Books.

Dunn, H. (2018). *Emergent legal pluralism: Legal consciousness and unanticipated outcomes of rule of law building in Eastern Democratic Republic of Congo* (doctoral dissertation). University of Minnesota.

Dunn, H. (2020). Research in the land of savages, victims, and saviors. In G. Hoogensen, P. Weitsman & R. Matthew (Eds.), *Women's perspectives on human security: Violence, environment, and sustainability* (pp. 154–182). Ohio University Press.

Dunn, H. (2021). Emergent hybrid legality: A study of legal encounters in the DRC. *Journal of Intervention and Statebuilding*, *15*(2), 201–220.

Ewick, P., & Silbey, S. S. (1998). *The common place of law: Stories from everyday life*. University of Chicago Press.

Haile, H. B., Bock, B., & Folmer, H. (2012). Microfinance and female empowerment: Do institutions matter? *Women's Studies International Forum, 35*(4), 256–265.

Heath, R. (2014). Women's access to labor market opportunities, control of household resources, and domestic violence: Evidence from Bangladesh. *World Development, 57*, 32–46.

Jacobs, C. (2018). Seeking justice, experiencing the state: Criminal justice and real legal uncertainty in the Democratic Republic of Congo. *The Journal of Legal Pluralism and Unofficial Law, 50*(3), 280–293.

Koddenbrock, K. (2012). Recipes for intervention: Western policy papers imagine the Congo. *International Peacekeeping, 19*(5), 549–564.

Lake, M. (2014b). Organizing hypocrisy: Providing legal accountability for human rights violations in areas of limited statehood. *International Studies Quarterly, 58*(3), 515–526.

Lake, M. (2018). *Strong NGOs and weak states: Pursuing gender justice in the Democratic Republic of Congo and South Africa*. Cambridge University Press.

Lake, M., Muthaka, I., & Walker, G. (2016). Gendering justice in humanitarian spaces: Opportunity and (Dis) empowerment through gender-based legal development outreach in the eastern Democratic Republic of Congo. *Law & Society Review, 50*(3), 539–574.

Lincoln, R. S. (2011). Rule of law for whom: Strengthening the rule of law as a solution to sexual violence in the Democratic Republic of the Congo. *Berkeley Journal of Gender, Law & Justice, 26*, 139.

Merry, S. E. (2009). *Human rights and gender violence: Translating international law into local justice*. University of Chicago Press.

Prinsloo, M. W. (1993). Recognition and application of indigenous law in Zaire, Rwanda, Burundi and Lusophone Africa. *Journal of South African Law, 541*.

Rubbers, B., & Gallez, E. (2012). Why do Congolese people go to court? A qualitative study of litigants' experiences in two Justice of the Peace courts in Lubumbashi. *The Journal of Legal Pluralism and Unofficial Law, 44*(66), 79–108.

United Nations Development Programme. (2011). *Strengthening the rule of law in crisis-affected and fragile situations*. United Nations Development Programme, Bureau for Crisis Prevention and Recovery. www.undp.org/sites/g/files/zskgke326/files/publications/UNDP_CPR_ROLGlobal ProgrammePhase2August2014.pdf

USAID. (2014). *Country development cooperation strategy, Democratic Republic of Congo (2014–2019)*. USAID. https://2012-2017.usaid.gov/sites/default/files/documents/1860/Democratic_Republic_of_Congo_CD CS_2014-2019.pdf

Verweijen, J. (2015). The disconcerting popularity of popular in/justice in the Fizi/Uvira region, eastern Democratic Republic of the Congo. *International Journal on Minority and Group Rights, 22*(3), 335–359.

Chapter 5

Legal Consciousness in Context

Statutory Rape and Early Marriage

In the early days of my fieldwork in 2015, I made a trip to Makobola with my interpreter, Marise, and an interlocutor, Denis, to meet the local *chef* and discuss research plans. As we approached home, we stopped by a restaurant beside the *cyber*[1] to get some refreshments. My colleagues ordered grilled goat served with a side of *bugali*, *pili pili*, onions, lime, and salt, while I stuck with the vegetarian option of fries. We sat at the small table in big plastic chairs, under an awning, sipping our Fantas and snacking. As we filled our stomachs, Denis began to explain some of the issues that he saw with the law in the Congo. He claimed that 80% of those in prison in Uvira were there for sexual violence, but incarceration does not help because it does not address their mental states. He made an argument for rehabilitation sessions, which Marise agreed with to a limited extent but also added her thoughts to the discussion.

Marise was concerned with addressing the underlying causes of sexual violence. However, she also argued that in cases where a young woman gets pregnant from rape, there are *arrangements à l'amiable*. The man can pay the dowry, so they will not bring him to court to go to jail. She added that, in any case, the most he would serve is six months and then the couple cannot get along. She noted that 25 years is too long to go to jail; how will the kid survive with the father in jail? "The punishment is disproportional to the crime"[2]. Admittedly, I was confused by Marise's stance. Although we had only known each other a few days, I knew that she had worked with a few local NGOs on women's rights issues. I was surprised to be hearing her arguments about justice for cases of rape. It was only through our continued discussion that I was able to contextualize these comments, and it became clear that she was talking about cases of statutory rape. As noted, her integration in the NGO world shaped the language she used, referring to sex with a minor as rape. At the same time, her statements reflect what I came to understand as a popular view that cases of what the law calls 'statutory rape' are often best dealt with outside of the legal system. In this chapter, I explore these ideas around both sex with a minor and adolescent marriage as areas that reflect contradictory legal consciousness.

I want to resituate my discussion with Marise and Denis into the context of legal encounters that I laid out previously. Over the past two decades, since

DOI: 10.4324/9781003289715-5

shortly after the Congo wars, much international activism, scholarship, and writing have tackled women's rights and experiences of SGBV in the DRC, often with a focus on the 'sexual' component. Indeed, Lake (2014) points out that ROL-oriented international programming in the eastern DRC has largely emphasized SGBV trials (see also Lincoln, 2011). In recent years, scholars have taken a more nuanced approach to understanding women's gendered experiences of conflict and law (eg. Jean-Bouchard, 2017; Lake, 2018), while some women have turned to a legal system that reflects great advances in prosecuting sexual violence—both in terms of applying international law and protecting and respecting survivors throughout the process (Lake, 2018). Research also reveals that survivors are mostly interested in the economic support and resources only made available to them when they pursue legal channels (Aroussi, 2018; see also Lake, 2018). Aroussi (2018) focuses on women's desire for and acceptance of customary justice and economic support and Lake (2018) on the link between the law and NGO support (including financial support). Scholars, including Aroussi (2018) and Lake (2018), have not extensively focused on the issue of statutory rape and how it fits with their arguments about law and justice and how popular understandings have been shaped by the messaging of ROL programmes and legal reforms. In part, this may be due to the difficulty in exploring this issue in particular because it is often translated simply as 'rape', even if not locally interpreted as such (Dunn, 2020). Yet, statutory rape is also a common source of harm or dispute in people's everyday lives. Homing in on the particularities of this issue lends insights into contradictory legal consciousness—the *disconnect in harm naming* and *different logics of justice*—and the production of *emergent hybrid legality*. In this chapter, I have disaggregated statutory rape from other forms of sexual violence to elucidate contradictory consciousness and the construction of legality.

Statutory rape and early marriage were identified by the population as frequent sources of harms and disputes. The local legal complex has also targeted these issues for *sensibilisation* as part of their broader SGBV programming. I examine these two phenomena together as they often, although not always, co-occur. Importantly, this chapter distinguishes between the legal harms of statutory rape and early marriage and the social understanding of sex with, or marriage to, an adolescent, as well as the disputes that may arise in these situations. I thus differentiate between legal harms, which are flat and categorical, and social harms, which are multidimensional and situational, and how this gap produces the *disconnect in harm naming*. My research suggests that people rarely interpret statutory rape and early marriage as harms in and of themselves, or *categorical harms*, as the law would prescribe. Rather, the harm is defined by the situation of the event and how various actors behave in response. This is the first dimension that is explored in order to delve into contradictory consciousness and *emergent hybrid legality*.

This chapter adds additional nuance to research on women's understandings and experiences of sexual violence and outlines the role of contradictory legal consciousness in how women understand, frame, and address harms and disputes around early marriage and statutory rape. As with other harms and disputes, contradictory legal consciousness is shaped through local NGO trainings, awareness raising, and socialization. Others have acquired legal knowledge through friends, neighbours, and radio programmes. However, while women's knowledge of the laws around sexual violence may have increased, this knowledge has encountered other aspects of legal consciousness, manifesting in contradictory legal consciousness. First, there is tension between popular understandings and what the law defines as the appropriate age to engage in sex or to marry. In other words, there is a disconnect between official and popular harm naming, the *disconnect in harm naming* theme. Second, there is a difference in popular and legal definitions of the appropriate legal-justice responses to these phenomena, which encompasses the *different logics of justice* theme. Further, this chapter addresses how and why disputes arise as a result of the situational understandings of harm and what they can tell us about legal consciousness.

Contradictory legal consciousness helps us understand why women might be more likely to turn to the legal system in cases of stranger rape or physical coercion, and less likely in cases of acquaintance statutory rape, and why early marriage is still practiced with limited social critique. This chapter also elaborates on the difficulties women encounter in terms of conceptualizing a particular experience as a harm and deciding what, if anything, should be done for redress.

As I will illustrate, the two legal consciousness themes—*disconnect in harm naming* and *different logics of justice*—are constructed through popular understandings and practices around statutory rape and early marriage that combine worldviews with knowledge, perceptions, and judgements about the state legal system and its representations of liberal legal ideology. Importantly, these themes serve to shape *emergent hybrid legality*. The state law has played some role in shaping popular understandings of justice, even if this has not led to people resolving these issues in the courts. Instead, it has reinforced ideas about rethinking what amicable settlements look like in situations of sex with a minor. Popular emphasis on marriage is being reconsidered in conversation with the law and changing ideas about girls' education.

I first lay out the formal legal context: What does the law say about statutory rape and early marriage? I briefly highlight the distinction between statutory rape and other forms of rape, highlighting that both the state and the population often prefer punishment in the latter cases. Next, I make the case that the state views the harms of statutory rape and early marriage as categorical, but the population frequently views them as situational, highlighting the underlying tension of the *disconnect in harm naming*. Finally, I explore the justice contradiction by looking at how adolescents and their families negotiate disputes around statutory rape and early marriage.

Formal Legal Context: Sexual Violence, Early Marriage, and the Law

As noted previously, the Congo has received much international attention because of the highly publicized accounts of wartime sexual violence. Officials modified certain legal codes as a result of these ROL-oriented interventions, programmes, and consultations. A major change was the creation of the 2006 law on sexual violence[3], which domesticated internationalized laws and norms on sexual violence, drawing on and modifying the definitions found in the Rome Statute of the International Criminal Court (Zongwe, 2012). While this legal reform did not specifically address age of marriage, which is outlined in the Family Code rather than the Criminal Code, this was also updated, albeit not until 2016. These reformed laws are described in more detail as follows.

The Laws on Statutory Rape and Marriageable Age

The 2006 law on sexual violence modified the 2004 Penal Code (Book II) to criminalize sexual relations with anyone under the age of 18 (Article 167[4]). As there are no 'Romeo-and-Juliet' laws—laws that reduce or eliminate the penalty for statutory rape if the age difference is minimal—in Congo, this means that any person under the age of 18 who has a sexual relationship with any person 18 years or older is considered a victim of statutory rape. This is further supported with other areas of law. For example, the Law for the Protection of Children, Article 2, states that a child is anyone under the age of 18 years old. Article 169 of the same code states: Paedophilic acts refer to any sexual attraction of an adult or adolescent to a child, including indecent assault, sexual intercourse, eroticism, pornography, sexual abuse, and rape[5]. Here, specifically, the definition between adolescent and child is not clarified. However, Article 2 suggests that a 'child' would refer to anyone under the age of 18.

One jurist[6] laid out some of the pertinent legal background for me. He stated,

> The age of minority is defined in the Constitution[7]. But, in contrast to history, it's a problem. Around 2000–2001, there was a big change from the time of the Mobutu regime, when there was not the same law and often women got married at fifteen years old. After Mobutu[8], there were two rebellions, the AFDL and RCD . . . RCD rebels began to use any practice, including rape as an instrument of war, so law was put in place to stop and address this offense. The law from 2001 was not comprehensive, so in 2006 they made laws that started to label the different forms of sexual violence. Then, they also had to teach men about sexual violence generally. . . . It was difficult for the community to understand and accept after having Mobutu's laws. Thus, conflict developed between parents and the

law. With *sensibilisation*, the community is trying to understand, but there are insufficiencies of follow-up and prosecution.

Indeed, since 1987, the Family Code[9] stated that women 15 and older and men 18 and older could enter into marriage; exceptions were also possible for younger individuals. The quoted jurist refers to the 2006 update to the Penal Code, defining the age of majority as 18, thus beginning to reshape domestic understandings of childhood. At the same time, the age at which girls can marry was only reformed in the Family Code in 2016, thus an internal conflict in the written laws persisted for ten years. The jurist quoted earlier suggests that people know the law, but they have a hard time accepting it; so, this knowledge of the law does not necessarily lead to changes in social practices. And, he believes that this increased knowledge appears to have been associated with negative judgements of the law—creating conflict between parents and the law. This is because the increased knowledge is conditioned by socio-cultural beliefs and practices and worldviews.

While the laws in the books have been updated to reflect global norms and standards around the age of consent and have been promulgated amongst the population, many cases of sex with a minor (both consensual[10] and non-consensual, meaning forced or coerced) are resolved outside of formal legal channels. Legal consciousness plays an important role in mediating between the act and how individuals and families choose to respond. Before continuing, it is important to note that, in Uvira, the population very much recognizes the difference between a child and a teen/adolescent/young person when framing their understanding of statutory rape. Although there is not necessarily a set age, the idea of sex with a *child* is largely unacceptable and reflects an area of overlap in categorical legal *and* social harm. It is the more fluid adolescent years that remain open for interpretation, with adulthood likely related to the beginning of menstruation. Unless otherwise specified, in this chapter, when I refer to minors, I am referring to adolescents under the age of 18, not young children.

One popular response to statutory rape is marriage. While not all adolescent marriages occur because of sex with a minor, it can be a precipitating factor. And, as a parallel with statutory rape, there is both a diversity of experiences and a disconnect between law and popular practices and worldviews that play a role in constructing contradictory consciousness around this issue. Additionally, there is another layer of complexity: Contradictory laws. The original Family Code, Article 352, states that the legal marriage age is 18 for boys and 15 for girls[11]. This law remained in place until 2016, even while the Penal Code was updated to recognize statutory rape as sex with someone under the age of 18. The Family Code was, however, updated. Law #87/010 of July 2016 modified Article 352 to make the legal age for marriage 18 years old for both boys and girls[12]. So, while laws have now become uniform, this is a more recent development and could play a role in different understandings and assumptions about what constitutes early marriage. Thus, it is notable that there have been conflicting laws around age of marriageability and age of consent until fairly recently, which add to the complexities of legal consciousness. Before delving further into those complexities, I briefly outline one area of overlap between the law and popular understandings of harm and justice for rape.

Rape and Punishment: Ideals and Realities

The bulk of this chapter will examine the *disconnect in harm naming* and the *different logics of justice* as forms of contradictory legal consciousness, but there is an important example of commonality between the formal law and popular harm naming: Stranger rape and rape with physical coercion. The analysis here is more limited than the other sections because I did not explicitly ask for interviewees to share experiences of sexual violence. However, it was mentioned in several interviews and discussions[13]. As noted previously, international and domestic actors have worked together to raise awareness about the updated laws around sexual violence. Both the law and the local population generally understand rape, specifically stranger rape, as a serious harm that cannot be addressed through reconciliation but should be reported to police or courts[14]. This may be a result of the active *sensibilisation* campaigns, or because of prior beliefs, but most likely it is the outcome of some combination of the two. For example, multiple people mentioned *sensibilisation* about sexual violence, such as Claude[15], who explained that little was known about rape or the laws surrounding it until *sensibilisation* activities. Indeed, Mireille[16] explained that it was only through the work of the NGO of which she was a beneficiary that she came to understand an experience she had as one of rape. Even a group of *chefs*[17] explained that before approximately 2012–2014, sexual violence used to happen a lot; but, there has been extensive *sensibilisation*, and it has declined. Thus, even if limited in some ways, it has indeed had an impact.

Yet, even in cases of rape, when people want some form of punishment, problems in the functioning of the legal system can still make people hesitant to use it. In this context, the popular wisdom is that if someone does not know who their attacker was, there is nothing that law enforcement or the courts can do. Additionally, there is limited understanding of the nuances of how the legal system works, leading to confusion, upset, and fear about the release of perpetrators when they are identifiable. Even though survivors and their families are aware that rape is illegal *and* they frequently, although not always, prefer punishment for their attackers, some perceive the state as having no ability to intervene and have mixed judgements about the efficacy of the legal system, even if they agree with its approach in principle. This theme emerged during group interviews in 2015 and was also reflected in individual interviews that I conducted in 2017:

> In the homes, rape is not normal. But, in cases of armed robbery, rape can often happen too. . . . Nothing can be done because the people (who

> commit the rape) are unknown and will flee. In this case the woman will go right to the hospital or city. . . . The family is informed and told what happened. . . . The family cannot have any reaction because the people (perpetrators) are unknown. All they can do is give support[18].

In a one-on-one interview, Naima[19] reinforced this discussion with a specific example. She shared that in April 2016 one of her neighbours had been raped while working in the fields. When I asked if she informed police, Naima explained, "Since the perpetrator was unknown, there was no follow-up." These examples highlight the lack of any recourse available to victims when the perpetrator is not known.

Civil society actors[20] in Makobola hit on another key issue—the release of suspects and perpetrators. When I asked how disputes were addressed locally, they explained, "Sometimes *la justice* doesn't work. For example, a raped woman goes to the police, they take the man, but then he is freed and can redo the same violence." This means that even if there is a preference for punishment, people may not feel that they can trust the legal system to deliver this to *their* standard. In other words, the situation in a particular case shapes broader perceptions of the functioning of the legal system, reducing its perceived relevance or appropriateness in other cases.

Further, survivors can be hesitant about the legal process for fear of reprisals. For example, Rose[21] did not want to go to the police for fear of violent retaliations when the perpetrator would be released from prison. Rose was a young woman who met with us in the office of her benefactor, MAP, an organization that provides legal aid and psycho-social support to women and girls who have survived SGBV. When I asked her how she had come to be a beneficiary of the organization, she explained that they had come to her village and offered support to survivors of sexual violence. Although she had not shared the incident with many, she offered us her experience of being attacked and raped by an unknown assailant when she was working in the field the previous year. I asked what she thought should happen to her attacker if he was caught by state agents[22]. She replied, "In my opinion, I would prefer not to bring him to *la justice.* I would suggest that we settle amicably." Jeanne, who was interpreting, added that this was likely because there would be something to gain financially through an *arrangement à l'amiable.* Still, I encouraged her to ask Rose. She provided a different reason, which was also more practical than ideological, but in a different way. She said, "We are afraid to bring people to *la justice* because, in our neighbourhood, there was a case of a guy who also committed this act. The girl's family brought him to *la justice* and the guy was arrested. He was a soldier, and when he was released from prison, he began to threaten the girl's family, which is why I prefer the amicable settlement." Rose provides a pragmatic reason for preferring to resolve outside of the courts due to the information that has circulated locally and popular wisdom. Although the other case she referenced was quite different, given that the accused was a soldier, it still shaped how Rose understood her situation.

Somewhat ironically, the release of accused perpetrators may actually reflect the proper functioning of the legal system. This is because of the liberal ideological underpinning of the legal system and what constitutes sufficient evidence. If the burden of proof is not attained, the defendant would be released, as per the law. There are also other mechanisms of the legal system that allow accused people to be released, such as on bail. However, these functions of the legal system do not necessarily build faith in its neutrality, even if from a liberal legal perspective this is seen as upholding the rights of the accused. Rush Smith (2015) observes a similar dynamic in South Africa and argues that this contributes to vigilantism because segments of the population view the state legal system as providing too many rights to the accused 'criminals'. I am not delving into vigilantism here, but the lack of confidence in the legal system *because* of elements that function as they should appears to be a similar trend in both Congo and this research on South Africa.

While punishment is not preferred by everyone in cases of stranger rape, it is more commonly preferred than in other cases of everyday harms or disputes. Yet, popular wisdom about the functioning of the legal system shapes some people's practical preference for reconciliation or restorative justice outside the state legal system. As I illustrate in what follows, this is quite different from how the population engages with statutory rape and early marriage.

Sex with a Minor: Categorical versus Situational Harms

As mentioned previously, the state's categorical approach to naming the harm of statutory rape is often divergent from the population's situational understanding, and this has implications for legal consciousness. For the population, sex with a minor may be framed as a harm and/or a dispute, but it depends on the nature of the encounter and its social reverberations. The legal framework does not map onto lived experiences and worldviews; hence, it reflects the contradictory consciousness theme of the *disconnect in harm naming*. The laws about age of consent may be known to the public, but that has not shifted perceptions or judgements about the appropriateness of turning to legal action in many of these cases. Worldviews and judgements about the legal system lead people to emphasize amicable settlements and reconciliation, which are in direct conflict with state legal procedures. This further reflects the legal consciousness theme of *different logics of justice*.

Disconnect in Harm Naming: *When Is Sex with a Minor a Harm?*

The idea that statutory rape is not always a harm is proffered by different segments of society. Reflecting this idea, one state official remarked on the relevance of making a distinction about cultural context—the local context versus the Western context from which the legal category of statutory rape was transferred are quite different. This topic arose when I went to a government office for a *document d'inscription* to show that I had informed the State of my presence and purpose in Uvira. I entered the director's office with two of my local interlocutors. Without prompting and as I have found to be relatively common when meeting with government officials, the director spoke of the problem of Western views on the DRC. He proceeded to describe how the context of Congo is quite unlike Western countries, and that is why people still do not follow or understand this law; he provided the idea of statutory rape as an example of this difference. He[23] said, "In the West, the age of majority makes sense. You start school at six years old. You spend six years in primary, then six years in secondary, which puts you at 18 years old when you graduate. But, here, some girls only go to school until they are 14 and then they get pregnant." This official was highlighting the different lived experiences of girls in DRC and how context influences popular views on age of consent. "Now, the law in Congo," he added, "puts the age of consent for girls at 18, but they often finish school at 14. They are not going to stay in their parents' home for much longer after they are done school, so they will likely get married." This official did not specify the age of the sexual partner, but his comments do provide important perspective all the same. Put differently, I understood him to be saying that starting a family makes sense once someone has finished her studies, which tends to happen at a younger age in the region. While the relationship between education and statutory rape is not widely studied, the relationship between education and early marriage has received attention. In analyses, to explore the contextual drivers of early marriage, it is noted that limited educational opportunities for girls can be both a cause and consequence of early marriage (Bunting, 2005). In other words, girls do not necessarily stop their education because they got married but may get married because their educational opportunities are limited, even at the high school level. At the same time, the social discourse on a girl's education in Uvira is in a moment of reflection and flux, and families are increasingly valuing female education, which I will detail a little later.

Part of what I took from the official's statement is that the harm of statutory rape is understood situationally, and this was confirmed by others. One discussion between a group of women[24] highlights this point. Following up on their thoughts on sexual violence broadly, I asked why sex with a minor is a problem. They responded,

> The problem is how the man behaves toward the woman. Even if the dowry is paid, the state considers it to be rape. Locally, if the man goes through the proper channels, the culture accepts it's ok and it is not considered rape. But, if he doesn't, it is considered rape.

Here, 'going through the proper channels' typically refers to paying the dowry and presumably getting married. This statement is thus an example of how, in popular discourse and practice, statutory rape becomes framed as the harm of rape *per se*, rather than a question of marriage; it is through the man's refusal to pay the dowry, not *the act* itself. Clearly, this is distinct from the law's categorial framing of statutory rape as a crime. This statement, which was accepted by the group of women, highlights the difference between categorical and situational understandings of rape.

Of course, as liberal legal ideology is integrated into legal consciousness, beliefs become muddied. For example, in a conversation with Claude[25] about his understanding of rape, I asked about sex with a minor, giving the hypothetical example of a 16-year-old. He responded,

> Sometimes I might say that it is rape because the girl has not yet reached the [legal] age. But, I could also say that they chatted and that they both consented. Now, if by bad luck they get caught, well . . . now that is the question I want to ask you, is it be rape or not?

It appears that, by talking through the situation, Claude was unsure what he thought, or what he *should* think in the presence of a Western researcher. This suggests that *sensibilisation* has had some impact in integrating aspects of the formal law into popular thought and discourse, affecting people's legal consciousness. Our conversation also serves as a reminder that my presence may affect how people reflect on disputes, harms, and laws.

These quotes are just some examples of how people have explained to me why statutory rape is not viewed as a categorical harm. The government official, cited earlier, made two important contributions that I explored through my research. First, he highlighted the continued norm that the *right* or *acceptable* response to teen pregnancy is to get married. Marriage provides the financial support and social acceptance or credibility. Second, he recognized the reality that if a high school girl gets pregnant, she is unlikely to finish her studies. Part of this, as I later learned, is often that schools do not allow pregnant girls to attend, and they rarely return after the birth. The other part of the equation is the expectation of marriage. These contextual factors remain pertinent in situations of statutory rape; thus, my argument about the disconnect between legal harm naming and the situational approach rooted in popular lived experiences and worldviews. This disconnect carries over to the issue of early marriage, at least in some cases.

Different Logics of Justice: *How Young Women and Their Families Understand and Seek Justice*

The disconnect in harm naming provides the backbone for understanding how and why harms and disputes around statutory rape are addressed in particular ways. In this section, I first explore why women did *not* bring disputes around statutory rape to the courts, highlighting their preference for bringing people together to find a solution. Second, I consider how adolescent women and their families actually chose to address disagreements in practice. Next, I outline how early marriage is negotiated to avoid or resolve disputes. Similar to the analysis of the disconnect between categorical and situational harm naming, this discussion shows the disconnect between the functioning of the courts and their alternatives in relation to the theme of *different logics of justice*, reflecting contradictory legal consciousness.

Cases of statutory rape are rarely brought to the courts in Uvira because people understand there to be more benefits in bringing families together to decide what to do. Statutory rape is not seen as inherently harmful, but harm can come if it is not dealt with according to local norms and practices. To explain why statutory rape is not brought to the courts, members of AA and their lawyer[26] explained that,

> If it goes to *la justice*, often people don't understand the process and procedures, the different components of the system. *La justice* takes the accused to see if it is actually him; there is an investigation, and he can be put in jail and required to compensate the victim. However, sometimes he cannot pay it, and it is seen locally as justice working for the perpetrator. This can be harmful to the victim. It is better for families to come together and provide the dowry if it's a minor, but when it becomes a problem of forced marriage, and if justice finds out, they will arrest the two families.

In this part of the interview, there were several important points being raised. First, it is evident that *knowledge* of the legal system is different from knowledge of the law. Here, the NGO members are arguing that people do not understand the legal process. Thus, even if people understand there to be a legal wrong or harm, uncertainty about the legal process plays a role in shaping their judgements of the system. Second, the interviewees emphasized the negative outcome of legal proceedings for victims and their families. In that sense, *practical* knowledge, or popular wisdom, of the system may also shape popular negative judgements. An amicable settlement, on the other hand, fits with popular worldviews about dowry payments and marriage being the appropriate response to what the law labels as statutory rape. Additionally, practical knowledge of socio-cultural processes suggests that it is easier to actually obtain the material benefit through this type of resolution when compared to the legal process.

Interestingly, AA's lawyer added,

> It [amicable settlements] is prohibited by the sexual violence law (of 2006)[27], but people were already doing it, so it is hard to stop. The sanctions were never determined in the law. There is no sanction for those who arrange the amicable settlements. Even if they are arrested, *la justice* won't win, and they won't go to jail. There is also the inadequacy of the justice authorities. The sexual violence law provides for a sanction of five to 25 years, and with minors at least seven years. But, when the judgement is given, the perpetrator only gets 12 months. The parents of the victim wanted a serious sanction but didn't get it. This upsets the population, so if the child is raped, they prefer that the family is given a cow.

Again, there are a number of points and elaborations to consider. In practice, although unacceptable according to the law, people continue to make arrangements between families after cases of sex with an adolescent under the age of 18. AA's lawyer may be discussing both statutory rape and forcible rape with a minor, which again highlights the necessity to continue to try to disentangle different types and experiences of sexual violence when thinking about the provision of justice. Cases of sex with an adolescent are often met with a desire to pursue an amicable settlement. Sometimes, it can be a result of the perceived insufficiencies of prosecution—perceptions—as the lawyer noted, even in cases where that might be the parents' first choice. At the same time, there are other reasons why people might prefer amicable settlements, which I elaborate upon as follows.

Another lawyer[28] highlighted the disconnect between liberal legal ideology and popular worldviews, noting the strength of local practices in terms of addressing statutory rape. He stated: "We can forbid amicable settlements or early marriage, but they still do it. As a jurist, we have the responsibility to use the right procedures and apply the rules (law) to bring the culture to good sense/reason." This jurist essentially described what recent legal reforms and ROL building efforts are attempting to do, which is to use the legal system and liberal legal rationality to 'tame' culture. However, culture is an ever-changing amalgam of international–local (and everything in between) entanglements. The attempts to 'bring culture to good reason' have thus already permeated cultural forms. However, the outcomes of these entanglements do not always reflect a shift to liberal legal logics and thus reflect the combination of *different logics of justice*.

Notably, legally defined statutory rape is not without repercussions outside of the law. Amongst much of the general population, dowry payment and marriage are the acceptable and necessary ways of addressing these cases. The underlying assumption is that the minor and the person she had sex with will either live together or have some relationship, even if he were to go to jail. In a group interview[29], participants voiced a concern for the relationship of the pair if she pursued legal action. "There are *arrangements à l'amiable.* In this case, if a young woman is pregnant from rape (in the sense of sex with a minor), the families can make arrangements for the man to pay the dowry, and they will not bring him to court. If they did bring him to court, the most he would serve is six months and *then they can't get along.*" People thus sometimes have the expectation that even if he goes to jail for having sex with a minor, they should get married or have some sort of relationship when he is released. In that instance, the concern is that the legal process will create greater disharmony in the family.

What happens when the man does not make these commitments? This is often the source of disputes, as he is not fulfilling the social expectations. When a marriage proposal has not been presented, or not accepted, a range of responses is possible. Still, going to court is rare. In a group interview with leaders of local NGOs[30], they emphasized that reconciliation was the best way to deal with these disputes. "With sexual violence, it means that it is forced. But, if it is sex with a minor, they can be brought together to figure things out. They can also arrest the man. Yet, if the problem is a pregnancy out of wedlock, reconciliation is the solution." Other women[31] informed me that,

> Rape[32] often happens because men want young girls. To resolve these cases, the two are invited to come together and talk. If they can find a mutually agreeable outcome, the problem is done. If not, the problem can be brought to the *chef de quartier* or *chef d'avenue* for a *baraza* meeting with *chefs* and *sages.* If no compromise is reached, then it goes to *chef de cité.* He can decide whether to send them to the *parquet* or to go put the man in prison.

I was further informed that, "When the rape is between a minor and a civilian, then they can come together for family negotiations." Compensation is a crucial detail to reconciling parties and addressing these cases amicably. In one case[33], where the minor was not forced, her father found out and was upset. Eventually, after being brought together with the girl's family for a discussion, the man agreed to pay 750 USD, but it was not the dowry; they did not get married. This is essentially compensating the family for the harm done to the girl's reputation in a context where women are still expected to be virgins when they get married and social status is greatly dependent on that marriage. It also speaks to the flexibility in types of arrangements that can be made.

Additionally, some people think that amicable settlements can also serve as a deterrent. In an interview with a group of local women[34], one explained that, "Yes, it [amicable settlements] can help reduce sex with minors because maybe the man is asked to pay three cows, and that is a lot. So, when others see that, they won't do the same thing." These women recognized that there is benefit linked to ending or reducing these sexual relations, even if they are seen as normal. In areas of everyday life that could be changed to reduce gendered violence or inequality, the legal system is not necessarily mobilized to enforce the change, but knowledge of the laws may instigate critical thinking about normalized social practices as a part of shifting legal consciousness. Modified laws can thus be useful for supporting socially catalyzed changes in gender norms and expectations. However, enforcing those laws before the normalization of new social practices could actually create more hesitation or uncertainty around the legal system as a result of the *disconnect in harm naming* and *different logics of justice* themes of contradictory consciousness. Notably, social change has indeed been developing in the area of early marriage and pregnancy, which predates, but also corresponds with, the legal change to marriageable age. As I discuss in the following, diverse families are recognizing that sex does not necessarily *have to* lead to marriage, even at a young age, especially due to shifting gender norms around high school and higher education.

Disconnect in Harm Naming and Popular Interpretations of Marriage Law Reforms

The disconnect between popular and legal naming and framing of early marriage shapes the contradictory consciousness that women (and others) experience. Definitions are a major component of this disconnect—the state's definition of early marriage, like statutory rape, is categorical. This is rooted in Western law and international human rights discourse and practice that understand any form of early marriage as inherently oppressive, abusive, and a violation of the rights of the child, regardless of context, history, and practice (Horii, 2020), and misses the complexity of the socio-economic conditions that affect options available to teen girls (Bunting, 2005). By contrast, popular definitions are situational, leading to different interpretations of events depending on different factors. As noted previously, in cases of statutory rape, the man's response is crucial in deciding whether or not a harm was committed. For early marriage, age, adherence to tradition, and socio-economic situation all play a role.

In some cases, adolescent marriage is a normal, taken-for-granted aspect of everyday life. It is neither viewed as inherently good nor bad, judgement develops mostly because of one's experience, although both cultural practices and *sensibilisation* around the issue also play a background role. Ophélie[35] who was 30 at the time of our interview, was married for the first time at 14. She went through the customary marriage process, and she and her family were happy because her husband was able to pay the dowry as well as take care of other basic needs, like food and clothing, as tradition dictates. "They brought the dowry—a cow, a goat, a case of Primus[36]—and there was a little party around the house. When it was over, a few people brought me to my husband's home." She explained that they had been good together; she specified that she never wanted for food. In a context where having basic needs met is difficult for any individual or family, socio-economic realities can make early marriage a strategic choice for some adolescent women and their families.

Ophélie added that she and her husband rarely had any problems. With small disputes, they would go to her in-laws who would advise them to not stay mad at each other. They showed the couple how to "live well together." She provided an example of a problem they had when she wanted a new *pagne*[37] because she did not have many clothes, and he said that he already had intentions on how to spend the money. In this instance, her in-laws brought them together and explained that it was his responsibility to provide clothing, and he "finally came to understand" and re-evaluate his spending. But, after a few years, she explained, he died from a fever and witchcraft. She stayed with her in-laws after his death.

This example illustrates that marrying at a younger age does not *necessarily* lead to regret, unhappiness, or abuse. If one's experience with marriage felt positive, knowledge of the new marriage law would not necessarily change one's perceptions or judgements of early marriage. One's personal experience and likely the experiences of neighbours and relatives, combined with what is understood to be normal and taken for granted, play a large role in shaping why people view early marriage as acceptable and under what conditions. Ophélie had a positive experience and was quite happy in her first marriage. This had much to do with the long-term aspects of the marriage, rather than how old she was. Her in-laws, as with many Congolese couples, were crucial arbiters in their relationship. Importantly, they did not only take her husband's side but attempted to maintain some gendered fairness in the home according to traditional practices.

There are other instances where young women have been strategic about early marriage. In Bisette's[38] life, marriage was a way to escape an abusive family. Bisette was an orphan who was taken in by a family. She said that the other kids in the family discriminated against her, which was at the root of why she got married at 13. In her adoptive family, she never went to school, while her adoptive siblings did. She was treated as a maid—sweeping, doing dishes, fetching water, weaving—and a work hand—tending and harvesting the field with *maman*. She explained that she did not really love the man she married, but she was suffering with her adoptive family. Based on her family life and the advice from a good friend, she judged that it was better to get married.

Bisette got married to escape the lack of love and support from her adoptive family. Interpreting early marriage as a strategic choice lies in stark contrast to the dominant international human rights understanding that views early marriage necessarily as a form of individual victimization or a violation of the rights of the child, ignoring the possibility of the individual autonomy or agency (Horii, 2020), further highlighting the *disconnect in harm naming*. Indeed, early marriage is one of the topics frequently raised in the human rights versus culture debates that define international feminist dialogues (Horii, 2020; see also Bunting & Engle Merry, 2007). Ironically, some countries that advance this kind of thinking actually lack those exact protections at home. In the USA, for example, the age of consent varies by state and is typically between 16 and 18[39], while the legal age of marriage is typically 18 or younger with parental and/or court approval[40]. Yet, these laws are rarely submitted to the same scrutiny by international human rights activists.

In the DRC, the possibility of applying for emancipation in cases of abuse or neglect exists, meaning, at least in theory, there are other options for children in difficult family situations. However, this is a more obscure area of law that has not formed a part of any of the *sensibilisation* work I was informed about; thus, youths are unlikely to have knowledge or access to information unless they are familiar with a legal aid organization. This point was never brought up in interviews with participants but was mentioned to me by one lawyer. Additionally, survival without parental support or marriage[41] would be immensely difficult given the gendered social structure and level of poverty, so applying for emancipation is likely the least desirable strategy.

In contrast to strategic reasons for early marriage, some younger women simply marry because they are in love. Soleil[42] shared how love guided her early marriage. At the same time, her relationship reflects some of the social shifts around marriage that have been taking place. She shared her experience of 'getting married' at 15 years old in a positive light. She met her husband on the shores of Lake Tanganyika, where she was collecting water and he was fishing. Soleil told me that, "He had courted me because I am Mutabwa and he is a Mufuleru [two different ethnic groups/tribes]. He loved me, so he came to my family [to ask about marriage]." He left a little money with her family as a pre-dowry. After asking follow-up questions—I asked if she quit school when she got married—I learned that she did not in fact have the marriage ceremony at 15 years old, even though her fiancé had come to talk with her parents about marriage. Her family, while accepting the pre-dowry, felt that she was too young to live with her 'husband'. She was pregnant and had her first girl that same year while still living with her parents. At 17 years old, they had the religious ceremony, and she moved into her husband's home. During these two additional years at home, she also had another baby with her husband, but her family still expected and encouraged her to live with them. According to Soleil, her family was happy with the situation because her husband had come to them immediately after she got pregnant, "to make the arrangements."

Soleil's experience reflects shifts and diversity in cultural practices, norms, and expectations. In keeping with tradition, the dowry remained an important aspect of their celebration; however, her family decided that she was too young to actually go through the marriage and move in with her fiancé at 15 years old. Even after she found out that she was pregnant, her parents welcomed her at home until she was older. She also completed more schooling during her time at her parents' home. Segments of the population support girls' education, even amongst poorer and less educated families.

That is not to say that all early marriages are positive and that no one is critical of their experiences. Camille[43] lived through a much more difficult situation. She got pregnant at 14 years old and then went to live with her 'husband'[44], a bodyguard of a military official, in a military compound. Camille survived forcible rape by her 'husband', which led to her first pregnancy. She explained,

> They [her family] told me to go live with my husband. When I did that, my mother fell ill from *la tension*[45] because of the situation. So, we had to take her to Bukavu for treatment. After that, *maman* said that I should return home because I was still young, and she would help me through the childbirth. But, I stayed with my husband.

Her 'husband' was 24 years old at the time that she became pregnant. They never had any marriage ceremony, and as the dowry, her family "only received a small symbol of a goat, a case of beer, and 100 USD." Disputes with her husband began immediately while she was pregnant; he was physically violent against her. She stated that, "Turbulence is the only thing that comes from getting married so young." Notably, the military official who employed her husband told her that she was too young and should return to her parents' home to finish school, perhaps signalling knowledge that she would not be safe with her husband, as well as shifting norms about the importance of girls' education. He asked how her parents could accept this arrangement. Camille's situation represents, not just a case of statutory rape and early marriage, but of forcible rape and domestic violence. While the former factors are also legal categories of harm, it is the latter factors that make her experience a situational harm and viewed locally as different from Bisette's and Soleil's experiences.

A further point of consideration that complicates the practice of adolescent marriage is the degree of freedom of the teen to choose to marry or refuse to marry. While none of the women I interviewed and discussed marriage with noted feeling familial pressure to get married, forced marriage was a concern noted by local organizations. In one meeting with a coordinator for a local organization that provides a variety of services for women[46], she said,

> [Regarding sex with a minor] We provide legal support. The problem here is parents prefer to resolve *à l'amiable*. The victim also often accepts this, and it sometimes leads to forced marriage. If you refuse this, you are not welcome at home.

This was further supported in an interview with a group of women[47] in Kiliba. In our discussion, they said,

> [Statutory] rape often happens because men want younger girls. To resolve these cases, the two are invited to come together and talk. If they can find a mutually agreeable outcome, the problem is done. If not, the problem

> can be brought to the *chef de quartier* or *chef d'avenue* for a *baraza* meeting with *chefs* and *sages*.

I asked if the girl is satisfied with this. They replied,

> The girl may not be happy, but she is obliged to do what the family wants because she is a minor. In some cases, there is consent on the part of the minor [to marry], and in some cases there isn't.

Both the local organization and this group of women highlight another layer of complexity to thinking about teen marriage. The adolescent girl is rarely in a situation to make the decision outside of the family dynamic. This can lead to very different outcomes, with some families pushing for marriage, while others don't, and may even emphasize education rather than marriage. Thus, making sense of when these marriages may reflect a harm again returns us to the situational character rather than a categorical harm framework. Additionally, it is possible that even if marriage is not the girl's preference, it may not be seen through the lens of a harm. As I noted, none of the women I interviewed about their marriage framed it as being forced, but some did highlight that their family was happy to receive the dowry. This may have created pressure on these young women to get married, even if they did not interpret this as 'forced' *per se*. The broader social context shapes the analytic frame through which harms are understood, again highlighting the *disconnect in harm naming* when the law is understood as categorical.

The cited examples illustrate how personal, familial, and social judgements regarding the appropriate age for girls to get married are situationally defined. In other words, making the age of marriage categorical, as the law does, reinforces the gap between the law and social norms and practices but still permeates social awareness. This is not to say that norms and practices are static. As noted previously, popular ideas about girls' education are shifting, which is affecting marriage practices. These women's experiences reflect the different ways women and their families come to define the appropriate age of marriage through an examination of personal circumstances in relation to broader socio-economic realities, not only or even primarily through legal frames or categories.

The distinction between categorical and situational interpretations of early marriage and statutory rape reflects a disconnect between the legal definition and the popular one; awareness of both is reflected in legal consciousness. The contradictory element of legal consciousness, here, is that legal definitions of early marriage and statutory rape are linked with liberal ideas about childhood, and they go against popular understandings, which one could place within 'worldviews' as a constitutive element of social experience[48]. Interestingly, the legal definitions were rarely explicitly condemned or seen as wrong but as irrelevant.

Negotiating Statutory Rape and Early Marriage: A New Emphasis on Education

As noted, early marriage holds an ambiguous space in legality, defined in law but not popularly assumed to be inherently harmful. Yet, there are segments of the population who want to reduce early marriage—which can happen because of statutory rape or independent of it—but they do not articulate legal prosecution as the best way to achieve this goal. Instead, education is becoming an additional factor that families consider in cases of sex with an adolescent woman.

Some women and families are starting to be more interested in their daughters receiving a high school education. In Songo, Celeste[49], a 16-year-old girl, got pregnant with an older man. He was actually arrested as a result of their relationship. However, the family did not want to follow up in the courts; instead, they did an amicable settlement through a local organization. It was decided that she would stay at home with her family, but he would pay her school fees and take care of her healthcare and other needs until she gave birth. In a similar case in Mulongwe, a 16-year-old girl, Alphonsine, got pregnant. It was unclear if the man was older than 18. However, again, instead of marriage, her family wanted her to stay at home to continue going to school. When I interviewed her, she was taking care of her young son and explained what life was like as a student and a mother. As a different example of changing norms, Ophélie was disappointed with the fact that she dropped out of school to get married at age 14. Now, as a 30-year-old woman, she is participating in a literacy programme for adults. Cases, like these, reflect popular engagement with the concept of early marriage but not necessarily through a legal frame. Girls' education is a changing aspect of the local worldview, bringing it closer in line with domestic laws and international standards, even if prosecuting men for statutory rape is not necessarily perceived as being the way to address the issue.

While in the past pregnancy meant the end of schooling, families' and the education system's responses are diverse. Schools are starting to let pregnant girls continue to attend, and this has at times reframed the discussion of what an amicable settlement should entail. Families and communities are placing value on girls' education, making early marriage less desirable. At the same time, incidents of sex with minors continue to be met with marriage proposals, as per the continued social practice. This shows how practices change, not necessarily as a result of legal reforms but in conversation with shifts in broader norms and expectations. In other words, it helps explain why social practices sometimes align with the law even when the law *per se* does not seem to have much influence in this change. This hints at the underlying problem with legal reform and ROL building; they expect to change legal consciousness by changing the law and educating people about those reforms. While legal reforms do affect legal consciousness, they do so in dialogue with broader social beliefs, practices, and norms. Thus, changes to law and *sensibilisation* do not necessarily lead to liberal legal outcomes. Instead, they become *a part* of legal consciousness and legality, and thus contribute to *emergent hybrid legality* rather than the transition to liberal legality.

Conclusion

In this chapter, I analysed early marriage and statutory rape and highlight the complexities of legal consciousness and gendered social norms and practices. I argued that reforming laws to promote gender justice and educating the population around those reforms, as aspects of building the ROL, may indeed shape legal consciousness but not unidirectionally in expected ways. Theories of legal reform to advance gender equality might not always be the most relevant or successful approach in different contexts.

Through ROL-oriented interventions and legal reforms, aspects of different legal codes that had been in conflict were unified. While changes to laws were in part a response to global pressures to advance women's rights, domestically, there is a wide range of acceptability regarding the age at which girls can and should get married that predates the change to the law. Age of marriageability also relates to the age of consent because teen girls' families often expect them to get married if they have sex with someone out of wedlock, especially if they get pregnant. Additionally, sexual relations are an essential part of consummating marriages at all ages.

Promulgation of new laws has made people aware of the possibility of punishment in cases of early marriage or statutory rape. However, popular knowledge of these legal reforms has done little to reframe these experiences broadly as harms or make families more likely to turn to the courts. Popular consciousness maintains an understanding of harms as situational and not categorical for statutory rape and early marriage. In cases of sex with adolescent women, the norm is still to propose marriage, but this is shifting. Broader changes in norms around girls' education, by contrast, have begun to reshape ideas about early marriage and how to address statutory rape cases. Teenage pregnancy is no longer a social death sentence or an end of schooling, and diversification of amicable arrangements has developed in response. Popular interest in girls' education has been influential in challenging the practice of early marriage. This in turn solidifies the informal realm as the appropriate space for addressing disputes.

My fieldwork further suggests that people have not fully accepted and integrated updated laws into their belief system. The law has not become the dominant social frame for defining early marriage because of its categorial approach to harm, even if it has been integrated in legal consciousness. Some older people find it difficult to accept the new law, which is so different from their lived experiences. Instead, a variety of other socio-cultural realities play a more important role in popular understandings of whether an adolescent woman is ready for marriage. Additionally, many women have had experiences of early marriage and view these in a positive light.

As this chapter makes clear, awareness of the laws can shape popular wisdom and practices in unanticipated ways. The next chapter explains a different example of how this happens by considering the laws around witchcraft and the role they play in the practice of popular justice.

Notes

1 Internet café.
2 Marise, fieldnotes, 11 April 2015.
3 Loi n° 06/018 du 20 juillet 2006 modifiant et complétant le Décret du 30 janvier 1940 portant Code pénal congolais. Law No. 06/018 of July 20, 2006 amending and supplementing the Decree of 30 January 1940 on the Congolese Penal Code.
4 "Tout attentat à la pudeur commis sans violences, ruse, ou « menaces sur la personne ou à l'aide de la personne d'un enfant âgé « de moins de dix-huit ans sera puni d'une servitude pénale de six « mois à cinq ans. L'âge de l'enfant pourra être déterminé par « examen médical, à défaut d'état civil." (www.leganet.cd/Legislation/DroitPenal/Loi.06.018.20.07.3006.htm). "Any indecent assault committed without violence, trickery, or threats to the person or with the help of a child under the age of eighteen will be punished by penal servitude of six months to five years. The age of the child can be determined by medical examination, in the absence of civil status" (author's translation).
5 "Les actes de pedophile s'entendentde toute attirance sexuelle d'un adulte ou d'un adolescent envers un enfant, notamment l'attentat a la pudeur, la relation sexuelle, l'erotisme, la pornographie, l'abus sexuel et le viol."
6 Interview, 30 January 2017.
7 As 18 years old (Article 41). The same Article states that, "The abandonment and maltreatment of children, in particular pedophilia, sexual abuse and the charge of engaging in witchcraft, are prohibited and punishable by law."
8 The first rebellion actually leading to end of the Mobutu regime.
9 Book III, de la Famille, Title 1, Ch. III, Sect. 2, Para. 2, Art. 352. "L'homme avant dix-huit ans révolus, la femme avant quinze ans révolus, ne peuvent contracter mariage. Néanmoins, il est loisible au tribunal de paix d'accorder des dispenses d'âge pour des motifs graves. Le tribunal statue à la requête de toute personne justifiant d'un intérêt." Loi n°87–010 du 1er août 1987 portant Code de la Famille.
10 Throughout the chapter, I will use consent in the way it is generally understood in Uvira, which is to say that it is possible for an adolescent under the age of 18 to consent to sex.
11 "L'homme avant dix-huit ans révolus, la femme avant quinze ans révolus, ne peuvent contracter mariage. Néanmoins, il est loisible au tribunal de paix d'accorder des dispenses d'âge pour des motifs graves. Le tribunal statue à la requête de toute personne justifiant d'un intérêt."
12 "L'homme et la femme avant dix-huit ans révolus ne peuvent contracter marriage."
13 At times, this may have been due to the expectations constructed through the saviour economic complex (see Chapter 3).
14 For example, this came up in multiple group interviews. Group interview, *chefs*, 13 April 2015. Group interview, security sector, 13 April 2015. Group interview, local women, 23 May 2015.
15 Interview, 24 March 2017.
16 Interview, 20 February 2017.
17 Group Interview, 25 April 2015.
18 Group interview with women, Kiliba, 23 May 2015
19 Interview, 7 March 2017.

20 Group interview, 14 April 2015.
21 Interview, 14 February 2017.
22 I would generally try not to lead or prime interviewees by asking questions that already hint in a certain direction, such as reference to 'state agents'. However, I was also aware that many survivors of attacks, including sexual violence, who do not know the assailant generally think that the state cannot do anything. Thus, to try to distinguish whether state justice/punishment would be her preference, I had to include the idea that the state could identify the perpetrator.
23 Interview (fieldnotes), 27 January 2017.
24 Group interview, 23 May 2015.
25 Interview, 24 March 2017.
26 Group interview, 30 January 2017.
27 While I cannot find direct mention of this in that particular law, it is possible that he was simply referring to the fact that statutory rape is defined as a crime, requiring a criminal investigation and proceedings.
28 Interview, 19 May 2015.
29 11 April 2015.
30 Interview, 24 April 2015. Note that these actors did not have formal legal training. Their understandings can thus be contrasted to the earlier statement of BB's lawyer, who emphasized that amicable settlements go against the law.
31 Group interview, local women, 23 May 2015.
32 I understood this to be statutory rape based on the fairly common understanding that statutory rape should be addressed amicably, whereas forced rape of a minor should not. However, it is also true that some people feel that all rape cases should be addressed amicably because it is the best way for the survivor to get something out of the violent experience and not feel threatened by the possibility of retaliation, as noted earlier in this chapter.
33 Fieldnotes, 23 May 2015.
34 Group interview, 23 May 2015.
35 Interview, 15 February 2017.
36 A domestic beer brand.
37 Local wrap clothing.
38 Interview, 7 March 2017.
39 www.ageofconsent.net/states
40 In recent years, there has been more attention and analysis of early marriage in the USA. Concerns and problems are remarkably similar to those in Congo, except the social context is extremely different, and this is not a generally accepted social practice that falls within people's worldviews.
41 Notably, According to Article 357, "Children, even if emancipated, may not enter into marriage. Loi no 16/008 du 15 juillet 2016 modifiant et complétant la loi no 87–010 du 1er août 1987 portant Code de la famille (Law No. 16/008 of 15 July 2016 Amending and Supplementing Law No. 87–010 of 1 August 1987 on the Family Code).
42 Interview, 12 April 2017.
43 Interview, 17 March 2017.
44 This was the expression she used, but as I came to learn, people can use the terms 'husband' and 'wife' to refer to a variety of relationships that are not all defined by a formal marriage, whether civil or traditional. Additionally, the term 'marriage' can be used just as loosely, with living together being one example.
45 High blood pressure.
46 Interview, 1 February 2017.
47 Group interview, 23 May 2015.

48 The tension between the global institutionalization of age-based childhood and special rights protections for children in contrast to diverse context-based understandings of childhood, specifically as outlined in the Convention on the Rights of the Child, has been subject to various discussions and critiques (ex. Pupavac, 2001; Schepler, 2005). In particular, this tension has been noted in conflict and conflict-affected areas where child soldiers have been used. When it comes to early marriage, some research explores the dynamics that lead to early marriage. For example, in different contexts, researchers highlight the role of poverty and gendered economic disparities, as well as educational opportunities as crucial factors in understanding early marriage (Bunting, 2005; Stark, 2018).

49 10 February 2017.

Bibliography

Aroussi, S. (2018). Perceptions of justice and hierarchies of rape: Rethinking approaches to sexual violence in Eastern Congo from the ground up. *International Journal of Transitional Justice, 12*(2), 277–295.

Bunting, A. (2005). Stages of development: Marriage of girls and teens as an international human rights issue. *Social & Legal Studies, 14*(1), 17–38.

Dunn, H. (2020). Research in the land of savages, victims, and saviors. In G. Hoogensen, P. Weitsman & R. Matthew (Eds.), *Women's perspectives on human security: Violence, environment, and sustainability* (pp. 154–182). Ohio University Press.

Horii, H. (2020). A blind spot in international human rights framework: A space between tradition and modernity within the child marriage discourse. *The International Journal of Human Rights, 24*(8), 1057–1079.

Jean-Bouchard, É. (2017). Sexual violence issues in eastern DRC: Processes of global and local co-constitution. *Canadian Journal of African Studies/Revue canadienne des études africaines, 51*(2), 257–273.

Lake, M. (2014). Organizing hypocrisy: Providing legal accountability for human rights violations in areas of limited statehood. *International Studies Quarterly, 58*(3), 515–526.

Lake, M. (2018). *Strong NGOs and weak states: Pursuing gender justice in the Democratic Republic of Congo and South Africa.* Cambridge University Press.

Lincoln, R. S. (2011). Rule of law for whom: Strengthening the rule of law as a solution to sexual violence in the Democratic Republic of the Congo. *Berkeley Journal of Gender, Law & Justice, 26*, 139.

Merry, S., & Bunting, A. (2007). Global regulation and local political struggles: Early marriage in northern Nigeria. In *Youth, globalization, and the law* (pp. 321–353). Stanford University Press.

Pupavac, V. (2001). Misanthropy without borders: The international children's rights regime. *Disasters, 25*(2), 95–112.

Rush Smith, N. (2015). Rejecting rights: Vigilantism and violence in post-apartheid South Africa. *African Affairs, 114*(456), 341–360.

Shepler, S. (2005). The rites of the child: Global discourses of youth and reintegrating child soldiers in Sierra Leone. *Journal of Human Rights, 4*(2), 197–211.

Stark, L. (2018). Early marriage and cultural constructions of adulthood in two slums in Dar es Salaam. *Culture, Health & Sexuality, 20*(8), 888–901.

Thornberry, E. (2019). *Colonizing consent: Rape and governance in South Africa's Eastern Cape* (Vol. 141). Cambridge University Press.

Zongwe, D. P. (2012). The new sexual violence legislation in the Congo: Dressing indelible scars on human dignity. *African Studies Review, 55*(2), 37–57.

Chapter 6

The Violent Side of *Emergent Hybrid Legality*

Popular Justice and Witchcraft

During my third field trip to Uvira, after months of hearing about witchcraft beliefs and cases of witchcraft, I had an opportunity to dive further into this phenomenon. I was invited by a local *mwami*[1] to learn about witchcraft and meet with his advisors, those with the expertise to determine if an act of witchcraft had occurred. This was a unique opportunity to gain first-hand knowledge about a phenomenon that I had heard much about but still did not fully grasp. When I returned home that day, I shared the generous offer I had received with Papa Félicien. Papa Félicien spent most of his days at work at the Port de Kalundu and most of his evenings sitting in a plastic chair in the courtyard with his portable radio glued to his ear. The most animated reactions I had seen from him up to this point were during political discussions with friends or occasionally when we discussed Rwandan or American politics. So, the reaction I received in response to my news about meeting with the *mwami* signified something. He displayed a sense of disbelief, combined with concern, protectiveness, and authority; I was essentially forbidden from going to meet with him.

Putting aside the cultural and gendered dynamics of being an adult woman *forbidden* from doing anything, his reaction was one of sincere concern. He was worried that these witchcraft advisors were 'brutal' and that once they shared their 'secrets' with me I did not know what they would do. He added, "They might want to see if a white person can absorb all their powers." Although I was still not set on cancelling the meeting, this is directly from my fieldnotes, "He said I really need to désintéressé[2] myself of those people." His reaction created some uncertainty in me, in my beliefs. In reflecting on that experience, my concern was more related to the possibility of poisoning[3] than of witchcraft. But, still, my resolve around the issue was shaken, even as I thought the meeting could enhance my understanding of this phenomenon. This was my third trip to Congo, and my stance on witchcraft—from non-believer to ambiguous sceptic—increasingly wavered with each visit. I had also discussed this with a friend who had been working in eastern DRC for over a year, and she had had a similar experience. When one is surrounded by unwavering certainty about something, it is perhaps not surprising that those beliefs start to affect your own

DOI: 10.4324/9781003289715-6

understanding of the world. Put differently, worldviews are profoundly social phenomena; while the researcher may enter the field with her own beliefs, she is not immune to the local context. Thus, while the reality of witchcraft may indeed be difficult to grasp from a Western worldview, the strength of those beliefs locally was enough to shake the confidence of this non-believer. In Uvira, belief in witchcraft and the harm it can do are powerful and widespread; they cannot be avoided, no matter one's socio-economic status, background, or education. With the pervasiveness of witchcraft fears in mind, the question of how accusations of witchcraft get addressed is obviously meaningful.

While ROL building efforts have not highlighted addressing witchcraft accusations to the extent they have cases of SGBV, the broader influence of international, Western legal standards has certainly been influential. The logic of witchcraft, typically known by its negative effects not an observable cause or act, does not easily fit with the ideology of liberal legalism and its emphasis on science and material evidence. Witness testimony may of course be used in a liberal legal system, but the possibility of witnessing magic or witchcraft is limited by a variety of factors, in particular its ethereal nature, but also the secrecy that surrounds it. Thus, the state law has maintained its stance of non-recognition of witchcraft, while the local legal complex has taken up the issue of witchcraft accusations in a way that walks the tightrope between state law and popular beliefs and practices. In other words, harms and disputes around witchcraft are positioned at the fault line of legal encounters and *friction* between internationalized liberal legal standards and more localized understandings of harm and justice.

In parts of Congo, such as Uvira, witchcraft is as real as any material reality. People have been told for generations that witches exist, what the signs are, and who the experts are. No one sees a witch in action, although there are accounts based in speculation; yet, everyone knows that these individuals have the power to kill their children, improve their neighbour's harvest, and generally influence everyday life. The population, based on their worldviews, understand witchcraft to be a real harm. Yet, the state and the state legal system do not. This is a clear example of a *disconnect in harm naming* in the opposite direction as the previous chapter; here, the population defines the harm, for which some recourse to justice is required, while the state does not recognize the harm.

While international actors raise concerns about the persecution and violence against accused witches, populations view a very different justice issue arising from the harm that witches themselves perpetrate (Ashforth, 2015). Witchcraft is an injury for which the population seeks punishment, and yet the state does not recognize the harm and thus offers no recourse to justice. Not only that, but the state legal system accepts that a witchcraft *accusation* may be an offence, a form of slander or libel. At the same time, the informal realm, namely chiefs and NGOs, makes some contributions to fulfilling people's needs for justice but has also fallen short by not punishing acts of witchcraft or by being too afraid to address cases. By contrast, *mwamis*, although possessing the power to determine if someone is actually a witch, will protect the witch rather than punish them as the population desires.

As I illustrated in previous chapters, recent reforms of state law fit imperfectly in the context of Uvira, but, with the help of the local legal complex, the situation has often created unique ways for the population to think about and engage with legal-justice. I have made clear that while people do not always follow official law, they often find ways to resolve everyday harms and disputes that integrate knowledge about the state law, shaping legal consciousness. This happens in some witchcraft cases as well. Yet, *emergent hybrid legality* is not always reflected in the use of mediation or amicable settlements. When punishment is desired by the population but not provided by the state or through other channels, the risk of vigilante justice manifests, which I understand to be an outcome of legal encounters, and the attendant shifts in legal consciousness. Vigilantism is hardly a new phenomenon, but understanding the complexity of its roots is a work in progress, with changing legal and political context increasingly recognized as playing a role (ex. Rush Smith, 2015; Verweijen, 2015). This is true in Uvira as well, where vigilantism is typically referred to as *justice populaire*—popular justice. Popular justice takes a variety of forms, from stoning to burning to the use of arms and is typically undertaken by local youths to correct a harm and ostensibly protect the community.

In this chapter, I argue that the witchcraft cases highlight the themes in contradictory legal consciousness—*disconnect in harm naming* and *different logics of justice*—and provide an additional form of justice to consider within the frame of *emergent hybrid legality*. The popular understanding that state-delivered justice can be hostile to victims of witchcraft tends to legitimize extra-legal-justice strategies. Popular knowledge of the law and legal system has reinforced negative judgements, as the law does not reflect lived realities of fear and harm as defined in this cultural milieu. The resulting practice, popular justice although not institutionalized nor widespread if one considers the extensiveness of witchcraft beliefs, has certainly become normalized as a way to achieve justice outside the more institutionalized realms of *emergent hybrid legality*.

The Harm of Witchcraft in Everyday Life

Witchcraft beliefs are deeply rooted on Congolese society; they are so pervasive in DRC that Schatzberg (2009) labelled witchcraft one of three forms of causality, the others being scientific causality and religious causality. This means that one of the main ways that people explain the world around them is through witchcraft. For example, a child falls ill and dies. This could be understood, depending on the individual and circumstance, as resulting from a disease that was not treated in time—scientific causality. Alternatively, it could be understood as God's will—religious causality. Finally, and a popular explanation for children's illness and death in Uvira, it could be explained as resulting from acts of a witch—witchcraft causality. Further, it is not clear that these forms of causality are hierarchically organized, meaning they all have more or less equivalent explanatory value to the population, although this may vary by region and individual.

Witchcraft beliefs do not appear to be linked with socio-economic or educational status; they appear to infuse the whole of Uvira's social world, as educated elites, such as lawyers, also recognize its power. Additionally, in the post-conflict era, where violence has become normalized, norms disrupted, trust destroyed, and traditional authority systems broken down, witchcraft accusations flourish (Verweijen, 2015; see also Lombard & Batianga-Kinzi, 2015). Witchcraft is a common-sense way to interpret the difficulties that define people's everyday lives. In other words, witchcraft beliefs are not an enigmatic, un-modern part of cosmology. They are a defining element of social life in many places across the globe (eg. Adinkrah, 2004; Ashforth, 2015; Schatzberg, 2009). In this section, I explore some people's ideas and experiences with witchcraft, also highlighting the significance of their fears.

Experiences with Witchcraft: Fear and Rumours

Through my fieldwork, I developed an understanding that the roots of injustice associated with witchcraft stem from its penetration into all facets of everyday life. Accusations of witchcraft often appear in instances where inequality has become more pronounced or evident. Income inequality or inequality in production capabilities, educational attainment, and infertility are all sources of difference, where gossip, rumours, and jealousy flourish as people struggle with basic subsistence. For example, in an interview with a group of wise elders[4], they explained, "When fishing is the primary source of income in a community and some men catch more than others, witchcraft is often understood to be the source of the different catches." Witchcraft is thus an explanation for divergent socio-economic outcomes. While other explanations can exist—chance or even the use of illegal nets that can easily trap more fish—witchcraft remains an important explanatory factor.

Further, witchcraft accusations thrive in a variety of contexts, where rumours and jealousy shape people's relationships and perceptions of one another. For example, Soleil[5] explained some tensions she encountered with her new neighbours who were threatening her because they viewed her as an outsider. She explained,

> During the time when my child was sick . . . he had diarrhea and was vomiting blood. When we brought him to the hospital, his stomach distended. In the neighbourhood, people were saying that I arrived [in town] with children, but I would leave with none. . . . Sometimes, they do witchcraft. . . . When I told my husband what the neighbours were saying to me, he told me that they cannot bewitch someone that they do not know, and my fortitude returned.

> Others said that they were saying that because I came from far away and married someone local, and they were jealous.

Soleil shared these threats with those close to her; they did not discount her fear but validated it and helped her understand the role of jealousy in witchcraft threats. This may be the most prevalent method of dealing with witchcraft that I encountered, getting advice from others—friends, family members, elders—but not making any formal complaints or seeking out mediation, in other words, finding a way to deal with it, coping. Popular understandings of how to address witchcraft are complex because belief that an act of witchcraft has taken place can be profoundly intertwined with jealousy and rumours, creating fears and misunderstandings between people. Of course, in the local worldview, it is important to note that the role of jealousy does not negate the possibility of witchcraft. In other words, just because jealousy plays a role in a threat or accusation does not mean the accuser is wholly fabricating the accusation or that the accused has not done *something*, but it is possible, which only adds to the complexity of trying to understand witchcraft allegations.

The linkages between jealousy and witchcraft may also occur if one's child is doing better in school than her neighbour's child or has a better job. When interviewing a group of women[6] in Makobola, they said, "it [witchcraft] is related to jealousy. Someone has nice kids, they progress and do well for themselves, then the neighbour wants to eliminate them." Naima, whose experience is described in detail as follows, thought that witchcraft was used against her because, "my husband cultivated a lot, and he hunted a lot of game." Essentially, it is a way of explaining social and socio-economic hierarchies as well as illness and death. It is used to make sense of phenomena that are not easily attributed to other types of causality. This not only relates to jealousy and gossip but also death and personal struggles.

Naima's[7] experience and interpretation of how witchcraft affected her life illuminate the gravity of the problem and provide a useful example of what Ashforth (2015) calls, "death needing narration" (p. 14). Naima's experience, as summarized from our interview, further illustrates the profound fear that witchcraft ignites in people, especially when trying to make sense of seemingly senseless death.

> Naima was a frail-looking petite woman approaching her 60th birthday. Jeanne and I met her in a home that we had access to for the purposes of conducting private interviews. The room was dark with clothes hanging and flapping in front of the windows and two large sofas and a chair placed around a large wooden table. We each took a seat, said our greetings and introductions, and I began to ask some questions. We did not get far before Genevieve, my interpreter, went mute, staring wide-eyed at a small green snake that was slithering about the corner of the room. Naima and I were

> not too bothered by it, but we eventually paused the interview to have a neighbour come and remove the snake, which Genevieve believed might be dangerous. I felt a sense of camaraderie between us as lots of smiles were shared after surviving the snake. Naima's frailty seemed to dissipate as she quickly opened up about her life and the difficulties she had endured. Indeed, she immediately shared with us that she had moved to Uvira as a result of ongoing problems with witchcraft being used against her and her family when she lived in Fizi decades earlier.
>
> Four of Naima's children had died in Fizi. The first died of measles. Naima explained that there are two types of measles: Measles that come from God and can be cured and measles that came from the 'dark hands' of men, alluding to dark magic or forces, and could never be cured. She elaborated that she had even gone to a medical doctor who could not save her child. The second died after being bitten by a dog and the third from diarrhoea. The fourth child died on Lake Tanganyika while he was fishing. His boat capsized, and he was killed by a crocodile. It was after this death that Naima and her husband sought the help of a féticheur. The féticheur described the person who was causing all the deaths and said that it was a family member. After determining who the nefarious family member was, the féticheur asked what Naima and her husband wanted to do. For the price of one cow, he said he was willing to kill the person for them. Naima and her husband could not bear to undertake such a drastic measure despite the suffering that her family endured; they feared the wrath of God. So, instead, without ever saying a word to this familial witch, they left their home, land, and family behind and moved to Uvira to restart their lives.
>
> Naima hoped for the witch's death, but she did not want to be responsible for it due to her religious beliefs[8].

Naima's narrative speaks to 1) the threat of witchcraft; 2) witchcraft causality in situations of 'death needing narration'; and 3) the measures necessary to maintain one's security vis-à-vis witches, in other words, the extent of disruption to one's life to escape a witch without turning to violence. Indeed, general options include trying to ignore the threat, trying to promote a dialogue between families, relocating to another town, or making other life-changing arrangements to reduce the threat. Naima and her husband left everything that they had worked hard for, as well as their family and community, because their experiences with witchcraft had been so grave; they could not fathom a different option. They did not want to harm another person, but this was the only other approach available. Bear in mind, her experience occurred decades ago, and NGO-run mediation services were not to be found to the extent they are today. Yet, her narrative exemplifies how witchcraft is viewed as a real and devastating harm that impacts people's lives and livelihoods. This is by no means the only instance I observed or heard about that illustrates the real fear that witchcraft instils in people.

By providing an example of the sacrifices that people are willing to make to escape the violence of witchcraft, Naima's story demonstrates that witchcraft accusations are not *just* used strategically or because of jealousy. Indeed, witchcraft is not experienced as a rare anomaly or as exceptional; rather, it is woven into the fabric of society and everyday life. People understand witchcraft as a real harm, but the possibility for addressing that harm proves limited. The arguments and cases I detail in the following sections illustrate contradictory legal consciousness around naming the harm of witchcraft, as well as justice for acts of witchcraft, structuring the nature of legality around this issue.

Witchcraft and the *Disconnect in Harm Naming*

The relationship between witchcraft and the law is different from the examples of harm explored in previous chapters. While areas of legal reform, such as statutory rape and early marriage, are relatively new, the status of witchcraft in the law is long-standing but rather ambiguous. There is no specific article outlawing witchcraft accusations; however, Article 78[9] of the Penal Code provides some important guidance. It essentially states that if anyone abuses the superstitious beliefs of another in a way that leads them to commit an act of violence, this is a punishable offence. However, more broadly, the state simply does not recognize witchcraft as a legal matter, which may be a remnant of the Belgian colonial system (see Diwan, 2004). At the same time, it could be a factor in other charges, including libel or slander. As I illustrate throughout this chapter, this formal legal context has been vernacularized into two main understandings amongst the population: 1) The state does not recognize witchcraft[10]; and 2) a witchcraft *accusation* is a punishable offence, likely through libel or slander laws, but also through the Penal Code Article 78 if it leads to another infraction.

Given the unquestionable and broad recognition of witchcraft in people's everyday lives and the non-recognition of witchcraft harms by the formal legal system, this is a clear case of *disconnect in harm naming*. And, although the disconnect is not the result of new legal reforms, it is an issue that has been subject to *sensibilisation* by the legal complex with internationalized training in legal and human rights issues. Indeed, insofar as international actors have become interested in witchcraft in Africa, it is generally as a human rights issue, with the understanding that greater protection is needed for those accused of witchcraft (Ashforth, 2015). The increased frequency of popular justice has led civil society to attempt to educate people on witchcraft and the law (Verweijen, 2015), also known as *sensibilisation*. In other words, the current context of internationalized local legal reforms has brought witchcraft; witchcraft accusations; and, most notably, popular justice into the spotlight.

Given the international, Western interpretation of witchcraft as 'not real' (Ashforth, 2015), it seems evident that it could not be a punishable offence in a system where criminal law is largely shaped by liberal legal tenets. Incongruence between the systems and logics of knowledge that define formal law and those surrounding witchcraft beliefs is used to justify the lack of regulation. AA[11] said, "There can never be proof of witchcraft in the law, although with custom there are ways." Jerome[12], a local lawyer, summarized how he understood the problems that enable popular justice. He stated, "There is no law to prosecute a witch, even when there is proof. It is a weakness of the justice system." The proof that he is referring to here is not legal proof but rather the proof provided by authorities on witchcraft, *féticheurs*, or the *mwami's* consultants. Jerome makes clear that, even from the perspective of a lawyer, the state laws provide a gap in justice delivery in cases of witchcraft. In one group interview[13], I was told, "The government manages things like they don't know it exists, but in some ways, they know it." One legal official at the Tripaix[14] explained to me: "No judges are witches, so they cannot say that it exists." I followed up on his statement: "But, most judges aren't rapists, but they can still recognize that rape exists." He responded by getting to the core of the issue: "Yes, but there is *proof*. There cannot be proof with witchcraft"[15]. In other words, the law cannot name the harm of witchcraft because it cannot be proven according to a particular form of rationality that characterizes the formal legal system, where scientific evidence, expert testimony, and witness accounts amount to proof. Notably, some other contexts where witchcraft is a problem have modified their legal system to start to be able to address the issue, such as Malawi, where investigations into witchcraft accusations are part of the legal system, and the accused are protected by the same legal standards or other accused individuals (Ashforth, 2015). However, in Congo, this has not been integrated into the law.

The standing of witchcraft in Congolese law has been the subject of interest for legal actors since independence. The newly independent formal legal system directly encountered the question of witchcraft and its legality in the mid-1970s. As explained to me by a prosecutor[16] from the Tripaix in Uvira, there had been a notable case that was brought before the court in Bas-Zaire (now Bas-Congo) province. A man had been fired from his job and, seeking to regain employment, tried to remove his replacement. Apparently, his attempts at poisoning and beating the replacement failed, so he went to a witch who performed incantations on a black cat (the case is known as the 'black cat case'[17]), but even this did not work, so the witch took a weapon and killed the replacement.

The prosecutor continued to explain that the case was brought before the courts and then went to the Court of Appeals of Bas-Zaire. The accused was initially charged with two infractions: Assassination and attempted murder *par moyen magique* (using magic). It was explained to me that this development was important "because the law is not just what is written, but judges can create law through their judgements, reasoning through the milieu in which they work." If he was convicted of attempted murder *par moyen magique*, lower courts could have referred to this judgement in future cases involving witchcraft. The case went to the Supreme Court of Justice, where they dismissed the attempted murder charge. An important Congolese jurist, Bayona ba Meya[18], argued that they had the opportunity to keep *moyen magique* as part of the charge. Therefore, this could have been a precedent setting case for integrating magic, and witchcraft, into the law. However, the removal of the aspect of the charge related to *moyen magic* in effect maintained and reaffirmed the idea that supernatural affairs were not to be mediated or punished by law.

At the same time, my discussion of the black cat case with the prosecutor shows that there is recognition amongst some legal professionals that witchcraft is indeed a harm that *could* have been regulated by law. Other countries, such as Tanzania and Cameroon, do regulate and punish witchcraft through their state legal systems, recognizing that there are indeed people who can provide expert opinion on these cases (Diwan, 2004). Interestingly, the outlawing of witchcraft and thus the courts' jurisdiction over witchcraft are remnants of the colonial system (Diwan, 2004). In this sense, the criminal law[19] in Congo stems from, and remains more aligned with, Western legal reasoning and values than domestic experience and context. Due to the *disconnect in harm naming*, people cannot frame their experiences of witchcraft as legal matter, thus reinforcing a distance between popular worldviews and the ideology of liberal legalism.

Notably, the *disconnect in harm naming* is an area of contradictory consciousness because people are aware of the status of witchcraft in state law or at least the popularized interpretation of its standing. The tension between liberal legalism and worldviews would not necessarily manifest in contradictory consciousness if people were not familiar with the law, as the legal complex often assumes. Although both domestic and international members of the legal complex have voiced concerns and doubts about the population's lack of knowledge of the law, as outlined in earlier chapters, it is significant to note that those I interviewed were strikingly aware of the official status of witchcraft and witchcraft accusations, even if they did not cite particular articles from the legal code.

Popular Understandings of Justice in Witchcraft Cases

While the formal legal system rejects the possibility of prosecuting acts of witchcraft, the population recognizes and experiences the harm of witchcraft, and some view punishment as the appropriate response. Although action is infrequently taken, in certain cases people will turn to mediation or popular justice. Interestingly, while people seemed open to the possibility of mediation for a variety of harms, such as those discussed in earlier chapters, this was not always the preference or norm with witchcraft. Indeed, people I spoke with often preferred punishment, and thus the *different logics of justice* theme of legal consciousness also emerges through the examination of witchcraft accusations. I highlight the population's desire for punishment in witchcraft cases, in contrast to the state's absence of justice, before turning to the practices that have emerged, both violent and non-violent.

Interviews with members of the population begin to provide some perspective regarding people's preferences and expectations of justice for witchcraft. Mireille[20] provides one example. When I asked her about security in her neighbourhood, Mireille responded, "In this neighbourhood, we are fine during the day, but at night, *maman*, you would cry. There are bad people, witches, murderers, because we are in a place that is still so backward." I followed up by asking specifically about witchcraft cases, Mireille replied,

> We are still so *reculées*[21] here. . . . And at night, you can't sleep. You hear sounds as if stones are being thrown on the roofs. I once saw the old man from over there, and they came and threw a dead person in front of him. They said, "our person, who you killed, you will eat him today. If not, you must bring him back to life, and if you don't, we will kill you too." Then, they started to talk in their traditional language.

My understanding, based on the question I asked, was that people assumed that the old man was a witch and the cause of the victim's death. I asked some follow-up questions about the case.

Holly: Have you ever heard that members of the neighbourhood attacked a witch?

Mireille: When you are a witch and you have already gone so far as to kill people, the young people wait for you; when you are alone, they shoot you with bullets.

Here, I asked some more specific questions about cases she was familiar with, then continued:

Holly: What do you think about that [the killing of witches]?

Mireille: I don't know, but it is good to discourage witches because we are always afraid, and with our children who are always here and there, God only knows.

Holly: Do you think there is something else that should happen to witches other than killing them?

Mireille: Killing them is the only thing that is right.

Mireille makes it very clear that she believes that punishment is the correct and appropriate response, even if that entails turning to popular justice. I understood her reference to youth attacks and shootings as manifestations of popular justice, which I explore in more detail later in the chapter. In conversations I had with a few people, they talked about the shift in popular justice from a form of mob justice to hired killings. Mireille's comments reflected the idea that punishment is not just an individual preference but a community need. The risk from witchcraft is understood as a broader threat to the community, not just an isolated case against an individual. As Mireille's interview illustrates, fear for the safety of children is one of those threats, thus reflecting concerns for the wider community, not just the individual. This also speaks to a less tangible understanding that witchcraft is a moral wrong. It is not just a crime but harm that can pollute the community, making public vigilance important. Camille[22] also spoke to the need and appropriateness of punishment.

Holly: You told us that there were also cases of witchcraft. What happens in relation to those?

Camille: I often hear about it, but I have never experienced it. There are times it can happen while you sleep at night; there are dogs barking outside, some cats. And we say these are the stories of witchcraft. But, I pray and go back to sleep.

Holly: Have you ever heard of a case of witchcraft or thieves being caught and injured?

Camille: We heard of a thief; we do not know which house he robbed. The youths pursued him until they reached the market and killed him. We do not know what he stole and which neighbourhood the young people who killed him were from. We only heard in the morning that a thief was killed, and that was it.

Holly: What do you think about that?

Camille: It is not good. But, when you have the problem of witchcraft, when you catch someone who has bewitched or killed, they must be killed.

When witchcraft is used for extreme purposes, a popular sentiment is that it should be punished in the most severe way. In both examples, Mireille and Camille highlight punishment, specifically death, as the correct response to witchcraft cases, especially if the witch is understood to cause the death of another. Notably, this does not mean that every individual who thinks that witches are a risk to the community would, themselves, kill the witch. This is likely why popular justice gets some community support; it puts the violent actions in someone else's hands. Although I did not specifically ask Mireille and Camille if they would be willing to use violence against a witch, Naima's narrative earlier in the chapter suggests that individuals, or even families, are not always willing to perpetrate or be responsible for violence themselves

In other interviews, I asked what people usually do when they suspect someone of witchcraft. Simon said that witchcraft is a common problem, "but you cannot bring that kind of problem to *la justice* because there is no proof." Ophélie said, "Nothing really. If you go attack the person, it is a mistake because they will imprison you. . . . They will tell you witchcraft does not exist." I asked, "But, do you think the state should imprison the witches?" She replied, "I can think it, but it won't happen." Ophélie's statement reflects the sentiment that there is nothing that a person can do in the face of witchcraft because the law is working counter to the victim's needs and the well-being of the community. In other words, she is arguing that if someone takes action against a witch they risk legal repercussions. These are a few examples illustrating popular knowledge of how witchcraft is situated in the formal law. The lack of 'proof' and the argument that witchcraft 'does not exist' fit with liberal legal ideology but clearly do not align with cultural beliefs and lived experiences. This scientific–legal rationality has not pushed people to reinterpret their deeply held beliefs. Knowledge of the law conflicts with beliefs and experiences and shapes negative judgements of the legal system as a space that does not protect communities and may even punish victims if they take action. Thus, not only is there a *disconnect in harm naming*, but *different logics of justice* are also at play.

Ironically, rather than the law helping to change popular perceptions of witchcraft, as numerous organizations, such as SKIR and DECFA, have attempted through *sensibilisation*, the population has come to view it as weak or irrelevant in its ability to protect them and provide justice. There is extensive popular knowledge that the state courts will not hear witchcraft accusations and that if one makes such an accusation, she could actually be prosecuted in the courts. In other words, people view the legal system as protecting the individual witch, not broader society. The state's logic of justice fails to provide justice to people who understand themselves to be victimized or under threat.

As I have begun to illustrate, people believe that punishment is at times the appropriate response to witchcraft, but the state does not deliver, creating the disconnect in *different logics of justice*. What does *emergent hybrid legality* look like in relation to these harms and the contradictory legal consciousness that surrounds them? The next section delves more deeply into the legal-justice practices that emerge, specifically techniques of mediation and popular justice.

Emergent Hybrid Legality and Popular Justice

How do people seek justice for witchcraft harms? Plenty of people choose to do nothing, or perhaps visit a *féticheur* to determine who is using witchcraft, but nothing beyond that. As noted previously, this may be a result of the impression that there is nothing that can be done. However, others try to seek justice, and the ways that witchcraft is addressed in Uvira reflect *emergent hybrid legality*. The first approach that I will address is mediation and dispute resolution. Although these are of limited use in cases of witchcraft accusations, they can and do play a role. I elaborate how mediator approaches can gain traction because they reflect popular contradictory consciousness. However, one limitation is that NGOs and other actors are focused on reconciliation when some people believe that punishment is the appropriate response to witchcraft. Thus, the second approach is popular justice, which, as discussed earlier in the chapter, is a form of vigilante justice/punishment. Liberal legal rationality, local worldviews, and restorative justice practices encounter each other and, contrary to the other examples I have provided, can produce violent justice practices.

NGOs, Elders, and Others

It is clear that the population cannot turn to the legal system in cases of witchcraft, but there is the option of trying to address the harm through other channels. Some witchcraft accusations are brought to village elders, chiefs, and other hybrid mediation mechanisms. NGOs and mediators often attempt to interpret cases strategically and with the goals of restorative justice and reconciliation. These interpretations provide a means to reduce the likelihood of violence against the accused. NGOs and other semi-formal spaces are accessible, but their outcomes are only acceptable under certain conditions, and their impact can be limited by fear on the part of mediators and lack of cooperation from the different parties to the dispute.

The logic of dispute resolution advanced by local organizations[23] was to show the parties involved that witchcraft is often linked with "psychological problems or disturbances, or that there are natural causes for an event that might appear to be the result of witchcraft. We do this because lots of things happen that people believe are the result of witchcraft, but they are actually normal." In other words, they attempt to shift disputants' perceptions of causality. This was a technique applied by various local NGOs and some other actors. For example, I was present for one *baraza* case, where a young couple believed they had been cursed so they could not conceive.

The dispute was between two couples: Jonathan and Marie—Isaac and Elizabeth. Jonathan and Marie had been unable to conceive and blamed Elizabeth for putting a curse on Marie. I was able to interview Jonathan, Marie, and Elizabeth. Over numerous *baraza* sessions, mediators heard the parties involved and then discussed what could be done to resolve the conflict. I attended some of these meetings, including the primary *baraza* gathering, where a resolution was reached, which included extensive discussion between mediators, which I observed.

Some relevant points of the case included: First, in this conflict, it was assumed by mediators and disputants that Marie was infertile, which is why she, as opposed to her husband, was perceived as the target of witchcraft. This is an important gendered component, as a woman's social and familial value largely revolves around her role as a mother; thus, infertility is a pressing concern. Multiple people I spoke with shared fears of witchcraft in cases of infertility. Women worried about being abandoned by their husbands if the couple did not conceive because of how normalized the expectation of having children is and because of the importance of having children for socioeconomic reasons.

Second, mediators cited official law and state rhetoric that witchcraft does not exist. At the same time, they did not affirm that they *agreed* with the official stance. In this case, mediators eventually established that the facts did not support the accusation of witchcraft, but they did not argue that witchcraft does not exist or that there cannot be proof . . . in other cases. Mediators raised concerns regarding a similar situation, where the accused was stoned to death after a woman with whom she had had an altercation died during childbirth, and they advised participants to respect one another and to avoid spreading rumours or gossip.

This suggests that mediators' awareness of local witchcraft practices and beliefs meant that they were acutely aware of the violence that might be perpetrated against the accused if some resolution was not established. Their analysis of witchcraft was ambiguous, reflecting popular contradictory legal consciousness by appealing to both popular beliefs and needs and the official state approach to witchcraft. It is meaningful that they did not explicitly voice agreement with the state interpretation of witchcraft, as that would have diminished their credibility in the eyes of disputants. As in many examples of mediation, they walked the line of *friction*, navigating a hybrid middle ground.

Third, mediators encouraged the couple to visit a doctor to determine whether there was a biological reason for the couple's inability to conceive. Jonathan stated that they had been to the doctor two or three times, referring to a 'traditional' doctor. They could not afford to visit a medical doctor. In this way, mediators sought to provide disputants the opportunity to make sense of the problem through one of the other lenses of causality, namely 'scientific causality' (Schatzberg, 2009). Of course, that intention encounters the realities of everyday life, where resources to pay for a visit to a medical doctor might be scarce.

In an interview with Jonathan[24], he made clear that he was content with the outcome because the conflict was over and everyone was friendly, although he still had concerns about his wife's health. Thus, although the conflict ended, Johnathan and Marie were left with no clear explanation for their inability to conceive. Marie[25] also said she was satisfied; the dispute had ended, and she accepted that witchcraft was not the cause of her presumed infertility.

Baraza helped reduce the intra-familial tensions and possibility of violence but did not have the means to provide the care from which Marie and Jonathan may have benefited. Mediators voiced disappointment at their lack of ability to provide resources, but their funding was limited.

In this case, mediators' approach reflected a version of *emergent hybrid legality*, where the law is cited, but informal mediation is advanced. They relied on getting disputants to accept, to a certain extent, the liberal legal understanding of proof while not challenging their beliefs in witchcraft, which would risk delegitimizing the whole process. Mediators made clear the official state stance on witchcraft, but they still heard the case, even though historically there has only been a select few people who would have the authority or ability to address witchcraft in any meaningful way. This case also highlights that, under the right conditions, punishment for assumed acts of witchcraft can be avoided if mediators are willing to hear cases. However, it is also worth noting that this case was an intra-familial dispute, and thus, the outcome may have been influenced by the familial relationship between the disputants, making them more willing to resolve the issue peacefully. In other words, those who were involved were less focused on punishment and more interested in being able to move forward.

Mediators and NGOs are not the only ones who can help diffuse a situation that involves witchcraft. When one is open to considering that they may not have been the target of witchcraft, other actors can help diffuse the situation as well. This is exemplified in part of my interview with Aline:

Holly:	. . . when your in-laws started to say that you were unable to conceive, what did you think?
Aline:	I thought a dark hand was present, or I had inadvertently left out my underwear and someone used it to make sure I could not give birth[26].
Holly:	Did other family members think the same thing?
Aline:	It was mostly his aunt and *maman*.
Holly:	They thought it was witchcraft, too?
Aline:	No. They said that I might be sterile because that exists with women.

Due to the emphasis placed on women's role as mothers in society, being unable to conceive may lead to social stigma and abandonment. This is true even if there is no evidence that it is the woman who is infertile. Aline[27] eventually sought mediation from a local NGO to help her and her husband accept the situation. The NGO mediators encouraged them to take a little more time and pray for a pregnancy; 'religious causality' (Schatzberg, 2009) frequently trumps scientific causality in situations related to health and death, where resources for healthcare are scarce. Shortly after, they conceived. Various actors, from family members to NGOs, can help diffuse the severity of witchcraft beliefs through the offering of an alternative narrative to explain the problem or source of suffering; thus, they can be helpful to people struggling to make sense of their life circumstances. At the same time, determining that one instance was not witchcraft does not reshape broader worldviews. It can, however, shape legal consciousness, normalizing positive judgements of mediation as a way to address witchcraft.

While NGOs have been successful in resolving witchcraft disputes some of the time, there are two main problems. First, people may not turn to them, possibly because they know there is no possibility of punishment. Others[28] do not believe that any sort of reconciliation is possible. Second, mediators might be afraid to hear and address cases of witchcraft. Mediators, *chefs*, elders, and others can be fearful of mystical or violent repercussions of these cases. For example, when I asked Anna if there was anyone in the community who helps with witchcraft disputes, she said, "Yes, but the parties have to agree to it. People do not want to get too involved in this problem." When I asked an organization[29] if they intervene in witchcraft cases, they said, "NGOs can be scared. Magical power is difficult to prove; it's mostly only known by its effects. Even police can know it is witchcraft but cannot accept this because there is no proof." Again, witchcraft is deeply ingrained in the popular belief system, and mediators, police, lawyers, and others are not immune to its influence.

It appears that good will on all sides of the dispute is helpful in resolving witchcraft cases, as are mediators who are willing to take some risks to see a peaceful outcome. Unfortunately, when this does not happen, people may live in fear or turn to popular justice to protect themselves and their families, or to seek revenge. At times, mediation may be viewed as an insufficient, ineffective, or inappropriate way to deal with the wrongs that were understood to have been committed. Popular justice is thus the ultimate form of punishment that people may choose to engage in.

Popular Justice

This chapter elucidates the *disconnect in harm naming* around witchcraft, which also corresponds to the *different logics of justice*. The particular combinations of these themes of contradictory consciousness create unique situations for legal-justice, including mediation. Yet, some people adhere to the idea that they need to find a way to execute punishment, which is not meted out through mediation or through the state legal system. They may turn to popular justice. Popular justice "evokes images of lawlessness and, especially when occurring in an African context, of barbarism and 'irrationality'" (Verweijen, 2015, p. 1). However, I propose that in the case of witchcraft accusations, popular justice can be understood within the parameters of *emergent hybrid legality*. I argue that popular justice is not a form of lawlessness[30]. The turn to popular justice is both a way of "coping with uncertainties" and "articulating a moral community" (Buur, 2008, p. 578). In Uvira, it emerges out of tensions between the state law and popular beliefs and falls within the realm of legality in the way that I conceptualize it throughout this book as "the meanings, sources of authority, and cultural practices that are commonly recognized as legal, *regardless of who employs them or for what ends*" (Ewick & Silbey, 1998, p. 22, *emphasis added*). Popular justice is a means for people to directly address the harm of witchcraft using violence.

Although popular justice is by no means a daily occurrence in Uvira, I was informed of several cases against witches during my fieldwork in 2011, 2015, and 2017. In one interview with a group of NGOs[31], they informed me that, "Witchcraft is a very repetitive problem. Three [presumed witches] were killed this month already, and there were two other cases of popular justice against witches where they failed to kill them." Research also suggests that cases in

Uvira may be on the rise (Verweijen, 2015). In one group interview[32], people provided a summary of how a witchcraft accusation develops into a situation of popular justice. They said, "[To identify a witch], first, someone accuses another. Then, they use special means to know if they are the one who hurt the other person. Next, people organize so that no one knows precisely who killed the witch." The examples that I discuss here explore this phenomenon while contextualizing and contributing empirical realities to the discussion of popular justice as a form of *emergent hybrid legality*.

While typical acts of popular justice might include burning or stoning the presumed witch, there have also been some shifts in technique. For example, Jerome[33] explained, "sometimes people find a criminal with [access to] arms to kill the person, instead of a big group doing it." One local organization that works specifically on issues of witchcraft also highlighted the shift in method. The director explained,

> In the neighbourhood of Kalungu, there was a case where they killed a woman who was presumed to be a witch. They had already killed her husband, who they also thought was a witch, two months earlier. He went to work around 19h, and he was shot. All the neighbours were disturbed by his activities in the community as a witch. When they killed his wife two months later, they said that the two had been working together as witches. She was also shot because now access to arms is easy, so hiring someone to shoot becomes the easiest way of doing popular justice. The service [police] arrived too late. There is no recognition of witchcraft at *la justice, that is why people do popular justice.*

This quote from the director points to several different issues. First, the circulation and accessibility of small arms in eastern DRC are not surprising and have been recognized[34]. This context has been shaped by years of violent conflict in combination with the limitations of demobilization, disarmament, and reintegration programming (eg. Richards, 2016). Second, the couple were seen as creating problems in the community due to their engagement with witchcraft. In the interview, it was ambiguous what exactly they were doing, but the notable point is that community members believed that they were causing trouble and were a threat to the community. Third, it was not necessarily clear why hiring someone to kill these individuals should be considered an act of popular justice. How can one conceptualize an individual's action with the '*popular*' aspect of popular justice? I would argue that this still counts as popular justice because it is locally conceptualized as such. However, these killings also rely on an understanding of threat to the *community*, as well as receiving some community support to legitimize the action. In these ways, individual perpetrators, rather than a group or mob, can still perform acts of popular justice. Finally, the director cites the lack of recognition of witchcraft by the state as the cause of popular justice.

Notably, the director I cited earlier, and others, make sense of popular justice in relation to the limitations of the state legal system. Linking popular justice to failures of the legal system finds support with some of the local organizations. For example, I asked the director of SKIR, a local organization that has done extensive research and *sensibilisation* to prevent popular justice, "Why do people turn to popular justice?" He said,

> There are three reasons. First, ignorance of the law. Second, the dysfunctional legal system. Congo does not convict of witchcraft, but everyone believes in it. But, because *la justice* does not take care of it, people go to the *féticheur*[35] and have the person beaten. Third, the proliferation of arms. There are fewer lynchings and burnings; now they pay someone to do the killing with guns[36]. Some are very happy about this. The perpetrator is unknown, and so there is no investigation.

Ignorance of the law is an interesting argument[37]; maybe people are unaware of the status of popular justice in the law, but my research suggests that people are quite aware that witchcraft is not prosecutable. I would argue, by contrast, that the turn to popular justice may actually be shaped by *knowledge* of the law. The general population seems to be acutely aware that the law and legal system do not work to protect people from witchcraft. His first point is even in tension with the second, where he does recognize that the population, whether they know the law or not, understands that the law does not punish acts of witchcraft. When he refers to the dysfunctional legal system, he does not follow up with comments about corruption; he follows up with the point about the *disconnect in harm naming* of witchcraft. That is the dysfunctional part; the state does not address a harm that the population experiences.

To illustrate the tension that I note in the director's comments, I return to some of my other interviews. For example, taken from a group interview with local women[38], they said, "The state doesn't recognize witchcraft. If a witch kills the child of another person, then they kill her child, then they will both stop because they will lose out in the end." An interlocutor[39] explained,

> A *maman* may do acts of witchcraft to kill a child. The witch doctor will be able to determine who did it. Then they will find a way to burn or stone the witch. Then they will continue in conflict. If you kill someone then you are brought to the state, but the state does not recognize witchcraft.

Mia said, "The *balala rondo* catch the witches and then release them because *la justice* in Congo does not recognize witchcraft." These are just a few examples that elucidate that people do indeed recognize this aspect of the law, reflecting the director of SKIR's second point that it is a failure of the legal system to do anything that leads some to popular justice. I would argue that the limitations of the formal system are interpreted and experienced in combination with the limitations of the other justice systems and practices.

The state's stance on witchcraft is certainly important in shaping the practice of popular justice, but as this chapter has illustrated, it is not the only element of significance. The combination of fear and desire for punishment rooted in worldviews and part of popular consciousness is disconnected from what the state has to offer in these cases, and people are very aware of that. This *friction* manifests in contradictory legal consciousness—*disconnect in harm naming* and *different logics of justice*—producing *emergent hybrid legality*, in the form of popular justice.

As I noted earlier in the chapter, the limit of state involvement in witchcraft accusations does not suggest that the state is failing in terms of justice provision according to its own logic, but that the *disconnect in harm naming* combined with *different logics of justice* creates a justice void that the members of the population fill in ways stemming from contradictory legal consciousness. Popular justice is rarely a relic of a distant and brutal past but a product of violent conflict and legal modernization. At its foundation, popular justice is—much like vigilantism—not rooted in anarchy but in injustice (Kucera & Mares, 2015, p. 171). Part of this problem was recognized by a group of *chefs*[40]. They explained some of the difficulties surrounding witchcraft when I asked about local disputes:

> Witchcraft . . . that is the important one! Just the day before yesterday, they [community members] came to the *chef* at 11pm because the house of a witch had been burnt and he [the witch] disappeared.
>
> "Why was he suspected?" I asked.
>
> So many people around him died and the same had happened in Sange. He was chased away from there for that reason. But, this problem cannot be resolved by *la justice* because *there is never any proof.* There is just one customary place you can go around Burambi to find out if someone is really a witch. When people commit witchcraft, they have to leave and cannot return to the same place. There needs to be *sensibilisation* to get people to abandon witchcraft.

The formal legal system functions according to a type of juridico-scientific rationality, for which proof that adheres to that evidentiary logic is paramount. By contrast, witchcraft functions according to rationality tied to mystical powers and beliefs. As the *chefs* pointed out, proof according to legal rationality cannot be met using mystical evidence. While there are traditional means of determining witchcraft, such as using a *grigri*, these do not hold up in a court of law because they do not constitute sufficient proof or hard evidence. Thus, the liberal legal ideology and local worldviews are in tension, and yet both are incorporated into legal consciousness, as the population has knowledge of the laws and the legal system's approach to witchcraft accusations. The turn to popular justice is the practice that stems from this contradictory consciousness.

The statements of the *chefs* point to another important idea. They argue that *sensibilisation* needs to be done to encourage people to abandon witchcraft. First, this is a reminder of how prevalent *sensibilisation* campaigns are in the post-conflict, legal reform context of Uvira. The other notable aspect of their reference to *sensibilisation* is that it should be done to encourage people to abandon witchcraft, not to change popular beliefs that witchcraft exists. This taps into how witchcraft is so profoundly situated in local worldviews, which, in turn, shape how it's addressed.

It may seem contentious to think about popular justice as a form of legality, or legal-justice, but punishment that includes physical violence or death is certainly not unheard of within the realm of legality. Indeed, some countries around the world maintain the death penalty as a form of official punishment. And, although some may view these regimes as illegitimate as a result, many do not. So, if killing in and of itself does not exclude an act from the realm of legality, why not think of popular justice in this way?

One response may be that popular justice is not officially state sanctioned, in contrast to the death penalty. However, as I argue throughout this book, the terrain of legality is not solely the purview of the state. This is especially evident in situations of legal pluralism, where the population and even official bodies recognize the work of those functioning outside the state legal system to address harms and deliver justice. So, although contentious, I argue that popular justice, in its current manifestation, arises out of the *frictions* associated with legal encounters, notably the two themes of contradictory consciousness, and thus can be understood as an area of *emergent hybrid legality*. This point also serves as a reminder that hybridity is not something to be romanticized; it is rather a reflection of the emergent, on-the-ground developments that result from shifts in legal consciousness and practical realities.

Manipulating Witchcraft Accusations

Although beliefs in witchcraft are undoubtably ingrained in popular worldviews and shape how people understand the world around them, including harms and justice, this by no means makes the subject immune to political manipulation. In fact, accusing someone of witchcraft can be quite expedient in power struggles because it plays on common fears.

During my research, I had the opportunity to talk with the family of one person who had been the target of popular justice. Her attack occurred about four months prior to my learning about the case in February 2017 and was still the topic of gossip around town; I had heard about it from a few different sources. Natalie[41], a woman who worked with SKIR so she was engaged in local cases of popular justice and witchcraft, was the first to provide me with information about the case. In the following, I paraphrase her narrative of the situation:

There was a case that occurred in Kabindula in October 2016, but she survived the attempts of popular justice and was able to flee town. Lucie was a girl who died, and people in the community said it was Martine, who was a witch, had caused her death. A group of youths took Martine and told her that she now had to resuscitate the girl. And it was when they were *en route* to Lucie, who was already deceased, that they poured litres of gasoline on her. They only had three matches, but when they tried to light them none of them worked. This reinforced the idea that she was a witch. Martine said the girl was dead, and there was nothing that she could do. Then, they all began throwing rocks at her, and it was a real miracle because none hit her. This also enhanced suspicions that the woman was a witch.

The *balala rondo*[42] tried to protect her until the police or soldiers arrived. The FARDC arrived and fired into the air. They finally got to her and then brought her to the *mwami*. The youths went to her house and pillaged it and destroyed everything; you could not even find a brick remaining. "I feel so bad; the son even lost all his documents and diploma." They even took the door and ceiling. It was actually three houses they raided because there were family members in the other two neighbouring houses.

The accused lived with three young girls, the daughters of her deceased daughter. She stayed for a while with her son in Nyamianda, but he was threatened. People told him that if his mother did not leave, they would destroy his property and home, and they would hire someone to kill Martine. It also had a negative impact on the three girls—they were discriminated against and left with nothing—no uniforms or notebooks for school; the other kids would run behind them yelling, "Witch!" The girls eventually had to leave too. Also, Martine was staying with the police for safety, but as the police also believe in witchcraft, they didn't want her to stay with them for long. MONUSCO eventually took her to Bukavu and then to Goma where she is hidden, and the kids are hidden in Bukavu.

As we spoke further, I learned some of the backstory to the case.

Martine was a leader at the Kimbanguist[43] church, which was the same church as Lucie. She was not a witch; the problem was that Lucie died because of a clandestine abortion. She had gone to [Dr.] Mukegwe, but it appears that something went wrong there, and when she returned she died. This is really a conflict within the church. Lucie's father is Bavira (natives of Uvira), and the Martine is Barega (group from around Bukavu and further north), and there was a conflict of leadership in the church.

So, when things like that happen, we do field visits and talk to all those involved. The Bavira from the church said that she is a witch to isolate her. At the same time, the family of the girl had gone to the *féticheur* and he had said that Martine was a witch and had killed the girl. Popular justice is often used against women, who are presumed to be witches. They are vulnerable to this accusation when they are old and have wrinkles on their face.

> Jeanette and I met with the son[44] of the accused witch to develop a more complete picture of the events. In summary (and paraphrasing), he explained that his mother was accused of witchcraft because there were some pastors who were against her, and they sought to get rid of her. They are a church that does not actually respect the norms of the Kimbanguist church. They make witchcraft accusations without even doing an investigation. Certain pastors were having clandestine meetings with neighbourhood youths against his *maman*[45]. Now, one day, a girl who lives in the parcel of the church dies. The pastor took advantage of this to tell the youths that it was his *maman*. The youths came and took her in the morning when he was not home. They went and got gas and said, "Today, we will burn you because it was you who killed the girl!" When they tried to burn her, it did not work, so they took her to the girl to try to bring her back to life. He received a phone call telling him what happened, so he went home right away. He found that they were burning his house, his mom's house, and his younger brother's house. (They were all on the same plot of land.) He called the police, and they divided between the houses and the church. The police took his *maman* and brought her to their office, where she stayed for a week before moving to Bukavu.
>
> The police did some investigations, but they did not arrest anyone. Even though they saw the people who were there, both at the church and the houses. During their investigations, they did however find that there was a document circulating in the church saying that the *maman* caused the girl's death.
>
> There is a file open with the Tribunal de Grande Instance, but he did not have the means to support the follow-up proceedings. I asked if there was anywhere else they could turn to. He said there are lots of NGOs that say they provide humanitarian aid, but they are just there to appease people. One organization did say they would pay for a lawyer, but he is still waiting for this to happen. He continues to receive threats, and all the police say is that they should get weapons to defend themselves.

Finally, I asked him if he believes in witchcraft. He replied, "No, because I cannot confirm it. There are no tests. All I can confirm is for *maman*." This answer is a little ambiguous. The argument that he does not believe in witchcraft because there are no tests seemed a little disingenuous, or that it may have been said for my benefit. It also came across as a way of affirming his mother's innocence. The idea that this is all he can confirm also leaves the space open for belief in the possibility of witchcraft. My scepticism comes from knowledge of how widespread beliefs in witchcraft are, as well as my feeling from the interview. However, it could also be that his mother's experience was a sort of wake-up call to question these beliefs.

Regardless of his personal beliefs, this case complicates the discussion of witchcraft and popular justice as it highlights how these accusations are bound up, not just in everyday understandings of causation but in localized power struggles. This case also signifies the point that popular belief in witchcraft is real, and this can have dire consequences when certain actors mobilize people based on those beliefs. Given that there are few other outlets for that fear, action in the form of popular justice is understood as a viable option. Thus, even when motivated by power struggles, popular justice emerges as an option because of tensions between popular worldviews and knowledge of the legal-justice options and the liberal legal ideology that undergirds the state legal system. If witchcraft were a part of the legal system, this could open space for investigations in cases of power struggles, such as this one.

Conclusion

Witchcraft is a common-sense explanation for phenomena from fishing success to infertility to death; yet, the state has ignored the plight of self-identified victims; sometimes, the laws even work against them. Verweijen (2015) argues that popular justice is rooted in the disruption of customary authority combined with dysfunctional formal justice. Yet, as this chapter has shown, sometimes it is the functioning of the legal system according to its own standards and logics that pushes people to seek justice through other means, which is also a type of dysfunction, although not the type Verweijen references. "As E.P. Thompson (1971) has elegantly illustrated, the customs, rules and moral codes people use to legitimize and/or ground their actions are more often than not at odds with the rules and laws promulgated by their rulers" (cited in Buur, 2008, p. 582). In practice, the legal system fails to provide justice for the population while being aligned with international ROL standards. This point of *friction* has produced two ways of addressing these harms and disputes. The first is the turn to informal and semi-formal systems and practices, essentially, mediation. This is generally more likely to be chosen and to work when dealing with family members or close neighbours where there is a strong desire on both sides to reconcile and maintain a relationship. However, sometimes, mediators avoid these cases due to the potential risks associated with getting involved in witchcraft cases. The second approach is popular justice.

Rather than affecting people's legal consciousness by validating the need to report those who make witchcraft *accusations*, the state's stance has validated popular violence in response to *acts* of witchcraft, shaping legal consciousness in an alternative direction. NGOs working on popular justice understand it to develop as a result of the insufficiencies of the legal system. Notably, the state and legal system are acting in accordance with international norms and expectations by attempting to protect the human rights of people, accused witches, from acts of popular justice. This very much puts the legal system at odds with popular beliefs, of which witchcraft is paramount, making the integration of liberal legal norms into popular consciousness more directly resisted. At the same time, few people stated that this reduced their trust in the state or the legal system; it rather made them seem less relevant.

The trend, in contexts that experience both witchcraft and international intervention in some form, is for international actors to interpret the violent treatment of witches as a human rights violation; there is an array of international organizations working to end violence against witches (Ashforth, 2015). However, little has been done on the part of international actors to develop a culturally sensitive understanding of the phenomenon of witchcraft that integrates social anxieties into their response. Instead, international organizations, strongly influenced by Western belief systems, have advanced scientific rationality and reason through a human rights approach (Ashforth, 2015). This has been accompanied by liberal legal interpretations of witchcraft and witchcraft accusations, which do not fit with local worldviews. This chapter thus explored how the phenomenon of witchcraft shapes both the *disconnect between harm naming* and the *different logics of justice* that produce *emergent hybrid legality*. Popular justice fits oddly with the other practices in the terrain of legality but is based in the same frictions of encounter that shape legal consciousness and *emergent hybrid legality*.

Notes

1 King or kin-based authority/leader.
2 Make myself disinterested in.
3 Witchcraft and poisoning are often discussed together. The one need not imply the other, but they are frequently discussed together or as component parts to a harmful act.
4 Group interview, Makobola, 15 April 2015.
5 Interview, 12 April 2017.
6 17 April 2015.
7 Interview, 7 March 2017.
8 From fieldnotes and interview, 7 March 2017.
9 "Quiconque abusant des croyances superstitieuses de la population, aura, sans fondement réel, imputé à une personne un acte ou un événement vrai ou imaginaire, sachant que cette imputation inciterait autrui à commettre une infraction, sera considéré comme complice de l'infraction ainsi provoquée." Anyone who abuses the superstitious beliefs of the population will have, without any real basis, imputed to a person a real or imaginary act or event, knowing that this imputation would incite others to commit an offense, will be considered as an accomplice of the offense thus caused (author's translation).
10 Confirmed in an interview with procureur at the Tripaix, Uvira, 11 February 2017.
11 Interview, 16 April 2015.
12 Interview, 30 January 2017.
13 Group interview, 23 April 2015.
14 Interview, 11 February 2017.
15 Yet, this is frequently the same issue in rape cases across the globe; they lack the kind of proof required by the legal system. Thank you to Dr. Monica Williams for pointing this out. The difference in witchcraft cases, I would argue, is that there is not even the *possibility* of legal proof that would meet the criteria of the legal system.
16 Interview, 11 February 2017.
17 The limited documentation I can find of the case provides somewhat different details but a similar analysis. The case was a missed opportunity for the Supreme Court to recognize the harm of witchcraft and integrate it into the law (eg. Kabesa, 2011).
18 Other documentation states that he was a judge in the case.

19 In contrast to family law, which is more mixed.
20 Interview, 20 February 2017.
21 Could be translated as remote, behind, or backward.
22 Interview, 24 March 2017.
23 Group interview with AA, Uvira, 16 April 2015.
24 Interview, 16 October 2011. The couple refused to be interviewed separately, so I interviewed them together and refer to the separate statements they made during the interview.
25 Interview, 16 October 2011.
26 I understood this to mean that she feared a curse had been done on them.
27 Both cases are about accepting that witchcraft was not the root cause of infertility. Although I do not provide a thorough examination of the gendered dimensions of witchcraft accusations—there is conflicting evidence about whether women are predominantly targeted as witches and why—it is notable that in both cases women were perceived as being infertile. This is because of the social importance tied to the family and thus the ability to have children. Indeed, women's power in the home and community is to a certain extent derived from their role as mothers. Aline feared that her husband would take another wife if she could not conceive, and that would likely have happened. Further, one key interlocutor argued that popular justice is often directed at women because they are seen as most likely to be witches (6 February 2017).
28 When I asked a group of NGOs if there were any conflicts that cannot be reconciled, some said witchcraft, elaborating that "you cannot even bring people together [in those cases]" (24 April 2015).
29 Group interview, 20 April 2015.
30 Although it may appear that popular justice *emerges* out of a lack of law (regulating witchcraft), as I have already outlined, there are a variety of ways in which witchcraft and the law intersect, especially around legal repercussions for making accusations. Therefore, I argue that popular justice neither emerges out of lawlessness nor reflects lawlessness.
31 Group interview, 24 April 2015.
32 Group interview, 15 April 2015.
33 Interview, 30 January 2017.
34 For example, one report found extensive small arms and light weapons trafficking along Lake Tanganyika and the Ruzizi River (Alusala, 2015), which are central to Uvira territory, and Uvira City sits directly on Lake Tanganyika.
35 Some people have said the féticheur can determine who cursed you [who the witch is].
36 Although the proliferation of small arms is not something I address in detail here, it is certainly linked with a sense of increased insecurity amongst the population, as well as the shifting nature of popular justice.
37 It reaffirms the common understanding by members of the legal complex that the population does not know or understand the law.
38 17 April 2015.
39 15 April 2015.
40 Group interview, 24 April 2015.
41 Fieldnotes, 6 February 2017.
42 Community-organized patrol.
43 Kimbanguism is a long-standing African church that was founded in Congo in the 1920s by Simon Kimbangu, who was arrested and imprisoned for life by Belgian authorities for insurrection (www.britannica.com/topic/Kimbanguist-Church).
44 Interview, 11 March 2017.
45 He received this information via an anonymous phone call and was told that he should move. He met with his family to discuss what to do, but no one wanted to. They stood by their innocence.

Bibliography

Adinkrah, M. (2004). Witchcraft accusations and female homicide victimization in contemporary Ghana. *Violence against Women, 10*(4), 325–356.

Alusala, N. (2015). *Assessment report on cross-border small arms and light weapons trafficking between the Democratic Republic of the Congo and the Republic of Burundi.* Action on Armed Violence. https://aoav.org.uk/wp-content/uploads/2016/02/AOAV-DRC-Burundi-Border-Assessment-Report-FINAL_en.pdf

Ashforth, A. (2015). Witchcraft, justice, and human rights in Africa: Cases from Malawi. *African Studies Review, 58*(1), 5–38.

Buur, L. (2008). Democracy & its discontents: Vigilantism, sovereignty & human rights in South Africa. *Review of African Political Economy, 35*(118), 571–584.

Carr, J. (2016). The lawlessness of law: Lynching and anti-lynching in the contemporary USA. *Settler Colonial Studies, 6*(2), 153–163.

Diwan, M. A. (2004). Conflict between state legal norms and norms underlying popular beliefs: Witchcraft in Africa as a case study. *Duke Journal of Comparative & International Law, 14*, 351.

Kabesa, J. (2011). Handling guilt under customary law-concept and basis. In H. Hamann, K. Ilunga-Matthiesen, & A. Mukalay (Eds.), *African law study library with specific emphasis on Democratic Republic of Congo* (pp. 113–144). Konad Adenauer-Stifttung.

Kucera, M., & Mares, M. (2015). Vigilantism during democratic transition. *Policing and Society, 25*(2), 170–187.

Lombard, L., & Batianga-Kinzi, S. (2015). Violence, popular punishment, and war in the Central African Republic. *African Affairs, 114*(454), 52–71.

Mambou Pembellot, A. F. (1985). La preuve des crimes de sorcellerie devant le juge penal congolais. *Revue juridique et politique: indépendance et coopération, 39*(1–2), 124–128.

Richards, J. (2016). Implementing DDR in settings of ongoing conflict: The organization and fragmentation of armed groups in the Democratic Republic of Congo (DRC). *Stability: International Journal of Security and Development, 5*(1).

Rush Smith, N. (2015). Rejecting rights: Vigilantism and violence in post-apartheid South Africa. *African Affairs, 114*(456), 341–360.

Schatzberg, M. G. (2009). Ethnography and causality: Sorcery and popular culture in the Congo. *Political Ethnography: What Immersion Contributes to the Study of Power*, 198–200.

Verweijen, J. (2015). The disconcerting popularity of popular in/justice in the Fizi/Uvira region, eastern Democratic Republic of the Congo. *International Journal on Minority and Group Rights, 22*(3), 335–359.

Chapter 7

The Rule of Law Revisited

Lessons from *Emergent Hybrid Legality* in the DRC

My final trip to Congo was in 2019; I organized a workshop to share my research findings and open them up to critique and discussion. The workshop participants had to be carefully curated to avoid having the event officially shut down, risking anyone's safety, making anyone a target, or creating a space of silence where no one felt free to talk. As such, we—myself and the organization I had partnered with throughout my research—focused on state officials and local organizations[1]. Given that these were the entities working on more formalized legal-justice, it was a good fit, even if it meant that many who had participated in interviews would not see how their participation contributed to my analysis. We had about 30 participants in the workshop, and they included most of the NGOs I had interviewed in 2017, local lawyers I had worked with, judges from the Tripaix, the *mwami's* assistant/advisor, and a visit from the *chef de cité*. In other words, there were still a variety of voices present to discuss the key themes I brought to the table: Legal pluralism, gender justice and women's rights, and witchcraft and popular justice. The dynamics of these various voices together in one room symbolized nuances of *emergent hybrid legality*—the overlap, tensions, and complements of different ways of thinking about harms and justice.

Of course, like with *emergent hybrid legality* and my research, the event was imbued with power dynamics, from the Western 'intervener' (me) setting the agenda to the special treatment of state actors, to the fees paid to speakers, to the present but non-professional interpretation services, to those excluded from participation. While those not in positions of power, most of the people I interviewed about their experiences of harm or dispute, were not present, they still played a role in shaping the discussion as they provided much of the information that shaped conference program. Similarly, while these same individuals do not set the agenda for legal-justice, they play an important role in shaping it through how they understand everyday harms and think about justice. At the same time, the workshop was itself a performance of legal encounters, with state and civil society actors engaging with each other, as well as traditional and local authorities.

DOI: 10.4324/9781003289715-7

As I have argued in this book, *emergent hybrid legality* is the outcome of legal encounters that occur as part of ROL building practices. Legal reforms that change domestic law and are often accompanied by *sensibilisation* activities have been important elements of ROL building and have ushered in a new wave of legal encounters that have played a crucial role in shaping popular contradictory consciousness. In Uvira, this has manifested in the two themes of contradictory legal consciousness that I outlined in the previous chapters: *Disconnect in harm naming* and *different logics of justice*. These two themes have been influential in shaping the terrain of legality—*emergent hybrid legality*. This book recognizes these dynamics by exploring legal encounters that manifest in both new laws and *sensibilisation* about the legal system and legal reforms. Thus, I make clear that international actors seeking to build the ROL have both directly and indirectly shaped the terrain of legality but not necessarily in the ways they expected.

My research disrupts the logic of the ROL cycle outlined in Chapter 1 by analysing the legal terrain through a focus on popular engagements with legal-justice. The cycle, by contrast, focuses assessments of success and failure on standardized ROL measures, such as specific indicators (Urueña, 2015). This book also moves beyond the standing critiques of ROL interventions, namely those that problematize the external imposition of a legal system, norms, and institutions that do not fit the local cultures and do not consider customary justice practices (Carothers, 2006; Channell, 2006; Grenfell, 2013; Hadfield & Weingast, 2014; Hertogh, 2016; Kleinfeld, 2006; Park, 2010; Peterson, 2010). The former has emphasized the need for continued resources, expertise, and education to ameliorate the outcomes. The latter either proposes a more serious role for customary justice and local engagement, or simply provides a critique. This book explores the emergent outcomes of legal encounters that occur as part of ROL building processes in terms of legal consciousness and legal-justice practices and institutions.

Thus, the questions I raised and sought to answer in this book are: What are the outcomes of legal encounters? What role do they play in shaping the legal terrain? How and why do they take the forms that they do? My focus on legal consciousness helps prioritize popular understandings and engagements with legality to move away from assessing legality in a top-down manner against ROL measures, which have been critiqued for their Western, liberal legal bias. I sought a better understanding of what the terrain of legality looks like, and why, rather than how, it does not measure up to interveners' standards. I also abandoned the romantic notion that traditional justice systems are inherently good or peaceful. I contextualize these systems and practices within the background of colonialism and current power dynamics.

Through my research, I find legality to be emergent and hybrid. It is not something that can be manufactured outside of the context in which it exists; thus, the results of legal encounters are to a certain extent unpredictable. Interveners and state actors cannot know in advance how globalized legal norms and practices will encounter local contexts—politics, actors, and other contingencies—or local worldviews. As I have noted, this may at times create space for violent reactions to certain harms, such as witchcraft. At the same time, legality is hybridized in ways that have not and probably cannot be engineered. The way mediators both use the law and reject the legal system is an important example. It is a means to raise popular knowledge of the laws and how the legal system works, but it also frequently plays a role in shaping perceptions and negative judgements of the legal system, often reaffirming beliefs in the benefits of restorative justice.

I do not make the argument that legal encounters are inherently bad; they are a reality across the globe, not just in transitioning contexts. They provide the opportunity to introduce new ideas or, if not necessarily new, ideas that gain traction through their international support. However, as the critics have suggested, conventional approaches to building the ROL abroad may be highly decontextualized, creating a gap between intent and outcome. My findings suggest that we need to shift how we assess and measure outcomes and, because of these assessments, rethink the way ROL building is done, from the underlying assumptions to best practices.

In Congo, for example, the surprising outcome of legal encounters, as they manifest in *emergent hybrid legality*, includes an increased awareness of the law; access to legal-justice; and constructive, although not necessarily explicit, social dialogue about what contextualized women's rights and gender justice should like. But, what are the implications of these findings for the ROL as both concept and practice? One shift that I propose is rethinking what the precepts of ROL mean in practice and how the goals of the ROL can be measured. I develop the following ideas as a way to continue to interrogate the meaning of the ROL and rethink the concept and practice for diverse settings. To do this, I first explore the ROL concept and its historical and ideological roots.

What Is the Rule of Law?

The ROL has been defined in several different ways; Kleinfeld (2006) argued that the concept manifests in academia and practice as "the proverbial blind man's elephant—a trunk to one person, a tail to another" (Kleinfeld, 2006, p. 32). Building on the important contributions of legal scholars, such as Fuller and Raz, the ROL is frequently defined by several precepts and characteristics. These can fall on a continuum from thin to thick, which parallels a range from procedural to substantive definitions (Tamanaha, 2004). In the more practical ROL industry and some scholarship, these continuums have amounted to a checklist of characteristics adding up to the ROL (Qerimi, 2020). At the same time, conceptually, there are a few main ideas undergirding the ROL. They include limiting government abuses of power, organizing everyday life, and justice provision. I elaborate on both the ROL characteristics and goals to illustrate the possibilities associated with *emergent hybrid legality*.

ROL Characteristics

The ROL is often presented on a continuum from thin to thick, meaning less to more requirements, or divided between formal and substantive variants (Tamanaha, 2004). The formal version includes ideas, such as laws that are prospective, public, clear in meaning, equally applicable to all, and created through the proper authorities, but the content of the laws is not considered (Tamanaha, 2004). This can also reflect procedural conceptualizations that refer to a form of rule-based governance structured by formally institutionalized rules (Narduli et al., 2013; see also Tamanaha, 2004) and focuses on the procedural aspects of justice (Stromseth et al., 2006). By contrast, thick/substantive ROL refers to the design and type of laws embedded in the legal order; it is concerned with notions of rights and justice[2] (Tamanaha, 2004; see also Carothers, 2006; Massoud, 2013; Stromseth et al., 2006), and sometimes advancing women's rights (see Lincoln, 2011). Amongst ROL scholars, there is more disagreement around the substantive definition, whereas the formal aspects are taken as widely accepted (Versteeg & Ginsburg, 2017) and universal. However, formal/procedural ROL still carries with it a particular standard of justice—procedural justice, defined by *a particular* process rather than content. In other words, the process is the content of justice, but processes need not be universal; a fair process may look different in different contexts.

The thin or formal understandings of the ROL, although seemingly more neutral and universal, actually encounter some of the same broad problems noted in critiques of the ROL building practice. Namely, they still tend to ignore local culture and beliefs. In other words, adhering to procedural aspects of justice can still be a problematic way to attempt to universalize the ROL because different populations may have different understandings of that define a fair process. For example, as noted in Chapters 4 and 5, many people do not view the adversarial approach to legal-justice as a 'good' or 'right' procedure. Through awareness-raising activities, knowledge about how the formal legal system works has become a part of popular legal consciousness, but this is in tension with the popular prioritization of 'bringing people together' to resolve disputes and address harms. Does the power of the ROL still hold when it is abstracted from people's understanding of a good/fair process? This is not to say that having a process and adhering to it is not important, yet, in ROL building, the nature of that process has largely been assumed.

At the same time, ROL building interventions done in conflict-affected/transitioning contexts often reflect more *substantive* versions of the ROL; this is likely because of the internationally recognized norms and institutions associated with creating a stable and peaceful society[3]. These interventions may, for example, have some substantive link with human rights or at least civil and political liberties (Carothers, 2006; Massoud, 2013). Other commonly referenced characteristics combine economic and political science understandings, including "effective security of the person, property, and contracting rights and arguably extends to basic civil and political liberties that guarantee the autonomy and freedom of the individual" (Haggard & Tiede, 2014, p. 406). This definition clearly speaks to the ROL's unabashedly liberal character, especially when combined with the goals of establishing order, justice, and peaceful liberal societies (Peterson, 2010); the ROL is at the core of the liberal state (Tamanaha, 2004).

It is not contentious to argue that substantive ROL overlaps with or takes the form of liberal legalism. "Liberal legalism . . . includes some commitment to rule of law practices and institutions, individual rights, free markets, and democratic government. . . . Liberal legal regimes provide a universal discourse that defines obligations, relationships and actors" (Engel & Engel, 2010, p. 3). Through attempts to modify local values and norms, substantive ROL interventions correspondingly aim at constructing liberal legal subjects. This is how legal reforms that bring state law in line with international human rights standards are then brought to the public. The production of liberal legal subjects is often an undertaking of transnational activists and human rights organizations and experts building the ROL domestically (eg. Grenfell, 2013; Massoud, 2013). The law transforms the political subjectivities of those who use it (Eckert et al., 2012), and interveners aspire to produce liberal legal subjectivities through building a ROL culture. One's legal subjectivity can be understood by how they interpret events, their actions, and the actions of others, and how they understand themselves in relation to the world around them, including the law, legal norms, and legal institutions (Engel & Engel, 2010). Basically, I understand liberal legal subjects to view themselves as rights holders and to view the legal system as the right and fair place to resolve disputes and seek justice. Notably, people have multiple and shifting subjectivities (Merry, 2009), so this would be only one constitutive part of a more complex whole.

Part of the ROL building project is to encourage people to engage with the law, to mobilize the law, in the hopes that this will promote the development of a particular type of legal consciousness. Throughout this book, I have made clear that in the Congo, this has been done through *sensibilisation* by local organizations, often partnered with international organizations and funders. Why is liberal legalism and the production of liberal legal subjects through ROL building important to my analysis of legal encounters? There are three main elements to consider as areas of tension: The individual as the basic unit of society, assumptions about the nature of law, and historical and spatial developments of liberal legalism.

First, liberal legalism includes liberal assumptions about the individual as the fundamental unit of society, existing prior to social organization, and the individual as rational[4] and self-interested (Scales, 2006). As a result, the law tends to focus on the individual—in terms of guilt or innocence, as well as victimhood—rather than social context or relations. The liberal legal subject is essentially stripped of all differentiated and embodied characteristics and exists simply as a decontextualized, rational, autonomous entity (Grear, 2011). Thus, formal equality—equality before the law—is often viewed as promoting substantive equality.

If we take the context of Uvira, we can observe why this may cause tensions in popular consciousness. The examples provided in both Chapters 5 and 6 highlight that the important harms and disputes surrounding adolescent sex and marriage, as well as witchcraft, are often not understood solely as individual problems. Adolescent sex and marriage are frequently understood within the family, and it is the family that is involved in determining the appropriate course of action, whether the payment of the dowry, school fees, or something else. The problem of witchcraft also reflects a similar tension. While an act may be perpetrated against a child, for example, the parents and whole family experience the harm as well and must determine what steps to take. Beyond that, acts of popular justice are at times taken for the stated reason of protecting the community. While individuals do matter as such, their experiences are entangled in their familial and community situations; harms and disputes are also seen through this broader lens, which is clearly in tension with the liberal focus on the individual. We need only look at the cases of witchcraft to understand that local rationality, one that accepts witchcraft causation, does not map onto the liberal rationality. Indeed, my analysis of why witchcraft cases are not heard in state courts buttresses this point.

Second, liberal legalism includes certain assumptions about the law. Hunt (1986) summarizes the features of liberal legalism as: 1) The separation of law from other forms of social control; 2) law as rules that define the correct sphere of their own application; 3) laws are portrayed as objective and legitimate, while other normative orders are seen as partial and subjective; and 4) laws produce predictable results through judicial processes. Hunter (2016) writes, "Liberal legalism posits law as an essentially benign, neutral and autonomous institution" (p. 19; see also Dossa, 1999). These ideas are crucial to understanding why particular forms of law, those that reflect the legal systems of liberal polities, are advanced in transitioning contexts. The (state) legal system is seen to exist and coordinate activities and resolve disputes according to shared values, universal principles, reason, and logic (Hunter, 2016). It is seen to exist outside of social influence while at the same time reflecting society and producing predictable outcomes even as they represent other forms of social control and normative orders.

However, one of the themes throughout this book is that legality is not separate from other forms of social control. Indeed, this is a point raised by scholars of legal pluralism since at least Falk Moore's (1972) work on semi-autonomous social fields. Thus, the separation of law from other forms of social control has limited applicability or relevance. Indeed, the concept of *emergent hybrid legality* recognizes the ongoing interactions between different realms of legal-justice, which is necessarily unpredictable as it emerges through legal encounters. Further, my analysis of legal encounters makes very clear that state law, although increasingly reflecting globalized liberal values, is not 'benign, neutral, and autonomous' or 'objective and legitimate'. Rather, it is very clearly embedded in international power dynamics. Thus, in practice, liberal legalism's assumptions about the law do not hold in spaces where it is advanced through ROL building that is largely shaped by external actors and factors. Finally, if we think about predictable results, state laws are not the only ones that can provide for such. Mediation through *chefs* and NGOs has also been accepted as relatively reliable and predictable.

Third, liberal legalism is a historical development that reflects how predominantly liberal states have created legal systems based on similar logics. In other words, not every component of a state's laws or legal system will reflect one version of liberal values, but there are strong similarities in many Western legal systems that developed alongside the liberal state. In recent decades, international and domestic actors have sought to transplant and adopt these legal systems that have come to be associated with the democracy and development.

As the critics of the ROL building enterprise have noted, these historical developments of liberal legalism alongside the development of Western capitalist, liberal democracies, reflect that liberal legalism is entwined with a particular culture and history. In other words, it is inherently particularistic and not universal. At the same time, we know that these developments have not happened in isolation from other countries that scholars do not consider part of 'the West'. In Congo, like many other countries, colonialism is a crucial period for thinking about the history of legal encounters. Belgian colonizers often engaged with and modified the role of local legal structures and authorities to align with the colonial mission (Dembour, 2000; Prinsloo, 1993). Further, the Cold War era saw the Western actors further shape the state structure and institutions by supporting the forceful removal of Lumumba and the installation of Mobutu's as leader. Finally, the transitional era after the Congo wars is largely defined by peacebuilding and ROL building interventions. Thus, liberal legalism as a historical development looks quite different in this context and is grounded in international power dynamics, rather than domestic developments.

As this section makes clear, the ROL, insofar as it reflects liberal legalism, is by no means a universal good. It is profoundly rooted in Western history, belief systems, and values. The three points outlined here—liberal legalism's focus on the individual, assumptions about the law, and Western historical roots—support this argument. My research suggests that instead of assuming that liberal legalism is a 'good' to be created through ROL interventions, we need to be more transparent about the tensions between liberal legalism and different social contexts. These tensions are what lead to the themes of contradictory legal consciousness—*disconnect in harm naming* and *different logics of justice*—that I outlined throughout the book. However, the issue is not solely a matter of 'fit', and interveners desire to change local *culture* and subjectivity to align with liberal legal values through *sensibilisation*, but to rethink the value that we have placed on building the ROL in a way that reflects liberal legal standards. This may lead us to the question: Is there another way to conceptualize the ROL?

While I do not provide a complete answer to this question, the next section explores *emergent hybrid legality* and the underlying goals of ROL building to begin to address this question.

Rule of Law Goals

What are the objectives that the ROL is meant to achieve that make it so desirable and associated with such a wide array of social goods, from democracy to development? When the norms and practices associated with ROL building are stripped away, we are left with three core goals: 1) Prevent or limit abuses of power[5]; 2) organize daily life[6], meaning knowing what is and is not acceptable and subject to sanctions; and 3) resolve disputes and get redress for harms[7] (Stromseth et al., 2006). I will address each goal in turn, exploring the possibilities of *emergent hybrid legality* to achieve these goals.

First, *limitations on abuses of power* is an idea that is conventionally conceptualized as *government* limited by law (Tamanaha, 2004). Thus, the ROL is typically defined by a set of institutional mechanisms meant to limit the government, such as judicial review and equal application of the law to everyone. Here, I commit to the idea of limitations on abuses of power but do not assume that these should apply only to *government* and its officials. Building on the legal pluralism scholarship, I recognize that there are various authorities that form the sources and enforcement of legality, all of which need to be 'checked'. This is especially important given that customary justice and localized justice practices are also subject to local power relationships and that they should not be romanticized (eg. Ubink, 2018). This means that limiting abuses of power by the government is still important, but also limiting other entities that regulate and provide justice for the community outside of the state should be taken into consideration. While this element is not the central focus of my analysis throughout the book, I provide some anecdotal insights.

Emergent hybrid legality can provide for this expanded conceptualization of limiting abuses of power. For example, it creates space to challenge abuses of power by allowing for different sources of justice and regulation from different authorities. In Chapters 4 and 5, for example, I engage with the variety of justice options available to the population generally and for addressing harms and disputes around marriage. If one space is experienced as being defined by abuses of power, people have other options and can avoid that space. This means that different authorities can serve as 'checks' on each other. Part of the power of mediation done by NGOs and *chefs* is that the population knows that if the process or outcome is unfair, if these leaders abuse their power, they can turn to the legal system or another organization or *chef*. So, limits on abuses of power can work on authorities within the state system. State and non-state actors can act as checks and balances on each other. For example, in Kiliba, a woman who was wrongly accused of cultivating someone else's land was arrested and imprisoned. *Baraza* mediators heard of the case, gathered the necessary evidence, and petitioned the courts to release her. They were successful. This illustrates that if the courts and legal officials are open to participating in *emergent hybrid legality*, checks on abuses of power can happen multi-directionally.

Second, *organizing everyday life* is about having a system of rules in place, conventionally understood as being codified by the government, to promote public order so that people can organize their daily affairs and have knowledge of what acts or behaviours are not permissible and may be met with sanctions. This also helps lay out the expectations of relationships, from marriage to business transactions. This core ROL goal is also present with *emergent hybrid legality*, if we do not assume that the regulatory framework is necessarily only emanating from the state. Scholars have, for a long time, recognized that other sources of social regulation can coexist with state law (eg. Falk Moore, 1972). If we accept that the structure of the system of rules may include multiple sources, this provides space for thinking about the possibilities of *emergent hybrid legality*.

One may challenge that *emergent hybrid legality* is antithetical to the goal of organizing everyday life precisely because it is *emergent*, meaning that legality is not completely pre-defined or written. However, if we think of the nuances of this point, it still fits well with the goal. Yes, legality is *emergent*, but, as I have argued throughout the book, the practices, mechanisms, and institutions that emerge are specifically shaped by popular shifts in legal consciousness combined with the practices of the local legal complex (as discussed in Chapter 4). Thus, changes in the systems of regulation emerge in dialogue with the population. Therefore, the ability to organize everyday life does not only stem from written laws, their equal application, and enforcement; it also stems from popular knowledge of how legal encounters are continuously (but slowly) changing the nature of legality.

For example, in Chapter 5, I elaborated upon the different regulatory systems of marriage, where they overlap, and what happens when there is a disconnect. People are still able to organize their marriage plans by choosing which system to engage with. At the same time, both parties in a situation of adolescent marriage or sex know that there is a tension between law and popular practice and can make decisions accordingly. To a certain extent, it gives people a degree of freedom to structure their personal lives. Justice practices are flexible and can be responsive to changing social norms, as I illustrate in Chapters 4, 5, and 6.

This leads to the third and final ROL goal, *resolving disputes and redressing harms*, which, I would argue, also extends to *access to justice*. In the ROL scholarship, justice provision is often viewed as the purview of state courts. Again, I maintain that the ROL requires justice provision, but I do not limit legitimate justice provision to the state. In a legally plural context, appropriate and legitimate ways of resolving disputes and redressing harms can come from different sources of authority, from community elders to NGOs. In Uvira, *emergent hybrid legality* means that the laws and legal institutions of the country engage with different aspects of the informal justice realm, producing new outcomes that are accessible to the population. Additionally, legal actors in the courts recognize their own limitations in terms of resources and their ability to address certain harms, and thus sometimes refer people to alternative justice systems. These emergent justice practices are relatively uncoordinated but have taken on certain patterns, as discussed in Chapter 4, that facilitate access to justice. Additionally, the new practices are reinforced as they become further entrenched in the population's legal consciousness. Thus, *emergent hybrid legality* addresses the socio-legal imperative of the legal system—to resolve disputes and redress for harms, and reflects the population's needs and desires in this area. In other words, people have different options that they perceive as fair for addressing harms and disputes, and *emergent hybrid legality* allows them to pursue these options.

My brief analysis of how *emergent hybrid legality* can align with ROL goals sheds a positive light on these on-the-ground realities. At the same time, I cannot romanticize the transitional legal terrain in Uvira. Violence still occurs, and people still experience problems in accessing justice. Violence, in the form of popular justice, has become accepted and normalized as a result of legal encounters and ongoing deficiencies of the terrain of legality for addressing witchcraft accusations. While the realm of legality has broadened in response to the shifting relationship between popular legal consciousness and legal pluralism, not all harms have been sufficiently addressed. Witchcraft accusations have potential legal ramifications, and informal systems have only had marginal success in addressing them. The strategy most sought within the realm of legality is to deny the existence of witchcraft, either indiscriminately or on a case-by-case basis. Rather than reshaping beliefs, the legal system's denial of witchcraft has created space for the legitimation of extra-legal violence. Thus, the encounter of global and local legal norms and practices has problematic outcomes as well.

I have put forth some ideas about how *emergent hybrid legality* maintains the possibility of advancing ROL goals. This is just the beginning of rethinking how these goals can be achieved outside of a state-only approach to ROL building. Shifting our focus away from standardized ROL measures and liberal legalism, which have largely shaped how scholars and practitioners think about the ROL, is a first step in reimagining what the possibilities are. One last major area of exploration remains, which is especially relevant in relation to the ROL building in transitioning contexts, where interveners view the transition as a space for advancing women's rights and gender justice, such as the DRC. What can *emergent hybrid legality* do for the goals of gender justice and women's rights?

Gender Justice and *Emergent Hybrid Legality*

From a conventional, liberal ROL perspective, the issue of gender justice is typically covered via legal protections and equality before the law because it is aligned with liberal legal values. As mentioned, liberal assumptions include the idea that the individual is the fundamental unit of society, existing prior to social organization, and the individual as rational[8] and self-interested (Scales, 2006). With the

ROL and liberal legalism, this translates as the liberal legal subject essentially stripped of all differentiated and embodied characteristics and existing simply as a decontextualized, rational, autonomous entity (Grear, 2011). As noted earlier, with liberal legalism, law is understood as neutral and autonomous. The (state) legal system exists; coordinates activities; and resolves disputes according to shared values, universal principles, reason, and logic (Hunter, 2016). Thus, formal equality—equality before the law—is often viewed as the best way to promote substantive equality. This has gendered implications in that the law is seen as (gender) neutral, which can reinforce substantive inequality (Ni Aolain et al., 2011), as it is not situated to recognize or address gender injustices.

By contrast, *emergent hybrid legality* shapes gender justice via an alternative logic, through ongoing engagement with this issue in a variety of spaces, both public and private. It is useful to consider the work of feminist transitional justice scholars, such as O'Rourke (2015), who is concerned with the period of transition, which scholars sometimes identify as a window of opportunity. While my research is not specifically about transitional justice, it is about thinking through justice in the transitional era through legal reforms. O'Rourke (2015) highlights three important areas for thinking about gender justice: Women's participation (in the transition), justice for harms against women, and transforming structural gender inequality. This is a useful lens for thinking about gender justice for women more broadly (see also Dunn, 2017). It considers participation, how harms are addressed, and broader structural inequality. How does legal consciousness and *emergent hybrid legality* reflect these elements of gender justice in contrast to liberal legalism?

One of the major strengths of *emergent hybrid legality* is its openness to shifts in social norms and practices and access to justice. The main characteristics of *emergent hybrid legality* are that it is emergent and hybrid. The hybrid aspect means that it integrates various ideas, norms, and practices, although sometimes there may be tensions within and between these elements. Given the important role of the local legal complex, this is often done in ways that integrate elements of the law and international human and women's rights ideas, with local beliefs and practices. Shifts have happened around women's participation in legal-justice, but tensions are still evident. For example, many of the NGOs who were working on justice issues had women in leadership positions and working as mediators. At the same time, sometimes, women's participation as disputants could still be limited by certain gendered expectations, such as in the case I cited where I intervened to ask why the female disputant's female representative was not afforded the same time to speak as their male counterparts. Notably, the context of *emergent hybrid legality* allows the space for rethinking gendered dynamics of participation in light of how the local legal complex engages with this issue and with the population.

Justice for harms against women is another key area to consider. Often, 'everyday' harms do not go through the legal system. But, with *emergent hybrid legality*, they can still be addressed in accessible forums. These forums integrate different ideas about gender justice. This has been an underlying theme throughout my analysis. In Chapter 4, I covered a range of justice possibilities and how the local legal complex is shaping them and the population's understanding of them through their *sensibilisation* activities. Chapter 5 explored the different understanding of justice and the options available to adolescents and their families in situations of adolescent sex and marriage. Again, the openness and flexibility of *emergent hybrid legality* allow people to make choices about what justice looks like for them, which can be shaped by popular wisdom about the terrain of legality.

Finally, considering the point of structural gender inequality, *emergent hybrid legality* also has something to offer. Rather than being the official word on gender justice, the formal law comes to serve as just one point in an ongoing social discussion about gender justice. In the context of *emergent hybrid legality*, the law can be referenced in the same discussion as culture, personal preferences, and practical realities. In spaces outside the formal legal system, this means that discretion on the part of the mediator is important but so is the voice of the different parties involved. Thus, there is no set way that cases must be addressed. Additionally, the formal legal system remains in place as a backup in some situations or as a threat in others.

Conclusion

If ROL scholars engaged more thoroughly with the socio-legal scholarship, they would encounter the long-argued point that for law to be viewed as legitimate and meaningful, it must bear some relationship to non-state orders (Ehrlich, 1936). For the law to be effective, "the diversity of individuals which compose the citizen body are the ones that need to define, structure, and thematically formulate the laws which are meant to govern them" (Gagnon, 2012, p. 24; see also Nicolaidis & Kleinfeld, 2012). In other words, a socio-legal bottom-up approach to law highlights that law is socially constructed and thus will likely look different across different social contexts (Kurkchiyan, 2011). However, the law advanced by interveners rarely reflects local beliefs and practices, as noted earlier. Socio-legal scholars, including the few who engage with ROL building, note the need to understand popular legal beliefs and practices, rather than assuming a need to change them.

Engaging with the extant socio-legal scholarship is useful for thinking through the variety of forms the ROL could possibly take. Hertogh (2016) has usefully done so by exploring Ehrlich's concept of 'living law' and considering the possibility of a 'living rule of law', which is defined not by social support for *the* ROL but rather the social definition of *a* ROL. This is precisely what my research has sought to advance. By examining the legal context that emerges out of legal encounters, I have provided a detailed account of the relationship between legal consciousness and the construction of *emergent hybrid legality*. Future research can build on this to explore these ideas in other contexts. Indeed, the concept *emergent hybrid legality* can be used in contexts around the world because, by its definition, it recognizes the possibility of different arrangements of legality across time and space. Scholars have already taken up the concept to explore transitional justice processes in Colombia (Bjorkdahl & Warvsten, 2021). Further engagement with the concept can provide the foundations for strengthening an alternative socio-legal theory of the RCL.

Notes

1 These individuals were also chosen for practical reasons. They would be easier to find and contact, and they would more likely be available to participate for the two days of the workshop.
2 It bears mentioning that other commonly referenced characteristics further reflect the liberal foundations of the ROL, such as "effective security of the person, property, and contracting rights," as well as "basic civil and political liberties that guarantee the autonomy and freedom of the individual" (Haggard & Tiede, 2014, 406; see also, Narduli et al., 2013). In these dominant framings of substantive ROL, other justice concerns, such as respect for cultural diversity or unique legal traditions, for example, are rarely, if ever, mentioned. Instead, the substantive concerns tend to reflect liberal values.
3 This argument dates as far back as John Locke, who argued that life without law was filled with insecurity and disputes; thus, individuals give up their natural freedom in order to live under a legal system provided by the government to maintain order (Tamanaha, 2004). More recently, a body of scholarship at the intersection of peacebuilding, statebuilding, security sector reform, and ROL construction has promulgated similar arguments. On the one hand, Stromseth et al. (2006) recognize that reaching the ROL ends—protecting people from arbitrary power of public officials, allowing people to organize their daily lives, and providing justice—does not necessarily entail the types of legal institutions and processes associated with Western legal systems. On the other hand, they argue that in a globalizing world, this is increasingly required; every prosperous, peaceful society has the same liberal legal institutions (Stromseth et al., 2006). They implicitly link the argument to dominant understandings of modernization, liberal peace and its implications for the legal system (see Chandler, 2015).
4 Imbued with a post-Enlightenment, scientific rationality.
5 This is near universal to all definitions of the ROL.
6 This idea is directly associated with Hayek. He argued that government rules (laws) needed to be stable and public in order to create a reliable framework so that people could plan their lives and organize social interactions and transactions in a certain way. Hayek was focused on augmenting individual liberty, a classically liberal goal. However, the idea of having rules that are widely known to facilitate the interactions of daily life—both by restricting and providing a permissive atmosphere—is by no means only for free market liberalism, but an assumed 'good' of the law.
7 This is developed indirectly in the legal philosophical texts. This component has also been key to more recent ROL conceptualizations, where it is often understood in terms of access to (legal) justice.
8 Imbued with a post-Enlightenment, scientific rationality.

Bibliography

Bjorkdahl, A., & Warvsten, L. (2021). Friction in transitional justice processes: The Colombian judicial system and the ICC. *International Journal of Transitional Justice, 15*(3), 636–657.
Carothers, T. (2006). The rule of law revival. In T. Carothers (Ed.), *Promoting the rule of law abroad: In search of knowledge* (pp. 3–14). Carnegie Endowment for International Peace.

Chandler, D. (2015). Resilience and the 'everyday': Beyond the paradox of 'liberal peace'. *Review of International Studies, 41*(1), 27–48.

Davis, K., Kingsbury, B., & Merry, S. E. (2012). Introduction. In Davis, K., Fisher, A., Kingsbury, B., & Merry, S. E. (Eds.), *Governance by indicators: Global power through classification and rankings*. Oxford University Press.

Dembour, M. B. (2000). *Recalling the Belgian Congo: Conversations and introspection* (Vol. 9). Berghahn Books.

Dossa, S. (1999). Liberal legalism: Law, culture and identity. *The European Legacy, 4*(3), 73–87.

Dunn, H. (2017). The transitional justice gap: Exploring 'everyday' gendered harms and customary justice in South Kivu, DR Congo. *Feminist Legal Studies, 25*(1), 71–97.

Eckert, J., Donahoe, B., Strümpell, C., & Biner, Z. O. (Eds.) (2012). Introduction: Law's travels and transformations. In *Law against the state: Ethnographic forays into law's transformations*. Cambridge University Press.

Ehrlich, E. (1936). *Fundamental principles of the sociology of law*. Harvard University Press.

Engel, D., & Engel, J. S. (2010). Tort, custom, and karma. In *Tort, custom, and karma*. Stanford University Press.

Ewick, P., & Silbey, S. S. (1998). *The common place of law: Stories from everyday life*. University of Chicago Press.

Falk Moore, S. (1972). Law and social change: The semi-autonomous social field as an appropriate subject of study. *Law & Society Review*, 7, 719.

Gagnon, J-P. (2012). Post-colonial public law: Are current legal establishments democratically illegitimate? *African Journal of Legal Studies, 5*, 21–43.

Grear, A. (2011). 'Sexing the matrix': Embodiment, disembodiment and the law—towards the re-gendering of legal rationality. In *Gender, sexualities and law* (pp. 48–61). Routledge.

Grenfell, L. (2013). *Promoting the rule of law in post-conflict states*. Cambridge University Press.

Hadfield, G. K., & Weingast, B. R. (2014). Microfoundations of the rule of law. *Annual Review of Political Science, 17*, 21–42.

Haggard, S., & Tiede, L. (2014). The rule of law in post-conflict settings: The empirical record. *International Studies Quarterly, 58*(2), 405–417.

Hertogh, M. (2016). Your rule of law is not mine: Rethinking empirical approaches to EU rule of law promotion. *Asia Europe Journal, 14*(1), 43–59.

Hunt A (1986). The theory of critical legal studies. *Oxford Journal of Legal Studies, 6*(1), 1–45.

Hunter, R. (2016). Contesting the dominant paradigm: Feminist critiques of liberal legalism. In V. E. Munro (Ed.), *The Ashgate research companion to feminist legal theory* (pp. 25–42). Routledge.

Kleinfeld, R. (2006). Competing definitions of the rule of law. In T. Carothers (Ed.), *Promoting the rule of law abroad: In search of knowledge* (pp. 31–74). Carnegie Endowment for International Peace.

Kurkchiyan, M. (2011). Perceptions of law and social order: A cross-national comparison of collective legal consciousness. *The Wisconsin International Law Journal, 29*, 366.

Lincoln, R. S. (2011). Rule of law for whom: Strengthening the rule of law as a solution to sexual violence in the Democratic Republic of the Congo. *Berkeley Journal of Gender, Law & Justice, 26*, 139.

Massoud, M. F. (2013). *Law's fragile state: Colonial, authoritarian, and humanitarian legacies in Sudan*. Cambridge University Press.

Merry, S. E. (2009). *Human rights and gender violence: Translating international law into local justice*. University of Chicago Press.

Narduli, P. F., Peyton, B., & Bajjalieh, J. (2013). Conceptualizing and measuring rule of law constructs, 1850–2010. *Journal of Law and Courts, 1*(1), 139–192.

Ni Aolain, F., Haynes, D. F., Cahn, N., & Fionnuala, N. (2011). *On the frontlines: Gender, war, and the post-conflict process.* Oxford University Press.

Nicolaidis, K., & Kleinfeld, R. (2012). *Rethinking Europe's "rule of law" and enlargement agenda: The fundamental Dilemma.* SIMA Papers No.49, OECD.

O'Rourke, C. (2015, July). Feminist scholarship in transitional justice: A de-politicising impulse? In *Women's studies international forum* (Vol. 51, pp. 118–127). Pergamon.

Park, A. S. (2010). Peacebuilding, the rule of law and the problem of culture: Assimilation, multiculturalism, deployment. *Journal of Intervention and Statebuilding, 4*(4), 413–432.

Peterson, J. H. (2010). 'Rule of Law' initiatives and the liberal peace: The impact of politicized reform in post-conflict states. *Disasters, 34*(s1), S15-S39.

Prinsloo, M. W. (1993). Recognition and application of indigenous law in Zaire Rwanda, Burundi and Lusophone Africa. *Journal of South African Law,* 541.

Qerimi, Q. (2020). Operationalizing and measuring rule of law in an internationalized transitional context: The virtue of Venice Commission's rule of law checklist. *Law and Development Review, 13*(1), 59–94.

Stromseth, J., Wippman, D., & Brooks, R. (2006). *Can might make rights? Building the rule of law after military interventions.* Cambridge University Press.

Tamanaha, B. Z. (2004). *On the rule of law: History, politics, theory.* Cambridge University Press.

Ubink, J. (2018). Customary legal empowerment in Namibia and Ghana? Lessons about access, power and participation in non-state justice systems. *Development and Change, 49*(4), 930–950.

Urueña, R., Merry, S. E., Davis, K. E., & Kingsbury, B. (2015). Indicators and the law. *The Quiet Power of Indicators: Measuring Governance, Corruption, and Rule of Law, 75.*

Versteeg, M., & Ginsburg, T. (2017). Measuring the rule of law: A comparison of indicators. *Law & Social Inquiry, 42*(1), 100–137.

Appendix A

Interviews and Narratives

Research into consciousness is not only about how people act; it is about how people understand and make sense of the law and justice in context-specific ways. This may be shaped by experiences, stories, knowledge, rumours, and belief systems. In my research, I used interviews as a main method of gleaning insights into peoples' legal consciousness, and I relied on similar but distinct interview methods for my four different rounds of fieldwork. During my first stint of fieldwork, I focused on interviewing participants of *baraza*, a traditionally informed, NGO-run justice mechanism in Kavimvira, a neighbourhood within the city of Uvira, Kiliba, and Makobola (towns/neighbourhoods in Uvira) (Map 3, Research Sites). I asked them about their experiences with conflict or harms and why they went to *baraza* instead of *la justice*, the state legal system. I conducted 29 semi-formal interviews with *baraza* participants and numerous informal interviews with mediators in the three different *baraza* locations: Makobola, Uvira City, and Kiliba. By semi-formal interviews, I mean that I had a list of guiding questions and topics, but I would not necessarily adhere to them strictly or in a particular order; I tried to follow the responses of interviewees more organically. Through these interviews, I was attempting to develop an understanding of: 1) Which problems brought people in for mediation? 2) Why did they choose *baraza* over other justice options, specifically, but not limited to the formal legal system? 3) What was the process like, and how did it differ from their understandings of the formal legal system? 4) Were they satisfied and has the issue been fully resolved? Given the gendered nature of some of the disputes I was researching, I began to further develop questions about gender roles, rights, norms, and expectations.

In the second round of fieldwork, I conducted semi-formal individual interviews with members of the legal profession, including judges and lawyers. Here, I asked questions to determine: 1) What problems were common in the community? 2) How do people address them and how *should* they address them? 3) When do people use the courts? 4) What are the successes and difficulties they have experienced being part of the legal system? I also held ten group interviews in Kiliba and Makobola. Groups were of anywhere from three to eight people and were divided up into different social groups, including local NGO members, women, chiefs, wise elders, teacher, and security forces. These were informal; sometimes people joined and others left. Throughout the book, when I 'quote' from group interviews, these are summaries of my notes, not directly transcribed from recorded material. By contrast, individual interviews were audio recorded and transcribed, and 'quoted' content is a translation, from interpreters and transcribers, of what the interviewee said. My interpreters and myself translated for the spirit of the content rather than to the letter, meaning 'quoted' material is not a verbatim translation but an interpretation meant to reflect the message of the interviewee.

Part of the reason I decided to hold group interviews that were focused on general questions about community harms or disputes and how people dealt with them was because, in 2011, I had found it difficult to conduct interviews in private. If I was seen in the community before the interview, people would be curious about what I was doing and who I was talking to, which raised ethical concerns around confidentiality. Sometimes, interviews would be interrupted, and I would have to pause, which disturbed the flow of the conversation. Additionally, group interviews created a space for people to have a discussion and build on or challenge each other's contributions. I found this method very fruitful for developing a sense of the harms and disputes in the community and how and why people make the decisions they do regarding how to address them. At the same time, group interviews may also create a scenario, where only some people participate and others just agree. However, when combined with the individual interviews I conducted in 2011 and 2017, I was exposed to a number of different people and their varied, and similar, understandings.

During my penultimate research period, I focused on individual interviews with local organizations and with the beneficiaries they referred me to. I conducted 46 interviews with members of the local population. I conducted ten interviews with local NGOs and nine interviews with other members of the local legal complex. The interviews with legal officials were of similar format as described previously. The interviews with NGO directors and staff were mostly informal and focused around their work. Some of them worked specifically in access to justice for women, another worked on a girls' education, another on early marriage, and a few worked on land disputes and other 'everyday' disputes.

The demographics of the individual interviews with members of the general public reflect, as I already mentioned, a bias towards female participants Almost all of the participants were married or at least cohabitated with someone for an extended period of time. Most had stopped school before graduating, some women specifically to get married or as the result of pregnancy. Most people worked as subsistence farmers with either their own land or a rented field. Others did petty commerce, and a few others were teachers. Few had electricity or running water in their home, but most had access to a cell phone and/or radio. Many said that at one point or another, they had problems paying their children's school fees (between 2000 FC and 8000 FC, or approximately 2–8 USD), medical bills, or their rent if they did not own their home. Generally, the interviewees could be understood as living in poverty and were 'average' people in the area.

In these interviews, I focused on building an understanding of their everyday lives—what a typical day was like; who they were close to; what they did in their spare time; and where they got their news/information about the community, country, and beyond. Then, I would lead into questions about harms or disputes in the community and how they are dealt with, then I would ask if they had any personal experiences that they would like to share. I would only ask questions specifically about *la justice* and other justice systems at the end of the interview if the interviewee did not raise these topics at some point. I would also rely on hypotheticals to distinguish what people would do in different cases and why. Direct answers are only a part of the data; silences, evasions, rumours, and different interpretations of events are equally important for analysis (Fujii, 2010; Schwartz-Shea & Yanow, 2013). Rumours are a major part of the social fabric and came up a lot in interviews, which I expand on more, when relevant, in the substantive chapters. Questions about everyday life often focused on marriage and work, mostly as subsistence farmers, lending insights into areas that are regulated by law, but that I had learned from previous research were often dealt with through other justice spheres, such as local *chefs*.

The individual interviews were partially focused on narratives and partially about people's perceptions, understandings, and judgements. The narrative sections typically developed from questions, such as: "Have you ever had a problem with someone in your family? A neighbour? What happened? What did you do?" Some women's narratives developed from questions about their marriage, what the marriage is like, and how it came about. Typically, interviews lasted approximately 45 minutes to an hour and a half and usually provided enough time to get background information, one narrative of harm or dispute and how it was addressed, as well as follow-up questions about the law and different justice practices. These narratives helped me develop an understanding of the subjectivity of the narrator and how she situates herself in the world around her and in relation to legal norms, practices, and institutions (see Engel & Engel, 2010). Additionally, these interviews provided contextualized nuance and challenged "taken-for-granted beliefs, assertions, and assumptions" (Thomson, 2013, np) associated with the dominant narrative about ROL failures and the so-called problem of local culture. They also lend insight into people's experiences with legal pluralism, assumptions about the law and legal systems, and interpretations of authorities and other actors—essentially, the information needed to develop a better understanding of what shapes and shifts legal consciousness in the wake of conflict and in a period of rebuilding.

Bibliography

Adinkrah, M. (2004). Witchcraft accusations and female homicide victimization in contemporary Ghana. *Violence against Women, 10*(4), 325–356.

Alusala, N. (2015). *Assessment report on cross-border small arms and light weapons trafficking between the Democratic Republic of the Congo and the Republic of Burundi.* Action on Armed Violence. https://aoav.org.uk/wp-content/uploads/2016/02/AOAV-DRC-Burundi-Border-Assessment-Report-FINAL_en.pdf

Aroussi, S. (2017). Women, peace, and security and the DRC: Time to rethink wartime sexual violence as gender-based violence? *Politics & Gender, 13*(3), 488–515.

Aroussi, S. (2018). Perceptions of justice and hierarchies of rape: Rethinking approaches to sexual violence in Eastern Congo from the ground up. *International Journal of Transitional Justice, 12*(2), 277–295.

Autesserre, S. (2010). *The trouble with the Congo: Local violence and the failure of international peacebuilding* (Vol. 115). Cambridge University Press

Autesserre, S. (2012). Dangerous tales: Dominant narratives on the Congo and their unintended consequences. *African Affairs, 111*(443), 202–222.

Autesserre, S. (2014). *Peaceland: Conflict resolution and the everyday politics of international intervention.* Cambridge University Press.

Baaz, M., & Stern, M. (2010). *The complexity of violence: A critical analysis of sexual violence in the Democratic Republic of Congo (DRC).* Sida: Nordiska Afrikainstitutet.

Benda-Beckmann, K. V., & Turner, B. (2018). Legal pluralism, social theory, and the state. *The Journal of Legal Pluralism and Unofficial Law, 50*(3), 255–274.

Björkdahl, A., & Gusic, I. (2016). Sites of friction: Governance, identity and space in Mostar. In A. Björkdahl, K. Höglund, G. Millar, J. van der Lijn, & W. Verkoren (Eds.) *Peacebuilding and friction* (pp. 98–116). Routledge.

Björkdahl, A., & Warvsten, L. (2021). Friction in transitional justice processes: The Colombian judicial system and the ICC. *International Journal of Transitional Justice, 15*(3), 636–657.

Bunting, A. (2005). Stages of development: Marriage of girls and teens as an international human rights issue. *Social & Legal Studies, 14*(1), 17–38.

Bunting, A., & Engle Merry, S. (2007). Global regulation and local political struggles: Early marriage in northern Nigeria. In *Youth, globalization, and the law* (pp. 321–353). Stanford University Press.

Buss, D. E. (2009). Rethinking 'rape as a weapon of war'. *Feminist Legal Studies, 17*(2), 145–163.

Buur, L. (2008). Democracy & its discontents: Vigilantism, sovereignty & human rights in South Africa. *Review of African Political Economy, 35*(118), 571–584.

Carlin, J. E., Howard, J., & Messinger, S. L. (1966). Civil justice and the poor: Issues for sociological research. *Law and Society Review*, 9–89.

Carothers, T. (2006). The rule of law revival. In T. Carothers (Ed.), *Promoting the rule of law abroad: In search of knowledge* (pp. 3–14). Carnegie Endowment for International Peace.

Carothers, T. (Ed.). (2010). *Promoting the rule of law abroad: In search of knowledge*. Brookings Institution Press.

Carr, J. (2016). The lawlessness of law: Lynching and anti-lynching in the contemporary USA. *Settler Colonial Studies*, *6*(2), 153–163.

Chandler, D. (2015). Resilience and the 'everyday': Beyond the paradox of 'liberal peace'. *Review of International Studies*, *41*(1), 27–48.

Channell, W. (2006). Lessons not learned about legal reform. In T. Carothers (Ed.), *Promoting the rule of law abroad: In search of knowledge* (pp. 137–160). Carnegie Endowment for International Peace.

Chanock, M. (1985). *Law, custom and social order: The colonial experience in Malawi and Zambia*. Cambridge University Press.

Chant, S. (2006). Re-thinking the "feminization of poverty" in relation to aggregate gender indices. *Journal of Human Development*, 7(2), 201–220.

Chua, L. J., & Engel, D. M. (2019). Legal consciousness reconsidered. *Annual Review of Law and Social Science*, *15*, 335–353.

CRG. (2016, 9 April). Press statement regarding the expulsion of Jason Stearns from the DR Congo." *Congo Research Group | Groupe D'Etude Sur Le Congo*. congoresearchgroup.org/press-statement-regarding-the-expulsion-of-jason-stearns-from-the-dr-congo/.

Davis, K., Kingsbury, B., & Merry, S. E. (2012). Introduction. In Davis, K., Fisher, A., Kingsbury, B., & Merry, S. E. (Eds.), *Governance by indicators: Global power through classification and rankings*. Oxford University Press.

Davis, L. (2015). *The EU and peacebuilding in the Democratic Republic of Congo*. Civil Society Dialogue Network Discussion Paper No. 9. European Peacebuilding Liaison Office.

D'Errico, N. C., Kalala, T., Nzigire, L. B., Maisha, F., & Malemo Kalisya, L. (2013). 'You say rape, I say hospitals. But whose voice is louder?' Health, aid and decision-making in the Democratic Republic of Congo. *Review of African Political Economy*, *40*(135), 51–66.

De Hamann-Legal. (n.d.). www.hamann-legal.de/upload/Handling_Guilt_Under_Customary_Law-Concept_and_Basis_- _Jean_Salem_Israel_Marcel_Kapya_Kabesal.pdf

Dembour, M. B. (2000). *Recalling the Belgian Congo: Conversations and introspection* (Vol. 9). Berghahn Books.

Derks, M. (2012). *Improving security and justice through local/non-state actors: The challenges of donor support to local/nonstate security and justice providers*. Netherlands Institute of International Relations 'Clingendael.

Diwan, M. A. (2004). Conflict between state legal norms and norms underlying popular beliefs: Witchcraft in Africa as a case study. *Duke Journal of Comparative & International Law*, *14*, 351.

Donais, T. (2013). Power politics and the rule of law in post-Dayton Bosnia. *Studies in Social Justice*, 7(2), 189.

Dossa, S. (1999). Liberal legalism: Law, culture and identity. *The European Legacy*, *4*(3), 73–87.

Dunn, H. (2017). The transitional justice gap: Exploring 'everyday' gendered harms and customary justice in South Kivu, DR Congo. *Feminist Legal Studies*, *25*(1), 71–97.

Dunn, H. (2018). *Emergent legal pluralism: Legal consciousness and unanticipated outcomes of rule of law building in eastern Democratic Republic of Congo* (Doctoral dissertation, University of Minnesota).

Dunn, H. (2020). Research in the Land of Savages, Victims, and Saviors. In G. Hoogensen, P. Weitsman & R. Matthew (Eds.), *Women's perspectives on human security: Violence, environment, and sustainability* (pp. 154–182). Ohio University Press.

Dunn, H. (2021). Emergent hybrid legality: A study of legal encounters in the DRC. *Journal of Intervention and Statebuilding, 15*(2), 201–220.

Dunn, K. (2003). *Imagining the Congo: The international relations of identity*. Palgrave Macmillan.

Eckert, J., Donahoe, B., Strümpell, C., & Biner, Z. O. (Eds.) (2012). Introduction: Law's travels and transformations. In *Law against the state: Ethnographic forays into law's transformations*. Cambridge University Press.

Ehrlich, E. (1936). *Fundamental principles of the sociology of law*. Harvard University Press.

Engel, D., & Engel, J. S. (2010). Tort, custom, and karma. In *Tort, custom, and karma*. Stanford University Press.

Ewick, P., & Silbey, S. S. (1998). *The common place of law: Stories from everyday life*. University of Chicago Press.

Falk Moore, S. (1972). Law and social change: The semi-autonomous social field as an appropriate subject of study. *Law & Society Review*, 7, 719.

Felices-Luna, M. (2012). Justice in the Democratic Republic of Congo: Practicing corruption, practicing resistance? *Critical Criminology, 20*(2), 197–209.

Freedman, J. (2016). *Gender, violence and politics in the Democratic Republic of Congo*. Routledge.

Fujii, L. A. (2010). Shades of truth and lies: Interpreting testimonies of war and violence. *Journal of Peace Research, 47*(2), 231–241.

Fujii, L. A. (2013). Working with interpreters. In L. Mosley (Ed.), *Interview research in political science* (pp. 144–157). Cornell University Press.

Fukuyama, F. (2010). Transitions to the rule of law. *Journal of Democracy, 21*(1), 33–44.

Fuller, L. L. (1964). *The morality of law*. Yale University Press.

Galanter, M., & Trubek, D. M. (1974). Scholars in self-estrangement: Some reflections on the crisis in law and development studies in the United States. *Wisconsin Law Review*, 1062.

Gallagher, M. E. (2006). Mobilizing the law in China: "Informed disenchantment" and the development of legal consciousness. *Law & Society Review, 40*(4), 783–816.

Godoy, A. S. (2006). *Popular injustice: Violence, community, and law in Latin America*. Stanford University Press.

Golub, S. (2006). The legal empowerment alternative. In T. Carothers (Ed.), *Promoting the rule of law abroad: In search of knowledge* (pp. 161–187). Carnegie Endowment for International Peace.

Goodale, M. (2008). *Dilemmas of modernity: Bolivian encounters with law and liberalism*. Stanford University Press.

Graham, A. (2014). One hundred years of suffering? "Humanitarian crisis photography" and self-representation in the Democratic Republic of the Congo. *Social Dynamics, 40*(1), 140–163.

Grant, H. B. (2021). The cultural ingredient to rule of law promotion. In *Building a culture of lawfulness* (pp. 1–9). Springer.

Grear, A. (2011). 'Sexing the matrix': Embodiment, disembodiment and the law—towards the re-gendering of legal rationality. In *Gender, sexualities and law* (pp. 48–61). Routledge.

Grenfell, L. (2013). *Promoting the rule of law in post-conflict states*. Cambridge University Press.

Hadfield, G. K., & Weingast, B. R. (2014). Microfoundations of the rule of law. *Annual Review of Political Science, 17*, 21–42.

Haggard, S., & Tiede, L. (2014). The rule of law in post-conflict settings: The empirical record. *International Studies Quarterly, 58*(2), 405–417.

Haile, H. B., Bock, B., & Folmer, H. (2012, July). Microfinance and female empowerment: Do institutions matter? In *Women's studies international forum* (Vol. 35, pp. 256–265). Pergamon.

Halliday, S. (2019). After hegemony? The varieties of legal consciousness research. *Social and Legal Studies, 28*(6), 859–878.

Halliday, T., Karpik, L., & Feeley, M. (Eds.), (2007). The legal complex in struggles for political liberalism. In *Fighting for political freedom: Comparative studies of the legal complex and political liberalism* (p. 1). Hart Publishing.

Hardesty, M., & Gunn, A. J. (2019). Survival sex and trafficked women: The politics of representing and speaking about others in anti-oppressive qualitative research. *Qualitative Social Work, 18*(3), 493–513.

Harper, E. (Ed.). (2011). *Working with customary justice systems: Post-conflict and fragile states.* International Development Law Organization.

Heath, R. (2014). Women's access to labor market opportunities, control of household resources, and domestic violence: Evidence from Bangladesh. *World Development, 57,* 32–46.

Hellmüller, S. A. (2016). Connections for peace: Frictions in peacebuilding encounters in Ituri, Democratic Republic of Congo. In A. Björkdahl, K. Höglund, G. Millar, J. van der Lijn, & W. Verkoren (Eds.), *Peacebuilding and friction* (pp. 172–187). Routledge.

Henry, N. (2014). The fixation on wartime rape: Feminist critique and international criminal law. *Social & Legal Studies, 23,* 93–111.

Hertogh, M. (2016). Your rule of law is not mine: Rethinking empirical approaches to EU rule of law promotion. *Asia Europe Journal, 14*(1), 43–59.

Hertogh, M. (2018). *Nobody's law: Legal consciousness and legal alienation in everyday life.* Springer.

Hilbink, L., & Gallagher, J. (2011). The state and law: A critical assessment. In K. Ansolabehere & R. Sieder (Eds.), *Handbook of law and society in Latin America.* Routledge.

Hilhorst, D., & Douma, N. (2018). Beyond the hype? The response to sexual violence in the Democratic Republic of the Congo in 2011 and 2014. *Disasters, 42,* S79–S98.

Hodgson, D. L. (Ed.). (2011). Introduction: Gender and culture at the limit of rights. In *Gender and culture at the limit of rights* (pp. 1–16). University of Pennsylvania Press.

Holterhus, T. P. (2018). A Theoretical introduction and legal perspective on rule of law transfers. *Goettingen Journal of International Law, 9,* 7.

Holzer, E. (2013). What happens to law in a refugee camp? *Law & Society Review, 47*(4), 837–872.

Horii, H. (2020). A blind spot in international human rights framework: A space between tradition and modernity within the child marriage discourse. *The International Journal of Human Rights, 24*(8), 1057–1079.

HRW. (2016, 9 August). DR Congo: Human rights watch researcher barred. *Human Rights Watch.* www.hrw.org/news/2016/08/09/dr-congo-human-rights-watch-researcher-barred.

Hunt, A. (1985). The ideology of law: Advances and problems in recent applications of the concept of ideology to the analysis of law. *Law & Society Review, 19,* 11.

Hunt A (1986). The theory of critical legal studies. *Oxford Journal of Legal Studies, 6*(1), 1–45.

Hunter, R. (2016). Contesting the dominant paradigm: Feminist critiques of liberal legalism. In V. E. Munro (Ed.), *The Ashgate research companion to feminist legal theory* (pp. 25–42). Routledge.

Isser, D. (Ed.). (2011). *Customary justice and the rule of law in war-torn societies.* US Institute of Peace Press.

Jacobs, C. (2018). Seeking justice, experiencing the state: Criminal justice and real legal uncertainty in the Democratic Republic of Congo. *The Journal of Legal Pluralism and Unofficial Law, 50*(3), 280–293.

Jean-Bouchard, É. (2014). The (in) visible subject: Women's normative strategies in eastern Congo. *The Journal of Legal Pluralism and Unofficial Law, 46*(3), 357–373.

Jean-Bouchard, É. (2017). Sexual violence issues in eastern DRC: Processes of global and local co-constitution. *Canadian Journal of African Studies/Revue canadienne des études africaines, 51*(2), 257–273.

Kabesa, J. (2011). Handling guilt under customary law-concept and basis. In H. Hamann, K. Ilunga-Matthiesen, & A. Mukalay (Eds.), *African law study library with specific emphasis on Democratic Republic of Congo* (pp. 113–144). Konad Adenauer-Stifttung.

Kelsall, M. S., & Stepakoff, S. (2007). 'When we wanted to talk about rape': Silencing sexual violence at the Special Court for Sierra Leone. *The International Journal of Transitional Justice, 1*(3), 355–374.

Kirby, P. (2015). Ending sexual violence in conflict: The preventing sexual violence initiative and its critics. *International Affairs, 91*(3), 457–472.

Kleinfeld, R. (2006). Competing definitions of the rule of law. In T. Carothers (Ed.), *Promoting the rule of law abroad: In search of knowledge* (pp. 31–74). Carnegie Endowment for International Peace.

Koddenbrock, K. (2012). Recipes for intervention: Western policy papers imagine the Congo. *International Peacekeeping, 19*(5), 549–564.

Koomen, J. (2013). "Without these women, the tribunal cannot do anything": The politics of witness testimony on sexual violence at the international criminal tribunal for Rwanda. *Signs: Journal of Women in Culture and Society, 38*(2), 253–277.

Kucera, M., & Mares, M. (2015). Vigilantism during democratic transition. *Policing and Society, 25*(2), 170–187.

Kurkchiyan, M. (2011). Perceptions of law and social order: A cross-national comparison of collective legal consciousness. *Wisconsin International Law Journal, 29*, 366.

Lake, M. (2014a). *Building the rule of law in fragile states: The role of external actors in shaping institutional responses to mass violence in the Democratic Republic of Congo and South Africa* (unpublished doctoral dissertation). University of Washington.

Lake, M. (2014b). Organizing hypocrisy: Providing legal accountability for human rights violations in areas of limited statehood. *International Studies Quarterly, 58*(3), 515–526.

Lake, M. (2018). *Strong NGOs and weak states: Pursuing gender justice in the Democratic Republic of Congo and South Africa*. Cambridge University Press.

Lake, M., Muthaka, I., & Walker, G. (2016). Gendering justice in humanitarian spaces: Opportunity and (Dis) empowerment through gender-based legal development outreach in the Eastern Democratic Republic of Congo. *Law & Society Review, 50*(3), 539–574.

Lemarchand, R. (2008). *The dynamics of violence in central Africa*. University of Pennsylvania.

Lincoln, R. S. (2011). Rule of law for whom: Strengthening the rule of law as a solution to sexual violence in the Democratic Republic of the Congo. *Berkeley Journal of Gender, Law & Justice, 26*, 139.

Lombard, L., & Batianga-Kinzi, S. (2015). Violence, popular punishment, and war in the Central African Republic. *African Affairs, 114*(454), 52–71.

Mambou Pembellot, A. F. (1985). La preuve des crimes de sorcellerie devant le juge penal congolais. *Revue juridique et politique: Indépendance et coopération, 39*(1–2), 124–128.

Mamdani, M. (1996). *Citizen and subject*. Princeton University Press.

Massoud, M. F. (2013). *Law's fragile state: Colonial, authoritarian, and humanitarian legacies in Sudan*. Cambridge University Press.
McConnachie, K. (2014). *Governing refugees: Justice, order and legal pluralism*. Routledge.
Merry, S. E. (1988). Legal pluralism. *Law & Society Review, 22*, 869.
Merry, S. E. (1990). *Getting justice and getting even: Legal consciousness among working-class Americans*. University of Chicago Press.
Merry, S. E. (2009). *Human rights and gender violence: Translating international law into local justice*. University of Chicago Press.
Mertens, C., & Myrttinen, H. (2019). 'A real woman waits'—Heteronormative respectability, neo-liberal betterment and echoes of coloniality in SGBV programming in Eastern DR Congo. *Journal of Intervention and Statebuilding, 13*(4), 418–439.
Mobekk, E. (2009). Security sector reform and the UN mission in the Democratic Republic of Congo: Protecting civilians in the East. *International Peacekeeping, 16*(2), 273–286.
Mutua, M. (2001). Savages, victims, and saviors: The metaphor of human rights. *Harvard International Law Journal, 42*, 201.
Narduli, P. F., Peyton, B., & Bajjalieh, J. (2013). Conceptualizing and measuring rule of law constructs, 1850–2010. *Journal of Law and Courts, 1*(1), 139–192.
Nelken, D. (2003). Comparatists and transferability. In P. Legrand & R. Munday (Eds.), *Comparative legal studies: Traditions and transitions* (pp. 437–466). Cambridge University Press.
Ni Aoláin, F. (2009). Women, security, and the patriarchy of internationalized transitional justice. *Human Rights Quarterly, 31*, 1055.
Ni Aoláin, F., Haynes, D. F., Cahn, N., & Fionnuala, N. (2011). *On the frontlines: Gender, war, and the post-conflict process*. Oxford University Press.
Nicolaidis, K., & Kleinfeld, R. (2012). *Rethinking Europe's "rule of law" and enlargement agenda: The fundamental dilemma. SIGMA Papers*, No. 49, OECD Publishing.
O'Rourke, C. (2015, July). Feminist scholarship in transitional justice: A de-politicising impulse? In *Women's studies international forum* (Vol. 51, pp. 118–127). Pergamon.
Park, A. S. (2010). Peacebuilding, the rule of law and the problem of culture: Assimilation, multiculturalism, deployment. *Journal of Intervention and Statebuilding, 4*(4), 413–432.
Peterson, J. H. (2010). 'Rule of law' initiatives and the liberal peace: The impact of politicized reform in post-conflict states. *Disasters, 34*(s1), S15-S39.
Phillips, A. (2001). Feminism and liberalism revisited: Has Martha Nussbaum got it right? *Constellations, 8*(2), 249–266.
Prinsloo, M. W. (1993). Recognition and application of indigenous law in Zaire, Rwanda, Burundi and Lusophone Africa. *Journal of South African Law, 541*.
Prunier, G. (2009). *Africa's world war: Congo, the Rwandan genocide and the making of a continental catastrophe*. Oxford University Press.
Prunier, G. (2009). *From genocide to continental war: The 'Congolese' conflict and the crisis of contemporary Africa*. Hurst & Co.
Pupavac, V. (2001). Misanthropy without borders: The international children's rights regime. *Disasters, 25*(2), 95–112.
Qerimi, Q. (2020). Operationalizing and measuring rule of law in an internationalized transitional context: The virtue of Venice Commission's rule of law checklist. *Law and Development Review, 13*(1), 59–94.
Rajkovic, N. M. (2012). 'Global law' and governmentality: Reconceptualizing the 'rule of law' as rule 'through' law. *European Journal of International Relations, 18*(1), 29–52.
Raz, J. (2017). The rule of law and its virtue. In R. Cunningham (Ed.), *Liberty and the rule of law* (pp. 3–21). Texas A&M University Press.

Reilly, N. (2009). *Women's human rights*. Polity.

Richards, J. (2016). Implementing DDR in settings of ongoing conflict: The organization and fragmentation of armed groups in the Democratic Republic of Congo (DRC). *Stability: International Journal of Security and Development, 5*(1).

Rubbers, B., & Gallez, E. (2012). Why do Congolese people go to court? A qualitative study of litigants' experiences in two Justice of the Peace courts in Lubumbashi. *The Journal of Legal Pluralism and Unofficial Law, 44*(66), 79–108.

Rubbers, B., & Gallez, E. (2015). Beyond corruption: The everyday life of a justice of the peace court in the Democratic Republic of Congo. In *Real governance and practical norms in sub-Saharan Africa* (pp. 245–262). Routledge.

Rush Smith, N. (2015). Rejecting rights: Vigilantism and violence in post-apartheid South Africa. *African Affairs, 114*(456), 341–360.

Santos, B. de Sousa. (1987). Law: A map of misreading. Toward a postmodern conception of law. *Journal of Law and Society*, 279–302.

Santos, B. de Sousa. (2006). The heterogeneous state and legal pluralism in Mozambique. *Law & Society Review, 40*(1), 39–76.

Sarat, A. (1990). The law is all over: Power, resistance and the legal consciousness of the welfare poor. *Yale JL & Human., 2*, 343.

Scales, A. (2006). *Legal feminism: Activism, lawyering, and legal theory*. NYU Press.

Schwartz-Shea, P., & Yanow, D. (2013). *Interpretive research design: Concepts and processes*. Routledge.

Shepler, S. (2005). The rites of the child: Global discourses of youth and reintegrating child soldiers in Sierra Leone. *Journal of human rights, 4*(2), 197–211.

Sieder, R. (2013). Subaltern cosmopolitan legalities and the challenges of engaged ethnography. *Universitas Humanística*, (75), 221–249.

Silbey, S. (2008). Legal consciousness. In S. Silbey, P. Cane, & J. Conaghan (Eds.), *New Oxford companion to law*. Oxford University Press.

Silbey, S. S. (2005). After legal consciousness. *Annual Review of Law and Social Science, 1*, 323–368.

Smith, N. R. (2015). Rejecting rights: Vigilantism and violence in post-apartheid South Africa. *African Affairs, 114*(456), 341–360.

Stark, L. (2018). Early marriage and cultural constructions of adulthood in two slums in Dar es Salaam. *Culture, Health & Sexuality, 20*(8), 888–901.

Stearns, J. (2011). *Dancing in the glory of monsters: The collapse of the Congo and the great war of Africa*. New York: Public Affairs.

Stromseth, J. (2008). Post-conflict rule of law building: The need for a multi-layered, synergistic approach. *William & Mary Law Review, 49*, 1443.

Stromseth, J., Wippman, D., & Brooks, R. (2006). *Can might make rights? Building the rule of law after military interventions*. Cambridge University Press.

Suarez, C. (2017). 'Living between two lions': Civilian protection strategies during armed violence in the eastern Democratic Republic of the Congo. *Journal of Peacebuilding & Development, 12*(3), 54–67.

Tamanaha, B. Z. (2004). *On the rule of law: History, politics, theory*. Cambridge University Press.

Tsing, A. L. (2005). *Friction: An ethnography of global connection*. Princeton University Press.

Tyler, T. R. (2021). *Why people obey the law*. Princeton university press.

Ubink, J. (2018). Customary legal empowerment in Namibia and Ghana? Lessons about access, power and participation in non-state justice systems. *Development and Change, 49*(4), 930–950.

United Nations. (2010, 27 April). Tackling sexual violence must include prevention, ending impunity—UN Official | | UN News. *United Nations.* https://news.un.org/en/story/2010/04/336662.

United Nations. (n.d.). What is the rule of law—United Nations and the rule of law. *United Nations.* www.un.org/ruleoflaw/what-is-the-rule-of-law/

United Nations Development Programme. (2011). *Strengthening the rule of law in crisis-affected and fragile situations.* United Nations Development Programme, Bureau for Crisis Prevention and Recovery. www.undp.org/sites/g/files/zskgke326/files/publications/UNDP_CPR_ROLGlobal ProgrammePhase2August2014.pdf

Urueña, R., Merry, S. E., Davis, K. E., & Kingsbury, B. (2015). Indicators and the law. *The Quiet Power of Indicators: Measuring Governance, Corruption, and Rule of Law, 75.*

USAID. (2014). *Country development cooperation strategy, Democratic Republic of Congo (2014–2019).* USAID. https://2012- 2017.usaid.gov/sites/default/files/documents/1860/Democratic_Republic_of_Congo_CD CS_2014-2019.pdf

Versteeg, M., & Ginsburg, T. (2017). Measuring the rule of law: A comparison of indicators. *Law & Social Inquiry, 42*(1), 100–137.

Verweijen, J. (2015). The disconcerting popularity of popular in/justice in the Fizi/Uvira region, eastern Democratic Republic of the Congo. *International Journal on Minority and Group Rights, 22*(3), 335–359.

Vinck, P., & Pham, P. (2008). Ownership and participation in transitional justice mechanisms: A sustainable human development perspective from eastern DRC. *The International Journal of Transitional Justice, 2*(3), 398–411.

von Benda-Beckmann, F. (1984). Law out of context: A comment on the creation of traditional law discussion. *Journal of African Law, 28*(1–2), 28–33.

Wojkowska, E. (2007). *Doing justice: How informal justice systems can contribute.* UNDP.

Zongwe, D. P. (2012). The new sexual violence legislation in the Congo: Dressing indelible scars on human dignity. *African Studies Review, 55*(2), 37–57.

Zurn, M., Nollkaemper, A., & Peerenboom, R. (Eds.). (2012). *Rule of law dynamics: In an era of international and transnational governance.* Cambridge University Press.

Index

Note: numbers in *italics* indicate a figure.